To Marry an Indian

D0337499

Cornwall Sep^t 1 – 1825

Mr H. L. Vaill Sir – after a length of th
time in your delay, things we have s
vidu – the sickness has been so great her
that we could not send sooner – if you a
thankful for them well – if not you will be
unthankful – I saw the long letter you o
Noiott – in which you throws out many
things against her & me & my wife – about
the Indian connection – which are altogether
uncandid, unjust, & untrue – where you show
us with deception – sin – y affidavett is viola
of truth &c &c &c – to all which I do not d
fitt to make any lengthy reply at present –
It is strength, pride & prejudice – that all
this clamour has been raised against Ind^n
And the least that can be said & done
against Christian connections of any d
lar I believe to be fitt – our whole famili
which have been together this summer have
become very harmonious on this subjec
together with Sally Hopkins – Mary Brinsma
& many other good people around us &
throughout the country – as you may
yourself perceive – is very great ha^pi I now
consider myself your Father & Friend

to give you any further times Benjn Gol
at present I have, without a little myst
for the sake of you . . . having enough spar

THE UNIVERSITY OF
NORTH CAROLINA PRESS

CHAPEL HILL
AND LONDON

To Marry an Indian

The Marriage of
Harriett Gold and *Elias Boudinot*
in Letters, 1823–1839

Edited by THERESA STROUTH GAUL

© 2005 The University of North Carolina Press
All rights reserved
Manufactured in the United States of America

Designed by Kimberly Bryant
Set in Quadraat
by Tseng Information Systems, Inc.

The paper in this book meets the guidelines for
permanence and durability of the Committee on
Production Guidelines for Book Longevity of the
Council on Library Resources.

Excerpts from Althea Bass, *Cherokee Messenger*
(Norman: University of Oklahoma Press, 1996),
© 1996 University of Oklahoma Press, have been
reprinted with permission.

Library of Congress Cataloging-in-Publication Data
To marry an Indian : the marriage of Harriet Gold
and Elias Boudinot in letters, 1823–1839 / edited
by Theresa Strouth Gaul.
p. cm.
Includes bibliographical references (p.   ) and
index.
ISBN 0-8078-2941-2 (alk. paper) —
ISBN 0-8078-5602-9 (pbk. : alk. paper)
1. Boudinot, Elias, d. 1839—Correspondence.
2. Boudinot, Harriett Gold—Correspondence.
3. Cherokee Indians—Georgia—Correspondence.
4. Women, White—Georgia—Correspondence.
5. Married people—Georgia—Correspondence.
6. Boudinot, Harriett Gold—Family—
Correspondence. 7. Interracial marriage—United
States—Case studies. 8. Cherokee Indians—
History—19th century—Sources. 9. United
States—Race relations—History—19th century—
Sources. 10. American letters—History and
criticism. I. Gaul, Theresa Strouth. II. Boudinot,
Elias, d. 1839. III. Boudinot, Harriett Gold.
E99.C5B7358   2005
974.600497'557'00922—dc22   2004024380

cloth   09 08 07 06 05   5 4 3 2 1
paper   09 08 07 06 05   5 4 3 2 1

Contents

A section of illustrations follows p. 144.

Acknowledgments

For grant support and research awards during the completion of this project, I thank the Texas Christian University (TCU) Research and Creative Activities Fund, Nokia Inc. and the TCU Women's Research Center, the South Central Modern Language Association, and the College of St. Catherine's Abigail Quigley McCarthy Center for Women. For assistance in the research that went into this book, thanks to Ann Schillinger of the Cornwall Historical Society, Danelle Moon of Yale University Library's Manuscripts and Archives, Gail Kruppa of the Torrington Historical Society, David Gomez of the New Echota State Historic Site, Bruce Reinholdt of the Gunn Historical Museum, and TCU's Interlibrary Loan Department. For their generous sharing of family lore and treasures, thank you to Jim, Henry, and David Boudinot, Judith Vaill Manchester, and Timothy Fetzer. My colleagues in the TCU Department of English have been ever generous with their support, interest, and encouragement; special thanks go to Linda Hughes for advice at key moments and Bonnie Blackwell and Karen Steele, who generously read drafts and contributed emotional support at various stages. Bruce Burgett provided crucial early assistance and advice, and Hilary Wyss gave much needed feedback and encouragement at the draft stage. Several graduate students helped greatly in the preparation of the manuscript, including Brian Fehler, Kathleen Johnson-Winston, and Talina Prow. And I'm very grateful to the University of North Carolina Press editorial staff, especially Sian Hunter, for their patience in guiding a novice through the publication process.

Two individuals deserve to be singled out for special thanks. Sargent Bush Jr. generously provided assistance and sound advice at every stage of this project until his death, and I wish very much that he could have seen the final product. His achievements in the editing of correspondence set a high standard for my work, and the mentorship he unstintingly provided me over the years was invaluable. Sharon M. Harris has been the guiding force behind the project since the day I, having just read the letters for the first time, excitedly went to her to ask her advice on how to proceed. She immediately sketched out a plan from start to finish that I have faithfully followed, with this result. Along the way, she answered an infinite number of questions and provided essential advice. I have been lucky to find early in my career two models of absolute professionalism, integrity, and generosity.

Family members and friends—too many to name here—have been enthusiastic cheerleaders for this project all along, and I thank them for their belief in me. Particular acknowledgment goes to my mother, Ruth Strouth, whose collection of nineteenth-century women's novels introduced me in childhood to the imaginative terrain that would become my intellectual and professional "home." And, finally, the biggest thanks of all go to Dave, Simon, and Sadie. They have endured countless sacrifices and been endlessly patient during the years of their lives this project has encompassed. They've done all of this freely for my sake, and with good humor besides.

Abbreviations

ABCFM	American Board of Commissioners for Foreign Missions
C.N.	Cherokee Nation
CornHS	Cornwall Historical Society, Cornwall, Connecticut
HLVC	Herman Landon Vaill Collection, Manuscripts and Archives, Yale University Library, New Haven, Connecticut
LM	Left margin
m	Manuscript
M	Margin
pm	Photocopy of manuscript
RM	Right margin
THS	Torrington Historical Society, Torrington, Connecticut
ts	Typescript

Editorial Method

Yale University Library holds the majority of the manuscript letters in the Herman Landon Vaill Collection (HLVC). Herman Vaill, the author or recipient of most of the letters, probably collected them and passed them down to his descendants. Ralph Henry Gabriel used the letters extensively in his *Elias Boudinot, Cherokee, and His America* and described the manuscript collection as residing at the time of publication in 1941 in the possession of Dudley Landon Vaill (1873–1967), the grandson of Herman and Flora Gold Vaill. Yale's records indicate that Dudley L. Vaill donated the collection to Yale in 1962.

The Herman Landon Vaill Collection includes typed transcriptions of the letters along with the manuscripts. Though librarians have no information on who prepared the typescripts, it is possible that they might have been prepared by or for the use of Gabriel. Though largely accurate, the typescripts do display regularization of some aspects of punctuation, spacing, and so forth, and sometimes present incorrect transcriptions of particular phrases and words. In two cases, the manuscript letters are missing from the Herman Landon Vaill Collection, and only typescripts remain.

The remainder of the letters in this volume are held by the Cornwall Historical Society (CornHS) or the Torrington Historical Society (THS). Cornwall possesses some manuscript letters and only photocopies of others, and curator Ann Schillinger has prepared typed transcriptions. Torrington's holdings exist only in photocopies and duplicate some of Cornwall's holdings. Neither Schillinger nor Gail

Kruppa, curator at Torrington, has any knowledge of the whereabouts of the manuscript letters of which they possess photocopies.

Though both the Yale and Cornwall collections include fragments of letters by Harriett, only complete letters are included here. I prepared the texts of the letters in this volume from the original manuscripts when available; when not available, I considered photocopies of the manuscripts the next most reliable source text and earlier typed transcriptions as the least. I sometimes consulted typescripts for assistance in deciphering difficult-to-read passages in the manuscripts or photocopies but did not rely on them. For letters in the Herman Landon Vaill Collection, I prepared initial transcriptions of the letters from microfilm. A graduate research assistant then proofread those transcriptions against the microfilm. Finally, I proofread the transcriptions against the manuscripts at Yale.

Before the text of each letter, a headnote indicates the collection in which the text resides, the form of the source text (manuscript [m], photocopy of manuscript [pm], or typescript [ts]), and the markings occurring on the outside of the letter, including return address, addressee, and postage. Because I contend that the placement of the exterior address material is crucial to the content of the letter itself (see the introduction), three asterisks set off on a separate line indicate the place in the letter where the return address, addressee, and postage appeared. If no asterisks appear, then the address material did not intrude into the body of the letter and was instead placed at the end or alone on a separate or back side of a page.

I have struggled to reconcile a desire for fidelity to the manuscript texts with the recognition that the text is already inevitably changed in the transition from manuscript to printed text. Except for the exceptions discussed below, this volume retains original spellings, punctuation, capitalization, abbreviations, and errors, even those that might appear simply typographic in nature. To enhance the accessibility of the volume for modern readers, I made the following changes.

The long s is represented with an s. Dates are set flush with the right margin, and indentations for new paragraphs are regularized. Line breaks are not reproduced unless they occurred at the end of a paragraph. In the letters proper, the salutation is set off on a separate line and made flush with the left margin, and the signature of the writer is set off on a separate line and made flush with the right margin. This regularization of salutation and signature does not occur in marginal insertions or postscripts.

Words rendered illegible or obscured by holes, fold-line tears, or damage caused by wax marks are represented in brackets. Strikethroughs represent ~~words canceled out~~, while interlinear insertions appear set ˢˡⁱᵍʰᵗˡʸ ᵃᵇᵒᵛᵉ ᵗʰᵉ ˡⁱⁿᵉ. Words given in brackets function in two ways: 1) as insertions by the editor to clarify aspects of the letter's form, such as "[Addressed to:]" or "[end of page 1]," and 2) as reconstructions of the original material with a fair amount of certainty. When followed by a question mark, the reconstruction is more tentative. "[Illegible]" or "~~illegible~~" marks words that cannot be read because of difficulties deciphering the handwriting or the effects of the strikethrough, while "[missing]" describes words that cannot be read because of holes in the paper or damage caused by wax marks. When words canceled out represent a slip of the pen (e.g., the clearly accidental repetition of a word or a misspelling of a word that is crossed out and then immediately corrected by the following word), they are silently corrected. When an interlinear insertion is corrective in purpose (adding a forgotten word or inserting a letter or two to correct a misspelling), it is also silently corrected. Any more substantive insertions, such as changes in word choice or additions for emphasis or stylistic purposes, are retained. All varieties of underlining, whether single, double, triple, wavy, or crosshatched are represented with a single line; instances of double and triple underlining for emphasis are registered in the notes.

All dashes are regularized in length. Dashes that duplicate existing punctuation in the letter—such as those that follow immediately upon periods, semicolons, exclamation points, or question marks or precede ampersands—are omitted, as are those which follow dates, follow lines in the superscription, and precede signatures in the closings of letters. Dashes following the salutation are changed to commas. Dashes that are meant to function as periods, as signified by the capitalization of the first letter of the next word or placement at the end of a paragraph, are altered. Dashes that are more ambiguous in their usage are retained. Curly brackets are omitted when they are seemingly decorative in purpose and replaced by parentheses when serving the function of parentheses.

I distinguish between two kinds of references to individuals by initials. One method uses the initial alone or with a period; this usage is retained as it appears in the manuscripts. The second method uses an initial and follows it with punctuation varying from ellipses to multiple dashes or several underlined spaces. In these cases, no matter what the following punctuation, the form has been regularized to the initial and one underlined space (e.g., "H . . ." or "H — — —" becomes "H_"). When one underlined space follows something other than an initial, the text here follows the original manuscript.

Marginal insertions are presented at the ends of the letters. Their original placement is indicated in brackets preceding the note, which include the following abbreviations: "[LM 1]" for left margin of page 1; "[RM 2]" for right margin of page 2; "[M 3–4]" for the margin between pages 3 and 4, and so on. In letters only one page in length, no number is placed after the abbreviation for left or right margin. Occasionally, some additional descriptive note is made in the brackets, such as "[LM top half of page]" to further clarify placement.

The 16 August 1836 letter written by Elias Boudinot to Benjamin and Eleanor Gold represents a special case in the volume. The source text for this letter is "The Death of Harriet Gold Boudinot," a 1979 reprinting in the *Journal of Cherokee Studies* of an article originally printed as "Last Hours of Mrs. Boudinott" in the 26 November 1836 issue of the *New York Observer*. The article as printed in the *Journal of Cherokee Studies* is replete with errors. It is my belief that most of these are printers' errors, introduced either at the time of the original printing or at the time of the reprinting. Despite extensive searching, I have not been able to locate an extant copy of the *New York Observer* for this date and thus have not been able to determine whether the errors were present in the original printing. Nor have I recovered the manuscript letter. Because Elias Boudinot's letters typically contain very few spelling errors and because some of the errors in the *Journal* are misspellings of names very familiar to Elias Boudinot (e.g., Burrick for Butrick), it is unlikely that the errors originated in his letter. For this reason, I have silently corrected the many errors in this piece.

To Marry an Indian

Introduction

In 1825, Harriett Gold, the youngest daughter in a prominent white family in Cornwall, Connecticut, wrote a secret letter to her older brother. In a scene worthy of an epistolary novel, the nineteen-year-old revealed her plans to marry a Cherokee man, Elias Boudinot:

> She knew her brother Stephen would feel worse over her marriage than any one else; he was eighteen months older than she; what one knew the other knew. When she let him know it she wrote a letter saying "She was engaged to Boudinot." One evening they were as usual together in the parlor conversing when she handed him the letter; there were two doors; one she locked before they went in, she went out and locked the other, and gave the key to her mother, telling her not to let him out until he became quiet. He screamed and called Harriett, Harriett like a madman. She locked herself in her room upstairs and would not come out until he promised to behave.[1] (qtd. in Starr 156)

A few days later, in front of friends and neighbors on the village green, Stephen lit a fire that consumed his sister's effigy. He also wrote a letter of his own, announcing the engagement to his siblings in a nearby town and thereby initiating the remarkable epistolary exchange that is the subject of this book. His heavy, large script communicated his agitation as effectively as did the letter's content: "The dye is cast, Harriet is gone, we have reason to <u>fear</u>. Yes. She has told Mr Harvy that she was engaged to that Indian E. and that she is determined to marry him. O!! dear!!!" (letter to Herman and Flora Gold Vaill and Catharine Gold, 11 June 1825). Stephen's dramatic announcement of Harriett Gold's engagement to Elias Boudinot marks a significant moment in the Gold family history. In the months to follow, no fewer than ten members of the Gold family scattered across Connecticut wrote eloquent and passionate letters that document their responses — ranging from articulations of racist outrage to reasoned argumentation — to Harriett's decision "to marry an Indian." [2]

Yet the significance of these letters cannot be measured only by their importance to a particular family. The moment, the participants, the subject matter, and the form of the exchange all indicate this particular correspondence's significance in national, historical, and literary terms. Written during the 1820s and 1830s, decades when politicians, literati, and ordinary Americans debated the terms of the relationship of Native Americans and Euro-Americans in the United States, the letters engage with topics of pressing national concern. The primary actors in the letters, white Americans and Cherokees, duplicated prominent interests in the national debate as whites clamored for Cherokee lands and the Cherokees took their case to the Supreme Court. Indeed, one of the central correspondents, Harriett's fiancé, Elias Boudinot, became a nationally known political personage and remains one of the most complex figures of the period. An ardent opponent of removal who eventually signed the treaty that set in motion the events culminating in the Trail of Tears, Elias was also an accomplished author whose extensive writings have not yet received sustained critical attention. Interracial marriage, such as the one proposed between Harriett and Elias, had long had the potential to ignite firestorms of debate in U.S. society because of the ways it intimately tested boundaries of racial and national identity, but firsthand documentation of perspectives of the involved parties is rare. Carried out in letters, perhaps the most widely accessible and practiced literary form in the nineteenth century, this exchange offers unique insight into how ordinary Americans negotiated fraught racial terrains. Equally important, half of the correspondents taking part in the exchange were women, who engaged in serious debate with their male relatives.

This volume traces the narrative of Elias's and Harriett's marriage through a correspondence spanning more than a decade. The first section presents the letters circulated in Connecticut among Harriett and members of her extended family during the period they debated the implications of the betrothal for their community and family. The volume reflects significant gaps in the material record of this time; I have not recovered any letters from Elias recording his attitudes toward his engagement or any of the letters that passed between Elias and Harriett during their courtship. Yet the letters that do appear here force a critical reconsideration of the operation of gender and familial dynamics in correspondence and the complex network of attitudes toward miscegenation held by individuals in early nineteenth-century New England. The second section of this volume begins after the contested marriage has taken place and presents the letters that Harriett and Elias write from the Cherokee Nation, where they have made their residence, back to Harriett's relatives in Connecticut. In addition to the daily concerns of domestic and family life, the newly married pair write about their increasing embroilment in Cherokee politics, contributing to the documentary record of this significant period in Cherokee and U.S. history. Preserved by family members because of their sense of the larger significance of the correspondence, these letters speak to readers across the passage of time with immediacy and urgency. Stephen Gold ends his letter announcing the engagement with the words, "Words cannot, no. let imagination only express, the feelings of my heart" (letter to Herman and Flora Gold Vaill and Catharine Gold, 11 June 1825). The imaginative identification for which he pleads becomes the task of the modern reader who, through these letters, becomes privy to the story Stephen and his family unfold.

CONTEXTS

Harriett Gold, Elias Boudinot, and the Foreign Mission School
Harriett Ruggles Gold—the nineteen-year-old daughter of a respected white merchant-farmer of rural Connecticut—found herself in the unique position to become engaged to a Cherokee man through a confluence of several factors shaped by the history of Christian ef-

forts to convert American Indians. Central among these was the presence of the Foreign Mission School in Cornwall, Connecticut, the town in which Harriett and her family resided. In the late eighteenth and early nineteenth centuries, religious revivals and governmental policies that emphasized "civilizing" and assimilating Native Americans into mainstream American society combined to create an encouraging atmosphere for those working to convert native peoples to Christianity. Illustrating this trend, the American Board of Commissioners for Foreign Missions (ABCFM), an organization formed mainly of Congregationalists and Presbyterians, hoped to spread Christianity across North America and around the globe.[3]

Founded by the ABCFM in 1817, Cornwall's Foreign Mission School had as its goal the education of "heathen" youth who would later return to their native lands to act as missionaries. The presence of several Hawaiians in Connecticut, most famously Henry Opukahaia, whose pious life and death were memorialized in Edwin Dwight's *Memoirs of Henry Obookiah* (1819), gave rise to the idea of establishing such a school. In addition, the ABCFM was not blind to other benefits of establishing a mission school in New England: instead of educating the young men at multiple missionary schools in their native regions, they could be gathered in a cost-efficient manner at one "central station" with ready access to books, lodging, and teachers (Harvey 22). As important, the young men would be removed from contact with their "pagan customs" and exposed to the civilized behavior of whites (Harvey 23). As one supporter explained, "A more thorough education may certainly be given to young heathen in such a school than in one instituted by missionaries in foreign lands; heathen youths may be more completely civilized, more thoroughly christianized, and their hearts more entirely won over to the Missionary cause; they may be made more efficient and more trustworthy aids in this great work of christian love" ("Journey" 464). The ABCFM settled on Cornwall, located in the northwestern part of Connecticut and with a population of around sixteen hundred in 1820 (Starr 62), as the most suitable place for the school because of both its isolated location and its representativeness as a typical American village of the time (Andrew 332–33). Over the school's nine years of operation, approximately one hundred students matriculated, most of whom were American Indian, though some white American students intent on becoming missionaries and students from such far-flung places as China, Greece, India, Java, the Marquesas Islands, New Zealand, and Tahiti also received educations there.[4]

Harriett Gold was the youngest daughter in a large family involved with and committed to the Foreign Mission School. Her sister Mary was married to an agent of the school, Daniel Brinsmade; the assistant principal, Herman Vaill, courted and married another of Harriett's sisters, Flora; and her father, Benjamin, was a staunch supporter.[5] Harriett herself attended the inauguration of the school's principal, counted among her good friends a white student at the school who later became assistant principal, and interacted with the visitors to the school whom her family hosted in their home.[6] As a pious young woman concerned with mission efforts and education, Harriett had ample opportunities to become acquainted with Foreign Mission School scholars.

Numerous among the American Indian students enrolled at the school were Cherokees, who hailed from Moravian and ABCFM mission schools in the Cherokee Nation. The embracing of the idea of education by some Cherokees was part of the larger cultural transformation the Cherokees experienced during the first half of the nineteenth century. Because of the effects of disease, war, and contact with Europeans and, later, Americans, the Cherokees' matrilineal, clan-based social structures increasingly eroded, upsetting the traditional gendered balances achieved through male engagement in hunting and warfare and female responsibilities for agriculture and domestic management. Exposure to Europeans' trading economy and the effects of George Washington's civilizing program resulted in profound changes in Cherokee life.[7] As William G. McLoughlin summarizes, "Each new generation—that born in 1789, in 1810, in 1831— grew up in a different order of relationships to nature, to one another, to the whiteman. First the communal villages broke up; then the clan ties waned; the family structure altered, and a new ethic of competition, hard work, barter, and trade for profit compelled a new orientation" (*Cherokees* 333).

Elias Boudinot's life exemplifies many of those changes.[8] Known during childhood by the name "Gallegina" or Buck, he was born around 1804 to Oo-Watie, also known as David Watie, and Susanna Reese at Oothcaloga in northwestern Georgia. His father and his father's brother, a Cherokee leader known as "The Ridge" or "Major Ridge," had established independent homesteads there in the wake of the Revolutionary War's decimation of traditional Cherokee towns. As Theda Perdue observes, Buck Watie's and his siblings' use of their father's surname and their close familial association with their father's brother and his family indicate the diminishing influence of matrilineality and an emergent patriarchalism that informed the child's earliest years (*Cherokee Editor* 5). Educated at mission schools from the age of six onward, Buck bonded closely with his educators (Wilkins 103), distinguished himself in his studies, and departed for Cornwall. On his way to the school, he visited a prominent benefactor of the Foreign Mission School, the elderly New Jersey statesman and philanthropist Elias Stockton Boudinot, and assumed his name in a common practice (Perdue, *Cherokee Editor* 3–6). After enrolling at the Foreign Mission School in 1818, he was viewed as one of the most promising scholars. Adam Hodgson, an English visitor to the school in 1821, reported that "[t]he principal of the school told me that Kalle-ga-nah had gone through a course of history, geography, and surveying, had read some books of Virgil, and was then engaged in studying Enfield's Philosophy; over which, indeed, I afterwards found him when I visited the school. I also saw his trigonometrical copy-books" (246). Another visitor to the school remarked that Elias, along with the other Cherokee students, "would have done credit to the best white young men of their age." Furthermore, the writer reported of a school examination, "Elias Boudinot, in a declamation, confuted the idea more completely by his appearance than his arguments, that savages are not capable of being civilized and polished" (qtd. in Perdue, *Cherokee Editor* 8). His educators published his letters in religious periodicals and sent his proof of a lunar eclipse to Jedediah Morse, geographer at Yale (Perdue, *Cherokee Editor* 6).

Elias and other students at the Foreign Mission School adhered to a rigorous schedule of study and agricultural work intended to accustom them, according to the school's principal, to "habits of industry" and other valued American traits. Though their movement through the town was restricted, it nevertheless was the intention of the school's administrators that students should have contact with Cornwall inhabitants.[9] The principal argued that "[i]t is highly important that at least some of the heathen youth . . . should be introduced into such society and educated in it; that they may see the operation of principles which they are expected to inculcate. We can never make skillful practitioners by mere theory. The keen eye of curiousity will mark many facts respecting social life." In particular, "[t]he situation and character of females in Christian society, is one important point of distinction between that and the society of heathen," and therefore the principal promoted students' exposure to white women as a means of acquiring the values of civilization (Harvey 23–24).

Within this latter point resides the contradiction that eventually destroyed the Foreign Mission School and revealed the notions of benevolence undergirding it as flawed. In her study of antebellum benevolence, Susan Ryan explains that while sentimental identification relies on a perceived similarity with the object of sympathy, benevolence conversely depends on "distancing rhetorics." In any interactions between benevolent donors and needy recipients—such as those occurring between Cornwall citizens and the Foreign Mission School scholars, most of whom were supported by Christian donations—"there had to be a concomitant recognition of difference, something that made one social actor the helper and the other a proper recipient of that help." An elision of that sense of difference would result in "a degree of social leveling that most donors would have resisted." As Ryan writes, "The simultaneous erasure and persistence of difference facilitates both the sentimental bond that creates the desire to give and the maintenance of hierarchy that suggests that such giving is safe, that it does not threaten the identity or status of the giver, that it does not, ultimately, make helper and helped the same" (19). Indeed, the relationships that would soon develop between two of the scholars and two local young women would dramatically upend the hierarchies and dissipate the differences upon which the structure of benevolence relied.

The Northrop-Ridge Marriage

Elias concluded his studies at Cornwall in 1822, when ill health forced his return to the Cherokee Nation, ending his hopes of studying theology at the Andover Theological Institute (Perdue, *Cherokee Editor* 8). After he left town, Elias and Harriett began to correspond, and their courtship progressed entirely through the exchange of letters, which I have not recovered. In the meantime, the marriage of another Foreign Mission School scholar to a white woman revealed local resistance to racial intermarriage. John Ridge, Elias's first cousin and son of Major Ridge, also attended the Foreign Mission School. While a student there, Ridge experienced an intensifying of a chronic hip condition and was sent to the home of the school's steward, John Northrop, to be nursed. In the course of his two-year convalescence there, Ridge and the Northrops' daughter Sarah requested permission to marry. The marriage eventually took place with her parents' permission in January 1824, and Northrop returned with Ridge to his home in the Cherokee Nation, where he went on to become a prominent political figure and wealthy plantation owner.[10]

News of the Northrop-Ridge marriage spread beyond the local community and reached the ears of a newspaper editor who had long been critical of missionary efforts. Isaiah Bunce, editor of the *American Eagle*, printed in nearby Litchfield, was quick to print harsh criticisms of the marriage that were laced through with racial bigotry. In an editorial printed in January 1824, after emphasizing the "affliction, mortification and disgrace, of the relatives of the young woman, who is only about sixteen years old," Bunce reflects that "[t]o have her thus marry an Indian and taken into the wilderness among savages, must indeed be a heart rending pan[g] which none can realize except those called to feel it." He declines to name the Northrops or "her who has thus made herself a *squaw*, and connected her ancestors to a race of Indians." But in a move contrary to much public conjecture on the pecuniary motives of her mother in the marriage, Bunce attributes its cause to "the fruit of the *missionary spirit*, and caused by the conduct of the clergymen at that place and its vicinity, who are agents and superintend the school." Though he "shrink[s] from recording the name of the female thus throwing herself into the arms of an Indian," he lists the agents of the school by name. His final indictment is direct: "And the relatives of the girl, or the people of Cornwall, or the public at large, who feel indignant at the transaction, some of whom have said that the girl ought to be publicly whipped, the Indian hung, and the mother drown'd, will do well to trace the thing to its true cause, and see whether the men above named, or their system, are not the authors of the transaction as a new kind of *missionary machinery*" (qtd. in Gabriel 61–62; italics in the original). In an article appended to a March reprinting of the above article, Bunce details more improprieties he believed were occurring in Cornwall:

> Have not the females in that place been seen to ride and walk out with them [the pupils of the Mission School] arm in arm, by night and by day—spend evenings with them—invite them to tea-parties —correspond with them by letters—and this by some who there called themselves the first, in short receiving them as the most favored gallants, and beaux, and the topknot of gentry; while the young men of the town, poor white boys, were often cast into the shade by their colored and tawny rivals? And this is known to more or less of the above named clergy and guardians of the school. . . . A gentleman from there since this took place, informs us that three other marriages with these natives, were supposed to be in treaty. (qtd. in Gabriel 62–63)

Ryan's consideration of the antebellum "culture of benevolence" helps to explain the vehemence of Bunce's attacks and the community's response to the marriage. The interactions that Bunce criticizes in Cornwall—the socializing and courting behaviors and particularly the act of walking "arm in arm" with its associations of intimacy and equality—do not correctly manifest the "recognition of difference" that Ryan describes as constitutive of benevolence (19). For this reason, these actions become threatening to the townspeople of Cornwall for the ways they upset what are perceived as rightful race and class hierarchies, since at this time in New England, Native Americans generally functioned as a dispossessed and servile underclass, which was hardly "the topknot of gentry" (Plane 148).[11]

Bunce's attacks were soon answered by a variety of people connected with the Foreign Mission School. The young white men of Cornwall formed an organization called the Bachelors of "Cornwall Valley" and wrote a letter to the editor in which they "spurn[ed] at the intimation that we have been cast into the shade, by our rivals, white or tawny" (qtd. in Gabriel 64). Timothy Stone, the minister of the local Congregational church and an agent of the school, submitted the Foreign Mission School's quarterly report to the *New Haven Register*. It was printed in that paper on 22 May 1824 and reprinted with additional comments in Bunce's paper on 31 May. The report denied the "malicious report" circulating in the newspapers:

> *Whatever may be our opinion* concerning such a connexion—the authority of the school should be wholly exempted from blame. Also the people of this village are to be entirely exonerated. Not a solitary instance is known of a female of Cornwall, who has been seen walking with a foreign scholar ("arm in arm") as it has been reported. It is true, our females are friends to the missionary cause; and these strangers are treated with civility and kindness, and deserve their esteem, as many of them are amiable and pious. But as for the repetition of the event, which gave occasion to so much slander, there is not as we believe, any distant prospect. ("Cornwall School" 1–2; italics in the original)

In addition, seven prominent men of Cornwall, including Harriett's father, Benjamin Gold, signed a letter they sent to Bunce in which they disputed his charges. Based on their proximity to and familiarity with the school and their standing in the community, the men stated that they "fully believe that such assertions as have appeared in your paper upon this subject are not *facts*; we deny that they are facts; and, in our turn, assert that they are *base fabrication*," and they challenged Bunce to publicly name his sources (qtd. in Gabriel 65; italics in the original). Bunce never printed the letter in his paper, though it ran in the *Connecticut Journal* on 10 August 1824.

Racial Attitudes in Connecticut

Two centuries of antimiscegenation sentiment in New England conditioned the sentiments of those who opposed the Northrop-

Ridge marriage. While white-Indian relationships and marriages had been a by-product of colonialism in New England since the beginning of European settlement, "powerful cultural and social sanctions worked against" such marriages, writes Ann Marie Plane in her extensive study of Indian marriage in the colonial period (146). Biblical prohibitions against marriage to non-Christians and aversion to the supposed barbarism of Native Americans made early settlers hesitant to enter into interracial marriages (Godbeer 92). As Richard Godbeer explains, "Any English man or woman who became sexually intimate with an Indian was liable to stigmatization as 'debased' or 'defiled'" (93). By the early nineteenth century, the increasing reliance on biological notions of race had rendered the idea of interracial sexual contact unnatural and repugnant. The publicity that resulted in 1802–3 when news of Thomas Jefferson's relationship with Sally Hemings became fodder for his political enemies, for example, emphasized the supposed perversity of sexually desiring a person of another race (Lemire 29).

In a striking manner, the gender configuration of the typical interracial coupling was reversed in the Northrop-Ridge union; rather than a white man initiating relations with a native woman, a white woman chose to marry a native man. While the white man/native woman relationship was consonant with the impetus of colonization, the converse posed an almost unrecoverable threat. Because of the ways that discourses of white superiority described racial identity in relation to gender roles, the status of white women functioned to stabilize whiteness as a racial identity. Only if white men preserved an ideal of themselves as elevating, idealizing, and protecting white women could those same men know themselves as belonging to the "superior" race. This identity relied on a contrast with native men, whom whites stereotyped as brutal and uncaring toward their wives, while native women, in contrast to white women, were viewed as degraded and virtually enslaved by their husbands, doomed to lives of unending labor. These conceptions had much to do with misunderstandings of the gendered division of labor, especially agricultural labor, in Native American societies, but they were highly influential among whites (Wallace 48). That a white woman would forsake her racial identity and choose to subject herself to an inferior man seemed apostasy of the highest degree.[12]

Two poetic effusions inspired by the Northrop-Ridge match give voice to racial attitudes in Cornwall.[13] Silas Hurlbut McAlpine's poem "To the Indians of Cornwall" presents the attempt of a Native American man to persuade a white woman to accompany him to his home and "[w]ith me my Indian blanket share." Replete with stock images of Native Americans as unsophisticated inhabitants of the forest and roaming hunters, the poem achieves its effect through the juxtaposition of the romanticized plea of the speaker with the titillating yet shocking references to interracial sexual intimacy. At exactly the halfway point of the poem, in the line which is the visual center of the poem on the page, an image of the native's arms "twin[ing]" around a white woman predominates; the repeated references to her whiteness in the earlier lines of the poem serve to create a visual image of dark-skinned arms twisting around — in passion but perhaps also with force — the "white girl fair." The poem, then, simultaneously taps into contradictory cultural anxieties that white women might feel sexual fascination for native men and that native men might sexually threaten white women, anxieties present in the captivity narrative tradition on which this poem relies.[14] The poet heightens the color imagery emphasized in the couple's embrace by highlighting in the next lines the Native American's "olive skin" and the girl's "lily" complexion. Here the poem registers the cultural shift occurring in theories of racial identity during the first half of the nineteenth century. The first stanza of the poem dwells on the cultural signifiers of Indianness — the "Indian blanket," the "bark canoe," the forest habitation — and is in line with theories of race, most prominent in eighteenth-century thinking, that focused on the environmental and cultural origins of racial identity. The second stanza's emphasis on skin color and the primitive ambivalence, part horror and part fascination, of interracial sexual contact voiced in a line alluding to the "colors mingled" in the couple's offspring brings into play emergent pseudoscientific discourses which biologized racial difference and which were beginning to circulate in U.S. culture by the 1820s, gaining full dominance by midcentury.[15]

Another poem achieved "considerable local fame" (Gold 32) at the time and entered into the folkloric memory of Cornwall (Gabriel 181). Written by Emily Fox of Cornwall, "The Indian Song, Sarah and John" depicts the romance of Northrop and Ridge. Ridiculing Northrop's purportedly elevated and mercenary notions of the "splendor" she would experience in the Cherokee Nation, the poem claims that Northrop would discover that life as John Ridge's wife would "sink her pride—'twould raise her shame," when she discovered that her destiny was to follow her husband on the hunt, carrying his game, while clothed in a "dirty blanket" and surrounded by "a savage whooping throng." This poem dwells less than the last on skin color, yet there is still a clear sense of racial hierarchy in place, particularly articulated through cultural and class differences. The poem ends with a caution to "young maids" to "take care / How Indians draw you into a snare." In its cautionary and punitive tone, it, like the last poem, performs the function described by Elise Lemire, who argues that writings about miscegenation tended to police the very boundaries of race that they were simultaneously creating (3). The final stanzas resonate with "a dreadful, doleful sound" representing the echoing tones of village gossip, which functions in the poem as a mechanism designed to control and punish transgressive behavior. As an interesting side note, the poem mentions by name Harriett's brother-in-law Herman Vaill as publishing the banns for the marriage and her father, Benjamin Gold, who "did them wait upon, / He waited on them most genteel too, / And seated them in his own pew." These references suggest that Herman and Benjamin had taken public stands to support Northrop and Ridge, a fact that would increase pressure on them when a member of their own family declared her engagement to a Native American.

The Gold-Boudinot Engagement

Harriett's announcement of her engagement to Elias followed the Northrop-Ridge controversy by almost exactly a year. Given the public humiliation the town and school had suffered at Bunce's pen and the school's agents' repeated assertions that another such marriage would not take place, it is perhaps no surprise that Harriett and Elias's plans for marriage would provoke a much more intense reaction. Within a week, in June 1825, the agents of the Foreign Mission School published a report in which they identified Harriett and Elias by name, proclaimed their "unequivocal disapprobation of *such connexions*," and branded "the conduct of those who have been engaged in or accessory to this transaction, as criminal; as offering an insult to the known feelings of the christian community: and as sporting with the sacred interests of this charitable institution" ("Foreign Mission School" 6; italics in the original). A few days later, Harriett's brother Stephen and the young people of the town gathered on the village green and burned images of Harriett and Elias in effigy, a scene Harriett witnessed from a neighbor's home where she had been secreted for her own safety. The humiliations continued: Stephen made threats against Elias's life, the minister's wife prevented Harriett from sitting with the young women's choir at worship services, and the minister canceled communion for the congregation.[16]

As in the case of the Northrop-Ridge marriage, the Gold-Boudinot engagement caught the eye of newspaper editors. Locally, Bunce renewed his verbal assaults, printing an article emphasizing the respectability of the Gold family and individually naming all Harriett's brothers and brothers-in-law, several of whom were ministers or prominent figures.[17] Papers as far away as Boston and Providence also picked up the story. One article proclaimed: "It appears that the *orthodox fair ones*, at Cornwall, have an overweening attachment to the *Indian dandies*, educated at that Mission School. Their love-smitten hearts are probably overcome by the *celestial charms*, which their *spiritual eyes* discover in those tawny sons of the forest; and in a *divine hallucination*, they calculate on pure, unearthly joys, in the *sanctified objects* of their choice" ("Cornwall Mission School" 383; italics in the original). As in Bunce's attacks on the Northrop-Ridge marriage, the writer in his ironic use of religious language critiques the mission project represented by the school. The proliferation of italicized words in the passage suggests how the idea of such an intermarriage seemed to exceed language's ability to express the antipathy it generated. In contrast, a more moderate editor wrote:

Why so much *sensibility* about an event of this sort? A gentleman who was thought fit, by many thousands of people, for the office of president, openly and frankly recommended an incorporation of the Indian race with the citizens of the United States, by intermarriages. . . . The proudest man, perhaps, in America, and as great a stickler for *dignity* as can be met with, boasts of the Indian blood in his veins. But the rev. doctor, who is at the head of the school, rudely exposes the name of the young lady who had found pleasure in the society of an Indian youth, and makes the affair "criminal." It is a strange world. If the persons are free to do as they please . . . we do not see why this fuss is made about them. (qtd. in Wilkins 151; italics in the original)

The writer here refers to eighteenth-century politicians' recommendation of intermarriage as a means to assimilate American Indians into American society. Nonetheless, the editor's naïve pose is striking; intermarriage had largely been rejected as a solution to the "Indian question" by this time, and ever greater focus on the biological differences between races would render it an increasingly repugnant option to most white Americans.

Cherokee Reactions to the Intermarriages

In contrast to the antimiscegenation sentiment cherished by many in Connecticut, attitudes among Cherokees toward interracial relationships had little to do with notions of racial or sexual purity. Unmarried individuals had greater freedom in sexual experimentation, and Cherokee women sometimes entered without social stigma into liaisons with white traders and adventurers for complex reasons having to do with politics and trade as well as desire and emotion. The matrilineal focus of Cherokee society ensured that the children of such unions would be incorporated into their mothers' clan, thereby minimizing any social disruption caused by these relationships.[18] The arrival of white missionaries in the Cherokee Nation provided new prospective mates, and missionary men married Cherokee women without commentary either from Cherokees or from the northern organizations sponsoring the missionaries (Wilkins 151). One hundred forty-seven white men were residents in the Cherokee Nation because of marriages to Cherokee women, according to statements made by John Ridge in 1826 (34). What seemed so shocking to white northerners, then, was not uncommon practice in the Cherokee Nation.

The reversal of gender in the pairing of white woman and native man did, however, provoke additional concerns in Cherokee culture, much as it did in white society, though for quite different reasons. Cherokees did not recognize as Cherokee children born of mothers who were not Cherokee. Because Cherokees traced family relationships through the mother's line, the children resulting from unions between Cherokee men and non-Cherokee women had no clan affiliations and thus no standing within the nation. The Cherokees addressed this situation by writing a law in 1825 that granted citizenship to children of Cherokee men and white women (Perdue, *Cherokee Women* 147). Clearly, the 1825 date of the passage of this law is not coincidental, following as it does in the wake of the Northrop-Ridge marriage and the announcement of the Gold-Boudinot engagement. While the legislation of these children into citizenship may seem a practical answer to a social conundrum, the ramifications of such an action were great. In undercutting long-standing traditions of matrilineality and thereby fundamentally disrupting the social order, the new law sanctioned the formation of patriarchal family units sundered from larger clan groupings.

Those in the Cherokee Nation who heard of the events in Cornwall following the announcement of Harriett and Elias's engagement displayed reactions ranging from amusement to outrage. Sarah Northrop Ridge, for one, "could not help laughing to think how foolish they [the citizens of Cornwall] act," reported Jeremiah Evarts, corresponding secretary of the ABCFM, in April 1826 (letter to Henry Hill). "Affairs in Connecticut relative to Boudinot's marriage have very much excited the minds of the Cherokees," wrote one missionary (qtd. in McLoughlin, *Cherokees* 189). David Brown, a Cherokee who had also attended the Cornwall school, wrote Evarts a lengthy and reasoned letter setting out the Cherokees' response. He reports that the Cherokees had heard about the threats made against Elias's life, the agents' public excoriation of Elias and Harriett, and the burning of the effigies, which the Cherokees interpreted as "an expression of abhorrence to the Indian character." He writes:

These things are the common topics of conversation among us & we know not how to understand them. Your missionaries have told us that the people of New England were our firm friends & that we might at all times lean on them for assistance; & we have felt peculiarly greatful for their kind offices. But you will not be supprized to hear that our confidence is now somewhat shaken. We are necessarily led to inquire, whether our friends in New England have always acted from love to us & a desire to do us good. If they loved us how could they treat us in this manner. They can not suppose it wicked for white people to marry Cherokees, because members of Baptists, Methodist & Presbeterian churches have married Cherokee ladies without censure. If white men may marry among us without offence, how can it be thought wicked for us to marry among them; especially if some of our white sisters are pleased with such connexions. Do our beloved friends in Connecticut say that such marriages will cast an indelible stain on their characters & be a reproach to their state? But if they loved us, won't they not be willing to stoop down & take a part of our reproach rather than add to the enormous weight under which we have so long been lying? If one of their dearest daughters should come & place herself on an equality with us in order to promote our eternal good, would she exercise greater condescension than our divine Redeemer did when he left the regions of bliss & came into our wicked world to seek a bride from among the apostate children of Adam? If our dear friends in New England loved us how could they treat us in this cold & unfeeling manner, especially at such a time as this when more than ever we need their prayers & increased exertions?

The sense of betrayal Brown articulates—the realization that Christian principles only thinly cover over firmly entrenched racism—had large-scale consequences for the relationship between Cherokees and missionaries. Historian William McLoughlin argues that the betrayal the Cherokees felt because of missionaries' reactions to the two intermarriages was a significant factor in increasing antimission sentiment and fomenting key transformations in Cherokee politics during the period 1821–27 (*Cherokees* 187–89).

Some missionaries in the Cherokee Nation shared the Cherokees' confusion and sense of betrayal. In his April 1826 letter, Evarts reports that John Gambold, a much respected Moravian missionary who had been Elias's first teacher, "was astonished that gentlemen of intelligence, the professed friends of the Indians, should have opposed a connexion with Boudinot on the single ground that he is an Indian." The ABCFM missionary Daniel S. Butrick wrote a long and passionate letter to Evarts in March 1826, in his hyperbole eschewing Brown's restraint:

> We understand that it is now stated in letters from the North, that if our dear br. Boudinot should appear in Cornwall, half the state would rise against him; and that his life would be in danger. Half the State Rise against him? that polished, that pious, that holy state? that state which gave birth, almost, to disinterested affection? that state which has so long, with a profuse hand, been throwing blessings to the ends of the earth? Rise against him? What! against our dear brother Boudinot? against the son of their own bowels? whom, by their prayers, and tears, and pains, they have brought forth into immortal glory? whom they have dandled on the lap of fond affection, and raised to an equality with the polished sons of Europe? whose learning, wisdom, virtue, & honour, deservedly place him in the first circles of civilized life? Half the state rise against our dear brother Boudinot? Even the heathen world blushes, and humanity sickens at the thought. (emphasis in the original)

In this passage, Butrick pinpoints the inconsistency—promising and then denying the rewards of civilized life to those who worked to assume its values—that would become glaringly apparent in the Cherokees' interactions with the U.S. government in the decade to come. Yet, at this moment, Butrick's concern is more immediately focused on the young men who were the potential victims of white racism; in a November 1824 letter written to Evarts in the wake of the Northrop-

Ridge marriage, he had criticized how the school in Cornwall had "plac[ed] the Cherokee youth in a very delicate situation. They must not look at a young woman, lest they should conceive an affection for her which could never be gratified, & might render them miserable through life. They must be viewed with suspicion & as a grade of inferior beings." After years of striving to articulate an egalitarian vision of Christianity and U.S. society to Cherokee converts, missionaries such as Butrick found their work undone (Andrew 339). The disillusionment some Cherokees felt had at least one concrete result: Evarts wrote in February 1826 that Elias reported "that the Cherokees will not send any youths to the school."

Elias Boudinot's Crisis

Of the reactions of the young man who did indeed find himself in the "delicate situation" Butrick described, we have little knowledge. Because his letters of this period have not been recovered, the only clues to Elias's reaction to events in Cornwall emerge in the correspondence of the missionaries who knew him. In his March 1826 letter to Evarts, Butrick describes Elias as having been "in great trouble" during the winter of 1825–26. In a December 1825 letter to Evarts, Butrick confessed to being aware of reports circulating that Boudinot had been accused of "attending a ball play on the Sabbath." Ball plays were a traditional Cherokee sport combining preparation for battle with ritual. Because at ball plays "the players are literally *naked* and yet a large proportion of the spectators are females" (qtd. in McLoughlin, *Cherokees* 208), missionaries were appalled and sought to prohibit recent converts from participating or attending. Elias's behavior thus incited questions about his Christian standing. In his 1825 letter, Butrick sympathetically accounted for Elias's act in his characteristically dramatic manner; Elias, he writes, had been distracted by the "the shameless conduct of the citizens of Cornwall, & the cruel treatment he had received from those who would claim to be his spiritual fathers. . . . [T]he smoke of his burning effigy, driven by the fiercest northern blast, had, for a moment, darkened his eyes, & occasioned this fall from which he would arise as soon as he had time for deliberate reflection."

Jeremiah Evarts discussed the issue with Elias, and his letter written in February 1826 reporting the conversation is one of the more detailed descriptions of Elias's state of mind during this time:

> Conversed at considerable length with Boudinot. He admitted that, being at the mineral spring, about 20 miles from his father's, he went out about a quarter of a mile and witnessed a ball play on the Sabbath. He had no thought of attending when he left his father's, (probably he did not know that there was to be a ball play,) nor did he go out because he expected to derive any pleasure from being present. He had no distinct object in view. He was very wretched, & did not care what became of him. It was just after he had heard of Cornwall himself, & had received anonymous letters, filled with the most [illegible] abuse, and threatening his life. He had never done such a thing before; and does not justify or excuse himself now. He only states the facts.

Evarts's revealing description of Elias's "wretched" state suggests that this young man, only around twenty-one years old, faced a significant dilemma. In his refusal to "justify" or "excuse himself," Elias rejects the missionaries' interpretation of his attendance at the ball play as a "fall" (Daniel Butrick to Jeremiah Evarts, 13 December 1825) or a "temptation" (Samuel Worcester to Rufus Anderson, 22 December 1825). Yet the absence of the structuring framework of Christian missionary attitudes to direct his actions leaves him, according to Evarts's description, with "no distinct object in view." Hilary Wyss's analysis of Native American converts is helpful in understanding the quandary Elias faced in positioning himself in relation to Cherokee and Christian belief systems. She argues that native converts crafted identities that "were neither strictly 'Native' or purely assimilationist but rather a hybrid of Anglo-American and indigenous cultures." The writings of such converts, according to Wyss, reveal the complex negotiations they enacted as they created identities that "marked them as different from missionaries as well as from other native Americans" (6). From all outward appearances, it would seem that until this point in his life, Elias had directed his energies exclusively toward differentiating himself from other Cherokees through his academic strivings, conversion to Christianity, and close association and identification with missionaries. Indeed, Theda Perdue, in her biographical interpretation of Elias's life, assigns him a wholly assimilated identity, arguing that "so completely did he embrace the tenets of Western culture that he seems to have accepted the dominant white attitudes toward Indians" (*Cherokee Editor* 10). Yet the opposition to his proposed marriage perhaps led him for the first time to differentiate himself from the Christians whom he had heretofore emulated. Knowingly disobeying missionaries' directives, Elias asserted his Cherokee identity by attending the ball play and refusing to apologize for it. Yet he nonetheless remains sundered from the Cherokees who participated in the ceremonial sport, a "witness" rather than a participant. Taking no enjoyment from the event that would temporarily drive a wedge between him and his Christian mentors, he could summon no concern over his own fate, torn as he was at this moment between two cultures and two destinies.

Being thwarted in love has been known to drive more than one heartsick youth to drastic actions, yet Elias's personal crisis had dimensions that were both personal and cultural. For this young Cherokee—eager, talented, ambitious, and rapidly distinguishing himself as part of an emerging biracial Cherokee elite—what could better prove his thorough inculcation of mainstream American values than to take a white, northern, Christian wife? If "the explicit purpose of much antebellum benevolence is the elevation of the helped, the reformation (not surprisingly) in the image of their benefactors," as Ryan claims (19), then Elias's engagement to Harriett marked the full culmination of this project in his life. But the reformers who educated Elias now insisted on the maintenance of the distance Ryan also describes as central to the exercise of benevolence (19); Elias's former teacher and Harriett's brother-in-law, Herman Vaill, a man fully committed to the ideals of missionary work, commented in outrage, "[T]o prove himself thus grateful to his friends, & faithful to Christ, it is not necessary that he should marry a white woman" (letter to Harriett Gold, 29 June 1825).

Yet it was necessary in ways that Herman did not and Elias perhaps only subconsciously understood. To fully become what the missionaries attempted to make him, Elias needed to take the final step: to anchor his domestic life fully in Western traditions of patriarchy by rejecting the matrilineal foundations of Cherokee life to become a Christian patriarch. Marriage to Harriett Gold would accomplish that in ways that marriage to a Cherokee woman, accustomed to the domestic and cultural power accorded her by matrilineality, would not. Yet his desire to carry out the act that would fully unite him with missionary and Western values also brought home to Elias in a potentially life-threatening manner the workings of the white racism that forever excluded him from that role. According to Perdue, the events that occurred in Cornwall profoundly changed Elias's worldview. His optimism that education and Christian conversion could result in equality between whites and American Indians dissipated; as she writes, "he found himself treated as an outcast by the very people he had tried to emulate." Because of the episode, he eventually came to a changed understanding of how Cherokees would function in relation to American society. Rather than unquestioningly accepting assimilation, Elias began to exhibit "racial consciousness" and envisioned the Cherokees as "develop[ing] their own separate 'civilized' institutions" distinct from white society. Perdue concludes that the discrimination he faced in carrying out his marriage led to a "resistance to the absorption of the Cherokees into white society [which] probably stemmed from a belief that Indians and whites could never be equals. At very least, Elias's encounter with . . . white racism reduced to an afterthought the idea of Indian assimilation" (*Cherokee Editor* 10–11).

Elias emerged from the momentary vacillation produced by this crisis with his determination unchecked and his goals clear. He would claim his wife and, if not fully reject, at least carefully distance himself from missionary efforts to control his life and, later, his work. Missionary Samuel A. Worcester, with whom Elias would forge a lasting working relationship and friendship, reported in December 1825 that Elias "will visit Cornwall and, I presume, does not intend to leave it without a wife" (letter to Rufus Anderson). Evarts further reported in February 1826 that Elias wrote an angry letter to Rev. Timothy Stone, which he wanted published, in which he "insisted on a public recantation of the letter of the agents [of the Foreign Mission School], so far as it inculpated him, or that they should prove that his conduct was criminal." He also "disclaimed any authority of the agents" over his choices or behavior (letter to Henry Hill).

CONNECTICUT LETTERS

Genre and Material Forms

Though Gold family members did not enter the extensive public discussion of the proposed marriage through publication, they did debate the issues surrounding the engagement in a series of letters. Following Stephen's announcement and the agents' public report condemning Harriett and Elias as "criminal," members of Harriett's extended family took up their pens and composed a flurry of thoughtful, sometimes passionate, and often eloquent letters to each other on what they soon came to call "the subject," a topic and discussion so momentous it needed no other name (Mary Gold Brinsmade to Herman and Flora Gold Vaill and Catharine Gold, 14 July 1825; Herman Vaill to Mary Gold Brinsmade, 2 August 1825). Indeed, this is a story of letters as much as human interests; letters were important players in the progression of events. The body of letters presented in this book reanimates a significant epistolary exchange that broadens current understandings of the letter's form, materiality, and cultural function.

Although critics have long approached the epistolary novel as an important genre, the epistle itself has waited until relatively recently for scholarly consideration.[19] Scholars of the past tended to view letters primarily as historical documents or tools revealing the characters of prominent personages (Decker 28), and the letters contained here do reveal much about racial intermarriage, Cherokees' resistance to removal, and Elias Boudinot as a man, author, and political figure. Ralph Henry Gabriel's *Elias Boudinot, Cherokee, and His America* (1941) exemplifies this use of the correspondence. Gabriel extensively quotes many of the letters collected in this volume, using them to piece together and vivify a portrait of Elias's life and times.[20] Today, critics increasingly accord letters a literary status, often independent of the reputation or importance of their authors, by considering them in relation to other forms of life-writing, the genres of which have lately experienced a surge in critical interest.[21] Even more than formal auto-biography, letters are quite possibly the literary genre that has been accessed by the most wide-ranging cross section of American society (Decker 60). As such, letters are uniquely situated to offer insight to scholars who are interested in the writings of members of marginal-ized groups who have had unequal access to more elite literary forms.

The endurance over time of particular conventions—such as date, salutation, conventional phrasings, and closing—identifies the let-ter as a recognizable genre (Decker 22). Yet letters' malleability ren-ders them flexible in accord with writers' and readers' varying and sometimes contradictory uses and interpretations.[22] Indeed, as multi-authorial, intertextual documents that resist closure of form and ad-dress multiple audiences, letters test the very boundaries of generic definition. Consequently, they pose a somewhat daunting critical task, "demand[ing] multiple frames" of interpretation (Gerber 42). As Toby Ditz explains, correspondents write "within the matrix of possibili-ties and constraints posed by the genre and narrative conventions, symbolic repertoires, discourses, and vocabularies that they mobil-ised and reworked in their letters" (62). The letters in the Gold corre-spondence reveal this matrix in complex ways. Multiple authors some-times contribute to the letters' composition in overt ways, such as when two writers divide the space of the letter or when a second writer adds a postscript or marginal insertion. At other times, corporate au-thorship is less obvious but still operant, such as when letters reveal that other family members had input into or helped to revise earlier ones or when writers incorporate others' sentiments by introducing them with devices such as "Mother says to tell you. . . ." The audience of the Gold letters is almost always multiple and extends beyond the formally named addressee—often male—to wives, sisters, and other relatives residing in the same household or beyond. The Gold letters reveal their intertextuality in their reliance on an often-dense layering of biblical passages, hymn lyrics, sermons, and quotations from con-temporary politicians. They resist the closure of the sign-off through the layering of postscripts, sometimes five or six deep, sometimes by different authors, and through the marginal writings that wind down the sides of the pages.

One significant moment in the Gold exchange reveals the importance of these characteristics and how the mishandling or misinterpretation of any or all of them could result in a breakdown of communication. Harriett's mother, Eleanor, sixty years old and the mother of fourteen children, became angry at the tone and opinions her minister son-in-law Herman Vaill expressed in a lengthy letter to Harriett written on 29 June 1825. Another son-in-law reports, "Mother said you had sent up one of your old sermons but she was glad you had paid the postage for it was not worth reading" (Daniel Brinsmade to Herman and Flora Gold Vaill and Catharine Gold, 14 July 1825). Here is an illustration of the multivoiced character of letters. A woman who writes no letters of her own in the exchange nevertheless voices her opinions through the retelling of a correspondent. She is responding to a letter written to her daughter, demonstrating the multiple audiences the letter reached, as does the correspondent's own apparent knowledge of the letter's content. The comment emphasizes the letter's overlap with the genre of the sermon. Indeed, this letter appears to have pushed the genre boundaries too far, for its homiletic qualities propel Eleanor's critique of it. There is the implication that the letter does not properly address its audience, treating family members like churchgoers, and that its content—heavily laden with scriptural references and religious argumentation—was also inappropriate to the context. Then, too, Eleanor might quite simply be commenting on the letter's length; written in a small hand over two full sheets front and back, the letter was uncommonly long and dense. Accordingly, her words might be concurring with the humorous critique Herman received at the hands of some vandal who inscribed in the back of a church pew in the local church, "The hissing goose has far more sense / Than Vaill with all his eloquence" (Starr 382). Additionally, Eleanor devalues his letter as an object of exchange, removing it from the spiritual realm where Herman situates it and placing it in a commercial one. When she says that she "was glad you had paid the postage for it was not worth reading," she is referencing the fact that in those days, the recipient paid the postage for letters received. As Earle notes, this arrangement "endowed correspondence with distinctive social and monetary obligations," placing one writer in the other's "debt" and creating expectations for epistolary conduct (8). Herman's unusually long, two-sheet letter would have cost a higher rate, and because it does not conform to Eleanor's expectations of a letter exchanged between family members, she deems it worthless.

The latter points about page length and postage highlight the importance of the material dimensions of letter writing. As Eleanor's comment indicates, letters cannot be divorced from the material conditions shaping their creation and reception. The genre's evolution has been affected by changes in the educational system, resulting in higher literacy rates across populations; the postal system, making the mail more affordable and reliable; transportation, rendering the population more geographically mobile and hence liable to be separated by large distances; and technology, leading to the invention, for example, of the durable and affordable steel nib to replace the quill pen.[23] Yet critics have paid less attention to such material aspects than to formal or content-related questions (Hall 83), perhaps because most readers encounter the letters of previous centuries in published collections rather than in manuscript form.[24] Certainly, when handling the holographs in an archive, one becomes acutely aware of the artifacticity of the letter. Yet the importance of materiality goes beyond the physical experiences of holding the sheets, squinting to discern the shade of ink and the width of the strokes made by the quill pen, registering the generational and gendered differences in the handwriting, noting the fold marks, or rubbing a finger along the rough texture of the wax seal. The material dimensions of the letter itself and its compositional context quite importantly shape its content and form.[25]

The simple matter of the number of pages, for example, has a profound effect on what is expressed in a letter. Postal rates calculated according to the number of sheets, established by the Postal Acts of 1792 and in effect through the period the Golds penned their letters (Fuller 43), led writers to regularize the length of their letters to the space of the front and back of a single sheet; hence the development of the writers' thoughts was inevitably shaped and bracketed by the sheet length. Rare in the Gold correspondence is a letter that does not fill all available space, though on one occasion Harriett confesses that

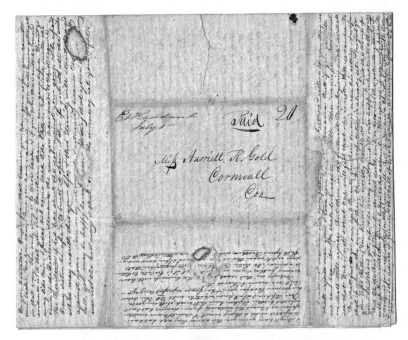

The last page of Herman Vaill's letter of 29 June 1825 to Harriett Gold displays how early nineteenth-century letter writers often filled the area surrounding the address. Herman Vaill, with his small, even script, makes use of every available iota of space. This letter, which drew criticism from his mother-in-law for its length, ran to nearly five thousand words over eight densely written pages and cost twice as much to mail as a typical letter. (Courtesy of Herman Landon Vaill Collection, Manuscripts and Archives, Yale University Library)

she fears she will not be able to fill her sheet, and so she searches for additional topics. She explains to Herman and Flora Gold Vaill in her letter of 29 March [1832], "I begin to feel almost ashamed I have written so much about myself & family—but when I began I was afraid that I should have to leave part of the sheet a blank & I knew Br. V. wouldn't like that, so I thought I would write down every thing just as it came into my head." Her reference to Herman's imagined displeasure registers the fact that he would be paying the postage on a letter whose sheet was not filled, an act he might have viewed as wasteful. This letter is one of the most personally revealing Harriett writes; the extra space seemed to allow her to explore her emotions to a greater degree. Her confession of shame suggests that such personal effusions were not conventional for writers, who typically filled their pages with news and had little room left over for reflection. Indeed, her comment indicates that she felt as if she had somehow violated the genre expectations of her readers, a surprising reversal of the view commonly held by modern readers who seek personal revelations in the correspondence of the past. Many readers will no doubt share my opinion that this letter is one of the most valuable and moving in the volume. Most probably, Herman Vaill's pecuniary concerns regarding page length and postage are to be thanked for its existence.

More common than empty spaces, though, were crowded pages, suggesting there was never enough room to fully express oneself. Writers reduced the size of their handwriting and filled every available space on the page, resulting in the proliferation of marginal insertions written crossways along the sides of the sheets and, less familiar to modern readers, the use of the area above and below the address area of the back sheet. Before the 1860s, letter writers did not use envelopes. The writers of the Gold letters tended to fold their sheets in half to form four writing pages, then to fold the edges of the paper over vertically before folding the letters into thirds again horizontally and, finally, sealing them with wax.[26] They usually placed addresses in the middle of the last page, and the writers often took advantage of the space above and below the address to continue their thoughts. Sometimes the formal letter ends in the first third of the page above the address, with a postscript or entirely different train of thought taken up in the bottom third after the address, sometimes with an additional sign-off in shortened form such as initials or first name only. Occasionally, a different writer fills the area below the address, just as other writers also penned marginal additions. If the address area had not intruded or the sheets had not offered open margins, the organization or development of ideas in these letters might have been very different.

Both the marginal insertion and the use of the area above and below the address, then, shaped in important ways how correspondents articulated their thoughts and filled various functions. In an early letter to his sister-in-law Harriett, Herman Vaill writes of instructional methods used in schools and her courting woes, situations geared toward her interests. But his marginal notes and postscripts below the address are addressed to her sister Flora, his wife, who is visiting her parents' home. The marginal addresses to his newlywed wife are a mixture of practical requests—"to send me one pair of Drawers" —and teasing, intimate, and even sexually suggestive comments. He writes, "I am well as usual; love my wife as usual, or rather more; wish to see her as usual, or rather more; & hope to see her before long, as usual" (letter to Harriett Gold, 22 August 1823). The innuendo of the final phrase and the tenderness of the entire passage work to soften and humanize the intellectual and rigid minister who later lectures Harriett in a letter on the selfishness of her desires. In the letter of 29 June 1825, the one criticized by his mother-in-law, Herman similarly uses the marginal insertions to speak more personally. Though the letter ends on a note of generalized religious rhetoric, the several marginal notations target Harriett in far more personal ways, driving home in particular how she had betrayed her siblings. In letters by Harriett's sister Catharine, the marginal notes and additions below the address contribute information or commentary that did not fit within the narrative scope of the letter proper. Her letter to Herman and Flora Vaill on 30 July 1825, for example, concentrates almost exclusively on updating them on reactions to the engagement in Cornwall. Her insertions and postscripts report and reflect on the death of one of the Hawaiian students at the Foreign Mission School, a somewhat unrelated topic. In a letter dated 1 September 1825, Catharine adds marginal insertions to an angry letter her father wrote to the Vaills. Her insertions in this instance work against the content of the letter to reassure them of her continuing affection and concern, which contrasts with her father's ire.

Familial and Gender Negotiations

Considerations of formal and material properties thus undoubtedly enrich understandings of the Gold family's letters, but equally important is attention to the ways that letters function as sites of contestation. Recognizing the important cultural function of letters, Susan K. Harris, for example, has argued that the aesthetics of letter

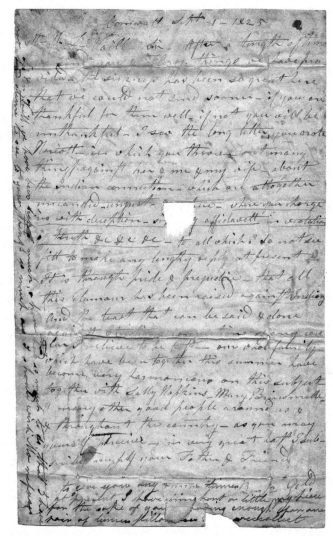

Marginal insertions were common in nineteenth-century letters as correspondents strove to fit as many words as possible into the space. Other writers sometimes penned the marginal notes, as in this case when Catharine Gold fills the margins of Benjamin Gold's letter of 1 September 1825 to Herman Vaill with affectionate messages designed to counteract her father's angry words. (Courtesy of Herman Landon Vaill Collection, Manuscripts and Archives, Yale University Library)

writing can be best understood as political strategies through which negotiations of race, class, gender, and other differential power relationships are carried out ("Personal Letters"). Harriett notes in an early letter that there is "a great division of feeling among many but especially in our family" (letter to Herman and Flora Gold Vaill and Catharine Gold, 25 June 1825). The Gold letters reveal the negotiations, based in gender and familial power relationships and the fraught terrain of race politics and miscegenation, following this "division of feeling." Through the letters, various family members resist, explore, test, and embrace the meanings inscribed in interracial marriage.

Interestingly, Harriett's voice is the most muted in the discussion. She writes one letter at the beginning of the controversy, in which she describes her experiences after the announcement of her betrothal. "Pen cannot describe nor language express the numerous & trying scenes through which I have passed," she writes as she paradoxically recounts in vivid detail how she witnessed her own friends, neighbors, and brother burn her image in effigy (letter to Herman and Flora Gold Vaill and Catharine Gold, 25 June 1825). Except through short postscripts she attached to others' letters or through other correspondents' reporting of her words, however, Harriett remains largely silent. Others relay her words and emotions, but her direct intervention in the epistolary conversation remains absent. Quite possibly, the public humiliations she endured as punishment meted out for her transgression of social mores — including her naming in the newspapers and the burning of her effigy — rendered her silent. Once the debate in the family has been resolved, however, Harriett resumes her correspondence, writing lengthy letters to her siblings.

Two of Harriett's brothers-in-law — General Daniel Brinsmade, husband of her sister Mary, and the Reverend Cornelius Everest, husband of Abbey — reveal the racist reactions her marriage inspired in some of the masculine portion of her family. In his first letter on the topic, Brinsmade cuts directly to the issue of interracial sexual contact, arguing that Harriett seeks only to "gratify" her "animal feeling" (letter to Herman and Flora Gold Vaill, 29 June 1825). His use of the term "animal" cannot be accidental, since American Indians were

In Harriett Gold's 25 June 1825 letter to Herman and Flora Gold Vaill and Catharine Gold announcing her engagement, the evenness of her script and her spacious use of the page contrasts markedly with letters she wrote after her marriage. (Courtesy of Herman Landon Vaill Collection, Manuscripts and Archives, Yale University Library) frequently compared with animals as inhabitants of the forest. In a similar vein, Everest writes, "Shame on such love," characterizing the proposed union as "unnatural" in its violation of racial boundaries (letter to Stephen Gold, 2 July 1825). In writing caustically of those who supported Harriett, Brinsmade blusters that they believe "no evil results from Indian marriages. . . . [W]e dont see and feel how good and how pleasant a thing it is to be kiss$^{\underline{d}}$ by an Indian—to have black young ones & a train of evils" (letter to Herman and Flora Gold Vaill and Catharine Gold, 14 July 1825).[27] In contrast to proponents of the marriage who they claim were influenced by sympathy for Harriett, Brinsmade and Everest portray themselves as maintaining community standards. Everest notes that he and his family "are not alone in our feelings. Nineteen twentieths of New Endland view the subject just as we do" (letter to Stephen Gold, 2 July 1825). Brinsmade concurs: "The good people in this place do oppose such connections and all who have express$^{\,d}$ an opinion favorable to them would revolt in a moment if it was brought home to their own firesides" (letter to Herman and Flora Gold Vaill and Catharine Gold, 14 July 1825).

Brother-in-law Herman Vaill masks under learned argumentation and pious sentiments what Brinsmade and Everest reveal more crudely. After receiving first word of her engagement, Herman sent Harriett the aforementioned eight-page letter of 29 June 1825, written in small script and presenting detailed arguments against the proposed marriage. In the letter, he claims repeatedly that he does not oppose intermarriages. Indeed, two years earlier, Herman had teased Harriett about her attractiveness to "every old bachelor who owns land near you, & every old widower that comes along." He concluded the earlier letter by advising her to "choose who you please, white, or black, or red" (letter to Harriett Gold, 22 August 1823). His opposition to the proposed marriage, he now emphasizes repeatedly, is inspired not by "dissimilarity of complexion, for that I care nothing about," but by his fear that the Foreign Mission School, missionary efforts, and the cause of Christianity in general will be damaged by the marriage (letter to Mary Gold Brinsmade, 2 August 1825). To prove his point, he provides lengthy analogies, scriptural quotations, and the ministerial argumentation his mother-in-law, Eleanor, found so irritating.

Yet just under the learned surface of the letter of 29 June 1825 lurks a more visceral response that has much to do with a rejection of the idea of sexual contact between a white woman and an American Indian. Herman cautions Harriett against mistaking her desire to live among the Cherokee as sign of a missionary calling or "because we love another object; & have a selfish inducement." Repeatedly using a metaphor comparing Harriett's sexual desire for Elias to fire, he warns her not to "kindle the fire, which if once kindled may burn, we know not how far." Given the recent burning of Harriett's effigy, the metaphor probes a sensitive wound even as it masks itself in the Christian rhetoric of damnation. Herman warns her against becoming that "one female enemy" who will end the existence of the Foreign Mission School, an allusion to biblical examples of women's traitorous sexuality. On 2 August 1825, after he has been chided by some female members of the family for being too harsh in his criticism of Harriett, he more clearly reveals his repugnance at the thought of her emotions for and sexual union with Elias:

> [C]an you find any motive that leads her but love. What other motive can she have? She may hope in vain to carry with her a heart that feels for the heathen, & for Zion. Her heart is engrossed with other feelings. . . . [I]f H. must die for an Indian or have him, I do say she had as well die, as become the cause of so much lasting evil as the marriage will occasion; better to die on the side of Xtian honour & Gospel sincerity than to pine away with satisfied love, & its consequences, on the bed of Love.

It is worth noting that during the period of controversy over Harriett's marriage, her sister Catharine met and married within the space of three months a man who was not a professed Christian, as Elias was, without any commentary from her brother-in-law on her wayward sexual desires. Her husband was, of course, white, though Harriett teasingly pointed out that his complexion was darker than Elias's (Flora Gold Vaill to Herman Vaill, [19] September 1825]).

When Herman's 29 June 1825 letter was shared among the larger family, it spurred intense debate. Though much of the discussion surrounded his harsh characterization of Harriett in that letter as "a hypocrite, & designed for a reprobate," a great deal of the controversy within the family centered on his accusations that Harriett's parents had been deceitful in their handling of the affair. In his castigations of the parents, it appeared to the women of the family that he overstepped the bounds of filial respect and duty. Eleanor Gold writes no letters to her children that have been preserved. Yet her opinions, such as her caustic evaluation of Herman's letter-writing abilities, echo through the writings of others. "Ma is almost worn out she feels as though her children had no tenderness for her & instead of comforting her were ready to fill up her cup of affliction till it is more than running over," writes Harriett (letter to Herman and Flora Gold Vaill and Catharine Gold, 25 June 1825). Catharine notes, "It is as much as ma can bear to be contradicted & it is more than she will bear, to be charged of telling a falsehood; especially by her children" (Catharine Gold to Herman and Flora Gold Vaill, 18 July [1825]).

Benjamin, a man characterized by his "cheerfulness," was also affronted (Harriett Boudinot to Herman and Flora Gold Vaill, 5 January 1827). Catharine recounts to the Vaills the reception Herman's letter received: "Pa was very much offended, he was outrageous—he could hardly speak peacibly about you" (letter to Herman and Flora Gold Vaill, 18 July [1825]). It is worth emphasizing that after initial reluctance, this patriarch, father of fourteen children and a deacon in the church, warmly supported his daughter in her unconventional choice. Accordingly, the Gold family letters force modern readers to reevaluate their views of the rule of the father in the nineteenth century. To be sure, Harriett's brothers and brothers-in-law act in far more tyrannical ways, acts of which the father disapproves. Benjamin states his view of his daughter's marriage choice succinctly: "And the least that can be said & done against Christian connections of any coular I believe to be best" (letter to Herman Vaill, 1 September 1825). A sentiment that quite possibly benefited his older daughters and their husbands at the time of their marriages, his comment registers the shift in the view of parental involvement in marriages in the United States during the late eighteenth and early nineteenth centuries. Numerous historians have noted that in the wake of the Revolution, parental control of children's marriage choices declined, symptomatic of a more general trend toward the loosening of parental authority influenced by the proliferation of democratic ideals (Norton, *Liberty's Daughters* 229). As in the novels of this period that Shirley Samuels considers, the "dramatic action" of the Gold letters revolves around "the frequently violent struggle for a democratic marriage," with the conflict manifesting itself as "competition among siblings" rather than through children's rebellion against parents (60).

In contrast to novelistic parents whom Samuels describes as "ineffectual fathers" and abandoning mothers (38), Eleanor and Benjamin wield power over their grown and married children through their withholding of economic and emotional support, thus revealing the operation of familial dynamics. The family at home in Cornwall had been engaged in procuring and making household furniture and necessities for the recently married Vaills; in the wake of Herman's letter, the parents threaten to withhold these items. As the women were spinning a carpet for Flora, Eleanor comments, according to Catharine, that "it may be Flora's if she behaves well, if she treats ma ill, she [ant] to have it." Catharine continues, "Yo[u m]ust both be very careful what you write to Harriet. if you write, Pa came very near saying you should not have another article sent you, & it would take but little now to make him say it. Pa & m[a say t]hat you must make some acknowledgment" (letter to Herman and Flora Gold Vaill, 30 July 1825). This exchange of goods for obedience and respectful treatment suggests one mode in which family relationships were maintained among the middle classes. Benjamin and Eleanor also refuse to receive visits from or make visits to their disapproving daughters, in effect using family contact as the axis of exchange, trading visits for accord. Herman Vaill shows the emotional pain such a trade-off could create when he writes, "This subject has been painful to us; we wish to visit Cl in Sept, but can't, because they say they don't wish to see us, as long as we feel so" (Herman Vaill to Mary Gold Brinsmade, 2 August 1825).

Eventually, the Golds send the items to the Vaills, and Benjamin writes a stiff and formal letter to his son-in-law. In this letter, Benjamin acutely comments that "[i]t is through pride & prejudice — that all this clamour has been raised against Indians" (letter to Herman Vaill, 1 September 1825). Certainly there was self-consciousness among the members of the family regarding the circulation of gossip, which Karen Hansen has described as "the mainstay of community discourse in antebellum New England" (115). The fear of gossip, which functions as "a medium for monitoring as well as negotiating community opinion" by "scrutiniz[ing] information and determin[ing] factual correctness and appropriate behavior" (115), seemed to propel at least some of the brothers-in-law's responses. Everest mentions how neighbors brought the paper in which the agents' report condemning the marriage was printed and began asking questions. He complains, "People are talking; many questions are asked. We are sick of answering. . . . We wish we had a cave in which we could hide away from the sight of man" (letter to Stephen Gold, 2 July 1825). Brinsmade notes that Bunce has published the names of all of the "Indians brothers in law" and comments wryly that Everest, who was left out of the list, "must consider himself slighted" (letter to Herman and Flora Gold Vaill and Catharine Gold, 14 July 1825). "[H]ow does Millington people like the idea of having a clergyman who is brother to an Indian," he needles Herman Vaill in the same letter. Herman's intention to publish his letter to Harriett emerges from a desire to "vindicate ourselves from all charges of knowledge or participation in it" (Herman Vaill to Harriett Gold, 29 June 1825). One can only assume that Stephen's role in lighting the fire on the town green and his continued threats toward Elias, which caused consternation among family members and friends who comment repeatedly on his "outrageous" behavior, perform a similar function (Bennet Roberts to Herman Vaill, 1 August [1825]). There were also concrete, worldly concerns at stake; Brinsmade worries that Benjamin's property will lose value and Everest wonders "what will become of that family! What are the prospects of the unmarried & unsettled children?" (letter to Herman Vaill, 14 September 1825).

"Let not pride have any hand is distressing us," pleads Harriett's sister Mary Brinsmade (letter to Herman and Flora Gold Vaill and Catharine Gold, 14 July 1825). In contrast to the brothers-in-law, who display lengthy and determined opposition based in racial antipathy, most of Harriett's sisters come to her support rather quickly. By the end of summer, Benjamin writes that the daughters who are in and near Cornwall "have become very harmonious" (letter to Herman Vaill; postscript by Catharine Gold to Flora Gold Vaill, 1 September 1825), and Harriett writes to her sister Flora, who lived some miles away, "You cannot think what precious interviews we four Sisters, (who are at present situated near each other), do enjoy" (letter to Herman and Flora Gold Vaill, 2 January 1826). Yet participation in this "harmonious" community opens the women to accusations from the men of being "turnovers," a charge that bears within it an implicit suggestion that they have betrayed their husbands' authority. In the midst of the debate, Herman Vaill pens a respectful letter to Mary Brinsmade explaining his continued opposition to the marriage. In its margins, he inserts a comment directed to her husband, Daniel: "We are all brothers of one mind I hope. I was sorry that Sister Mary had so [enco]uraged H. as to express approbation. I hope they will not make you into a turn over, & I hope that Mary will turn back again. Brother Everest [and Sister?] Abbey are as yet 'Cakes not turned;' & we must all show that when John Randall spoke of Yankee 'dough faces,' he did not mean us" (letter to Mary Gold Brinsmade, 2 August 1825). In this statement of gender solidarity, Herman—who had to be aware that Mary would also read the marginal note, incorporated as it was in a letter addressed to her—taunts Daniel Brinsmade with his wife's independence of opinion. Herman's reference to "dough faces" brings into play contemporary politics; he refers to politician John Randolph's belittling reference to northerners who supported southern interests in the Missouri Compromise of 1820. By introducing a sectional conflict into the discussion as an analogy for family members who support the union of (northerner) Harriett with (southerner) Elias, Herman reveals what Samuels claims for the novel, that it "played out national conflicts" through the interactions of a "flawed family grouping" in which sibling rivalry flourishes. The interested parties in this epistolary debate similarly operate, then, on some level as a "functioning allegory for the nation" (60).

While the men's rigid responses seem to be formed in response to outside concerns—worry over their public reputations, social attitudes toward intermarriage, or concern for the Foreign Mission School—the women's shifting responses emerge from a need to gather information, a willingness to suspend judgment, an obligation to an ideal of familial cohesion, and the sense that the family is a place within which to exchange opinions freely. Mary Brinsmade explains that talking with Harriett and reading the relevant correspondence formed the groundwork for her change in opinion, and Harriett's sister Catharine returns home from visiting the Vaills specifically "to find out how it had gone on." She changes her position "[a]fter hearing their statements" (letter to Herman and Flora Gold Vaill, 18 July [1825]). Catharine also passes along the view of Harriett's sister Sally Hopkins, who does not write any letters in the exchange. Though her husband treated her mother quite rudely, Sally, in contrast, "appears very friendly, to her parents, & to Harriet. She does not think it worth a while, to forsake her parents, because they differ in opinion from her." Catharine shares Sally's view of the family as a sphere in which divergent opinions can be tolerated and judgment suspended, continuing, "I do not intend forsake them. I love them as well as I ever did. I believe they have acted conscientiously. Whether they have been in an error, or not, is not for me to say, I do not feel disposed to condemn their motives, nor do I Harriett's" (letter to Herman and Flora Gold Vaill, 30 July 1825).

All the women hoped to extend the process of information gathering and exchange to the men. Mary Brinsmade pleads with Herman Vaill to "tell us all your concerns as far as possible" (letter to Herman and Flora Gold Vaill and Catharine Gold, 14 July 1825). Flora Vaill writes her husband when she is visiting her parents that "you had better come & talk the matter over" and reiterates that she is sure he would change his mind, too, "if you could talk the matter over" ([19] September 1825). Of Harriett's sisters, one, Abbey Everest, continued to oppose the marriage and refused to visit. Her sisters recognize that it is her inability to exchange information with them that causes her to maintain her opposition. Flora believes that "Abbey will feel much better satisfied & relieved if she will but come home and learn the truth. . . . I am confident should she come & be candid she would not long retain the impressions she now has of her parents & Sister" (letter to Herman Vaill, [19] September 1825). The sisters cast a degree of blame on Abbey's husband, Cornelius Everest, for her seclusion.

When he visited Cornwall earlier in the fall, he gave rise to gossip when he did not call on his in-laws. The sisters suspect that his rigidity is compelling Abbey's absence from home, and they say they "pity" her (Harriett Gold to Herman and Flora Gold Vaill, 2 January 1826). Whatever Herman Vaill's and Daniel Brinsmade's views, neither of them prohibited their wives from visiting their parents; indeed, Herman writes a letter apologetic in tone to Benjamin and Eleanor which "prepared the way" for Flora's visit to the family, resulting in her change of opinion (Flora Gold Vaill to Herman Vaill, [19] September 1825). In this, his letter fulfills the mediatory function Janet Altman describes as characteristic of the epistolary form (22).

In some cases, the differing response between Harriett's sisters and brothers-in-law pitted wife against husband. In one particularly noteworthy instance, the letters themselves became the space of negotiation and resistance. On 14 July 1825, Mary Brinsmade mails a letter to the Vaills and Catharine Gold in which she explains the reasons for her new acceptance of the marriage. In the margins of all the pages of this letter, heavy marks obscure lines of script beneath. Only by reading her husband's letter to the same parties, dated the same day and mailed separately, can one understand the significance of those lines. Daniel Brinsmade explains, "Mary has written a letter to you to which I beg leave to dissent—and have written two or three small notes on the margin at which she seems to be wrathy and will probably scratch them out before she sends it." In her "wrathy[ness]," the wife obliterates her husband's words and forces him to write his own letter to articulate his "fix^d & unalterable" position of "opposition to the marriage." She grants his opinions no space in her letter, thus claiming it and the opinions she expresses in it as her own.

The sisters all comment on Herman Vaill's lengthy letter. In the letters of the Gold women, there exists no obsequious diminishing of their own status as they address the men to whom they write. They state their opinions openly and confidently, sometimes softening the impact of their critique by assuring the addressee of their affection, but in no way lessening it. Susan K. Harris has pointed out the importance of the "relative social standing of the correspondents: their consciousness of their own status, along an almost infinite number

Heavy lines obscure the words written in the margins of each page of this letter from Mary Gold Brinsmade to Herman and Flora Gold Vaill and Catharine Gold, written on 14 July 1825. Daniel Brinsmade's letter of the same date reveals that his wife had angrily crossed out his marginal insertions expressing opposition to the marriage. (Courtesy of Herman Landon Vaill Collection, Manuscripts and Archives, Yale University Library) of grids, in relation to that of the person to whom they are addressing their letter" in determining the tone and content of letters (Cultural Work 56). While to some extent the Gold sisters occupied the same social standing as their male relatives by privilege of their family relationships, the men's status was significantly elevated in important ways by gender, education, and public station. The wife of a minister did not occupy the same status position as the minister; a pious but not formally educated young woman differed in standing from a Yale-educated minister. Yet these factors do not seem to impact the Gold sisters' willingness to articulate their opinions with confidence. Flora Vaill, while visiting her parents, writes to her husband, "Come to read over your letter of 2 sheets to H. I think it is hard to bear, H. says it cuts the hardest of anything she has ever received from anyone, but she is willing to forgive. I know you would not have written so if you knew the circumstances as I do now" ([19] September 1825). She seems to agree with Harriett that he requires forgiveness for what he wrote, yet she deftly maintains wifely loyalty while implicitly criticizing him for having written as he did. Herman's sisters-in-law also showed little hesitation in taking on the minister. Mary Brinsmade writes, in an almost scolding tone, "Permit me to tell you, my dear brother, that I was sorry to see some expressions which I saw in the latter part of the letter which H. received from you last week" (letter to Herman and Flora Gold Vaill and Catharine Gold, 14 July 1825). Twenty-one-year-old Catharine, who, like Flora, was present while Herman wrote the letter, dares to tell the learned minister that he should not have made one of the statements he made: "[Y]et I do think myself—it would have been better, had that part been omitted" (letter to Herman and Flora Gold Vaill, 18 July [1825]). In buttressing her arguments, Catharine refers to her elder sister, rather than a male family member: "I believe it is not thought best by any one that has seen your letter, that you should publish it. Mary says unless you wish to disgrace yourself; you must not publish it" (letter to Herman and Flora Gold Vaill, 30 July 1825). The letter that matriarch Eleanor memorably characterized as an "old sermon" that was "not worth reading" is roundly criticized by her daughters as well. Toby Ditz has noted that "the definitions of self, other, and situation that they [letters] contain are acts of power" (63). The Gold women's letters assert their power to make such definitions independent of men.

In the end, Harriett and Elias married quietly in her parents' home nine months after they announced their engagement. Most members of the family had reconciled themselves to her decision in the intervening months from betrothal to marriage, with the exception of Abbey and her family, who appear to have remained estranged from Harriett. Even Stephen came to accept Harriett's choice, putting the maintenance of his relationship with her ahead of his principles on intermarriage. As Flora describes, "Stephen feels strenuously opposed to indian connections, but has given it up & sings with Harriet as usual, rides & walks with her & is as chirk as ever. He has just told me that he is not troubled on account of pride in the least" (letter to Herman Vaill, [19] September 1825). Indeed, Stephen soon took a public stand for Harriett that might have functioned as atonement for his lighting of the effigy fire. Soon after the news broke, Harriett had been asked not to join the choir so that she would not "disgrace" the other girls; late in the summer, she returned to her seat in the gallery (Harriett Gold to Herman and Flora Gold Vaill and Catharine Gold, 25 June 1825). Flora recounts what happened: "Every one of the young men left the seat, in the morning for fear, & Stephen sung alone all day. I have not heard better singing in a year" (letter to Herman Vaill, [19] September 1825).

Late in her life, a distant relative of the family, Eunice Wadsworth Taylor, dictated to her daughter her reminiscences of the events surrounding Harriett and Elias's marriage (Starr 154). As a romanticized retelling of the events described in the letters, the narrative provides additional details surrounding the wedding:

After the town of Cornwall had become quiet over the marriage of Sarah and John, there arose another tumult, and the social life of the parish, usually so quiet, arose to fever heat over the announcement that "Elias Boudinot (John's cousin) was about to marry Harriett, daughter of Col. Gold," one of the fairest, most cultured young ladies of the place, a very pious, amiable girl, the nearest of perfection of any person I ever knew. She was the youngest of fourteen children; the others all married except two brothers. One brother was a Congregational Minister. Her sisters all married in high rank; some rich, one a Cong. Minister, one a lawyer, another a Judge, &c. All had married so well that it was a dreadful stroke to have Harriett marry an Indian. She was the idol of the family; they tried to persuade her not to marry him, but all in vain. Not only was her own town stirred but one Minister came from another town to try and persuade her not to marry Elias Boudinot. They talked to her half a day, but she would argue them down, and they would say; "she must have him; no other way." She would say, "We have vowed, and our vows are heard in heaven; color is nothing to me; his soul is as white as mine; he is a Christian, and ever since I embraced religion I have been praying that God would open a door for me to be a missionary, and this is the way." She thought she could do more good to be one of them; they would not be jealous and think she looked down upon them.

After it was known that she must and would go the "roughs" in town burned her and Mrs. Northrup and Sarah in effigy; they used a barrel of tar. While they were burning, Harriett's friends carried her one mile away; the house, in which she was, stood on a high hill, she looked out of the window and said, "Father, forgive them; they know not what they do." Sure enough, for they afterwards repented of it; could not forgive themselves. . . . Many said Boudinot would never come into the town alive, but if he did he never should go out alive. Such excitement was never in town before. Six months after the engagement was publicly known they were married. Excitement ceased and he came into town unmolested; had a splendid wedding at two o'clock p.m. My father and mother attended the wedding; no young people invited; only the married friends and relatives of Harriett's parents were present.

Boudinot had been there a week and Stephen had not seen him. When his sister and husband came, whom he had not seen for some time, he came rushing into the room. "How do you do, Flora?" "How do you do, Boudinot?" The next morning he came to the breakfast table and waited upon us and upon Boudinot also. But he could not see them married. He worked in the saw-mill all the afternoon. I was making Harriett's wedding outfit at the time, (no sewing machine or ready-made garments in those days). I was in the room with them until I almost forgot that he was an Indian; he prayed so fervently; sang so sweetly. . . .

[Later, Mrs. Gold said that Harriett had] "a kind, good husband, and the smartest grandchildren we ever had; Harriett had married as well as any of her children, and you know how our children have married well." (qtd. in Starr 155–56)[28]

After the wedding, Harriett accompanied Elias on some of his northern tour, during which he delivered addresses to audiences in cities including Charleston, New York, Philadelphia, and Boston to gather funds to purchase a press for the establishment of a Cherokee newspaper. He published as a pamphlet the speech he delivered on these occasions, "An Address to the Whites," and the *North American Review* printed excerpts from it (Review of "An Address to the Whites"). The couple then turned south toward the Cherokee Nation. What opponents of the marriage feared—that, in Herman Vaill's words, it would "annihilate the Institution" of the Foreign Mission School—proved to be true (letter to Harriett Gold, 29 June 1825). Though the official reason for the closing of the school was that it would be more effective to educate the youth in their own home regions, most observers understood that the two "Indian marriages" had too clearly revealed the intolerance and racism of even the most benevolent New Englanders and that the school at Cornwall would no longer garner the support of the community (Andrew 340–42).

CHEROKEE LETTERS

Negotiating a Married Correspondence
Harriett's and Elias's married correspondence included in this volume begins less than a year later with Harriett pregnant with their first child and Elias poised to become editor of the *Cherokee Phoenix*. In their shared first letter dated 5 January 1827 and addressed to the Vaills, both Elias and Harriett take on the role of ethnographer, providing information about the Cherokee way of life to New Englanders who are unfamiliar with it yet curious. Elias explains the work-

ings of the Cherokee language, and Harriett describes Elias's family, the food they eat, her domestic conditions, and the climate. One can sense in Elias's elaborate wordplay, expression of lofty sentiments, and pointed barb about people who commit the "gross crime of matrimony" a certain anxiety in establishing correspondence with the man, Herman Vaill, who had been the assistant principal at the school where Elias was educated and who had so strenuously opposed their marriage. Elias signs himself "Your Indian Brother," and when read within the context of recent events, emphasis seems to fall on the word "brother" in an attempt to cement the new relationship in which he finds himself with Harriett's family.

Harriett signs off in two different places. After the body of the letter, she writes "Your Cheerful & affectionate Sister," intended probably to assure her family that she is not regretting the drastic step she took in marrying Elias. After a postscript, she signs herself "Your Cherokee Sister," mimicking Elias's farewell, yet with the emphasis falling on the word "Cherokee," the newly emerging aspect of her identity. While Elias uses the nomenclature of "Indian" to characterize himself, indicating that he understands the ways whites view American Indians generically no matter what their tribal affiliation, Harriett particularizes herself not as a missionary to the Cherokee or as a woman married to a Cherokee but simply as a Cherokee. She thus identifies herself with a particular people and set of interests that exist outside white conceptions of "the Indian." In another letter, not collected here, written soon after her marriage, she indicates that she has a Cherokee name, "Kalahdee," about which she writes, "I am pleased with my Cherokee name, it already sounds very natural to me" (qtd. in Church 15). She describes her affection for Elias's family: "I love them all much & I may say—we love each other," as well as her feelings about the choice she made: "I can truly say I am contented & never passed my days more pleasantly than while I have been in this Nation" (Elias and Harriett Gold Boudinot to Herman and Flora Gold Vaill, 5 January 1827). Soon after, in a subsequent letter, she comments that she is "more attached to this than my native home. The place of my birth is dear to me but I do love this people & with them I wish to live & die" (letter to Herman Vaill, 21 November 1827). The letters

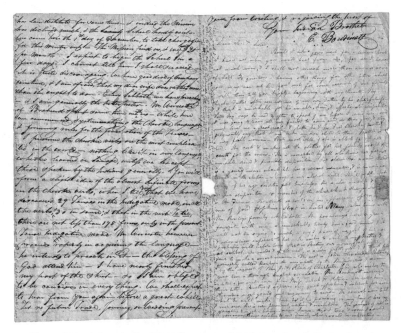

Elias and Harriett typically shared the space of the letter after their marriage, as in this 5 January 1827 letter to Herman and Flora Gold Vaill. In this letter, Elias writes first, his bold handwriting sprawling capaciously across the page. Harriett's handwriting and use of space are noticeably more cramped than in her before-marriage epistles, reflecting the change in the material conditions of her letter writing. (Courtesy of Herman Landon Vaill Collection, Manuscripts and Archives, Yale University Library)

written soon after her marriage thus chart her evolving enmeshment in the Cherokee surroundings in which she now resides.

At this point, Harriett's and Elias's correspondence with Harriett's relatives takes on the key quality William Decker cites of epistolary exchanges: the effort to overcome the distance that is the precondition for the letter writing (15). The earlier exchange about the engagement had the intensity of a debate between people who were also periodically seeing each other, whereas now the distance of a thousand miles and extended absence imprint themselves on the sentiments penned by the letter writers. In addition, the sense of a conversation or debate is no longer present. This section of the preserved correspondence is one-way, comprised mostly of letters from the Boudinots to the Vaills sharing details of their lives. The letters' pages are now shared between Elias and Harriett, with Elias writing first and Harriett second. Whereas before marriage Harriett wrote lengthy letters, often a full four pages, that were entirely hers, after marriage she is restricted to smaller spaces. Elias's bold, large handwriting sprawls capaciously across his pages, while Harriett writes in tiny, sometimes almost indecipherable script, a marked contrast to her even and spacious before-marriage hand. She attempts to compress as much information into the small space allotted to her as possible, explaining, "I have many things to say—but must make my sentences short" (letter to Herman Vaill, 21 November 1827). As she comments in her first letter, while she is adjusting to this new hierarchization of the space of the page, "I have confined myself as it were in fetters." Yet Elias seems to feel a similar concern, writing in the same letter, "I have nearly finished, my part of the sheet—so I am obliged to be concise in every thing" (letter to Herman and Flora Gold Vaill, 5 January 1827). The two mutually negotiate their division of the space of the page in a way satisfactory to both. Although Harriett might have wished for additional space, she also had an investment in seeing her husband forge a relationship with members of her family through correspondence.

Editor of the Cherokee Phoenix

The Cherokees were entering a period of their struggle with the United States government that marks a watershed in the history of Indian-white relations. Rapidly increasing populations in the states and territories bordering on the Cherokee Nation heightened demand for the fertile lands held by Cherokees. A complicated history of land cessions and treaty making stretching back to the turn of the century induced white Georgians to pressure the U.S. government to fulfill earlier promises to buy all Native American landholdings in Georgia. After ceding large tracts of land in earlier treaties and watching some of their numbers emigrate west to Arkansas, however, the Cherokee remaining in the Southeast became more adamant in their desire to retain their lands. Attuned to the government's interest in civilization programs, some Cherokees increasingly adopted white ways, an effort that many believed would result in retention of their land. By 1826, when Harriett and Elias entered the Cherokee Nation as a married couple, some Cherokees dressed in Western-style clothing, lived in frame houses with their nuclear families, practiced agriculture using such implements as the plow, spun and wove, planted cotton and owned slaves, operated taverns and ferries, and sent their children to missionary and white schools. Many Cherokees were literate in Cherokee, owing to the invention of a Cherokee syllabary, and some could read in English. The Nation had established a system of written laws and would soon write a constitution modeled on the U.S. Constitution and publish a bilingual national newspaper.[29] In all these areas, Elias, in his role as clerk to the National Council from 1825 to 1827 and as editor of the Cherokee Phoenix from its inception in 1828 through 1832, would play a central role.

After serving as clerk to the National Council and teaching briefly at a mission school in Hightower in northwest Georgia, Elias assumed editorship of the Cherokee Phoenix, and he and Harriett settled in 1827 in New Echota, the new capital of the Cherokee Nation and the site of the printing office of the newspaper. The bilingual Cherokee Phoenix, which had columns in English and Cherokee, published material relevant to Cherokee politics as well as miscellaneous material gathered from other newspapers. The goal of the paper, as Elias states in the prospectus in 1827, was the "benefit of the Cherokees," and he notes that "a paper published exclusively for their benefit, and under their direction, would add great force to the charitable means employed by the public for their melioration" (Boudinot, "Prospectus," 89). In addition to readers in the Cherokee Nation, Elias hoped to obtain subscribers sympathetic to the Cherokees throughout the northern states, even, as he writes pointedly to his brother-in-law, in "Connecticut, the land of <u>intermarriages</u>" (letter to Herman Vaill, 21 November 1827). The letters contained here give new insight into his editorial duties, as when he writes: "Perhaps few will properly know the extent of my duties, by merely seeing the Phoenix, which carries but little evidence of much labour. But I can assure you I have no time to be idle. My duties are complicated" (letter to Herman and Flora Gold Vaill,

23 January 1829). Harriett notes, "He works very hard. . . . His salary is also small, considering his expenses—but he is willing to makes some sacrifice for his country" (letter to Herman and Flora Gold Vaill, 7 January 1831). He supplemented his income by taking on translating jobs in collaboration with Samuel A. Worcester, an ABCFM missionary who hoped to translate the Bible, sermons, and hymns into Cherokee.[30]

There is remarkably little scholarship on Elias's role as editor of the Cherokee Phoenix or the work he produced as a prolific author. Despite the availability of many of his writings in Perdue's Cherokee Editor, he has not shared in the critical attention accorded other American Indians who produced texts during this period.[31] Possibly the neglect stems from a generic cause, since most of his writings were journalistic, a form of writing often ignored by literary critics. Perhaps the perception of him as an entirely assimilated and Christianized Cherokee does not attract critics interested in "authentic" Indian voices, or maybe the historical infamy attached to his subsequent role in the Cherokee removal proves problematic to modern scholars.[32] Critics' work on Elias's contemporary, Pequot William Apess, who also published impassioned defenses of native rights, suggests useful approaches to Elias's oeuvre. Caroline Haynes, for example, claims that Apess's familiarity with Euro-American discourses, far from disabling critique, actually allowed him to "adopt a new, more accepted form of rhetoric that could work to counter the powerful anti-Indian, expansionist rhetoric and the growing conception of the U.S. as a homogeneous Anglo-Saxon nation-state" (27). Like Apess, Elias in his writing displays not so much an unthinking internalization of Western values as a redeployment of them in strategic and resistant ways as he criticizes the acquisitiveness and greed driving white Americans' treatment of Cherokees. In an editorial published in 1829, for example, Elias uses constitutional and legal discourses of rights and laws to critique the race theories of the day and the rhetoric used to undergird the myth of Indian extinction. "The causes which have operated to exterminate the Indian tribes that are produced as instances of the certain doom of the whole Aboriginal family," he writes, "did not exist in the Indians themselves, nor in the will of heaven." He thus rebuts notions of biological inferiority and manifest destiny. Instead, he argues, the United States created the situation "by infringing upon their rights." With this, he links the United States' treatment of Cherokees with England's oppression of the American colonies, thus redeploying the rhetoric of the American Revolution. He furthers this parallel when he discusses the negative consequences of "tak[ing] his rights away . . . invest[ing] him with oppressive laws, grievous to be borne" (Editorial 105).

In an 1831 editorial, Elias ironizes the language of Christian benevolence, which he shows to be as damaging to the Cherokees' interests as more forthright aggression. After denying a published report that Cherokees were starving and thus should be removed from their lands as an act of charity, Elias writes, "We beg our compassionate friends, therefore, not to put their benevolent purposes into effect right away, but to permit us a little longer to subsist on sap and roots. We are endeavoring to procure something more substantial. But if, with the aid of providence, we shall fail, we will then go to a land flowing with milk and honey" ("Georgia" 131). Ably countering the article's reference to "sap" and "roots" with the biblical allusion to "milk and honey," Elias demonstrates that the "benevolent" haste to improve the Cherokees' circumstances served to mask the desire of their less than "compassionate friends" to remove them more quickly from their land.[33] These two brief examples must serve to illustrate the richness of Elias's rhetorical maneuvering in his editorials. Though outside the scope of this introduction, a consideration of his work as an editor, writer, and translator is crucial to understanding American Indian textual production during this period in U.S. history and Elias Boudinot as a significant figure within that history.

A Cherokee "Squaw"

Elias jokingly calls Harriett a squaw in two letters, explaining, "All our wives are known in Georgia by that name" (letter to Herman and Flora Gold Vaill, 1 July 1831). His comment indicates that white Georgians leveled the pejorative title at all Cherokee wives, regardless of racial identity, and the term functions, therefore, as a useful access point into Harriett's adjustment to her life in the Cherokee Nation.

While she encountered some challenges not so different from those her sisters might have faced when they married — shouldering the responsibilities and increased workload of directing a household and bearing and raising children — she did so within radically different social and political contexts. Though their letters produce the illusion that Elias and Harriett have successfully re-created a New England home, their household was situated in the Cherokee Nation on land that was the focus of increasing political strife. Harriett was simultaneously the pious and genteel wife of a man who had remade himself in the image of a New England patriarch and, in the eyes of white Georgians and perhaps even some of her relatives, a woman who degraded herself by becoming the "squaw" of a Cherokee man. Her letters reveal her negotiations of these roles and offer compelling insight into her marriage.

On the occasion of a visit to his daughter in 1829–30, Harriett's father wrote a vivid account of their circumstances:

> Mr. Boudinot has much good company and is as much respected as any man of his age. His paper is respected all over the United States, and is known in Europe. . . . She has a large and convenient framed house, two stories, 30 by 40 feet on the ground, well done off and well furnished with the comforts of life. They get their supplies of clothes and groceries — they have their year's store of teas, cloths, paper, ink, etc. — from Boston, and their sugars, molasses etc. from Augusta.[34] They have two or three barrels of flour on hand at once. This neighborhood is truly an interesting and pleasant place; the ground is level and smooth as a house floor, the center of the Nation — a new place laid out in city form — 100 lots one acre each — a spring called the public spring about twice as large as our sawmill brook, near the center, with other springs on the plat; six new framed houses in sight, besides a Council House, Court House, printing office and four stores, all in sight of Mr. Boudinot's house. . . . The stores in the Nation are as large as the best in our towns in Litchfield Co. (qtd. in Church 17–19)

In this setting, the new capital of the Cherokee Nation planned to resemble the New England towns Benjamin used as a reference point,

Harriett found herself adjusting to a life for which her privileged up-bringing in Connecticut had in some ways hardly prepared her. Indeed, Harriett's extensive workload inhibits the letter writing she had more time for as a single woman, illustrating another way that material conditions impinge on correspondence; as she writes to her sister, "Should I like you, wait for a leisure hour I know not when you would hear from me" (letter to Herman and Flora Gold Vaill, 5 January 1827). In addition to the domestic duties of maintaining a household for Elias and herself and eventually their children — she bore her first child in 1827 and went on to have five more children in the next nine years — she oversaw a household that frequently housed members of Elias's family, children attending the missionary schools, and visitors on official business in the Cherokee Nation. Elias comments, in a mastery of understatement, "I am afraid, that my dear wife does rather more than she aught to do" (letter to Herman and Flora Gold Vaill, 5 January 1827). She found that her skills in sewing were much in demand among the Cherokees, who were increasingly dressing in Western attire but did not necessarily have the domestic skills to match their desires.[35] On one occasion, she describes hosting a quilting bee for the women while Elias holds a corn husking for the men. In these acts, Harriett and Elias were participating in the civilizing efforts of whites who attempted to train Cherokees in domestic and agricultural skills and the proper gendered division of labor.

In addition to providing information about her life, Harriett's letters have an emotional component. She expresses her affection for her distant family and her longing to see them, yet she is always careful not to imply that she in any way regrets her controversial decision to marry Elias and move to the Cherokee Nation, as when she writes, "Neither time or absence has or ever can diminish my affection for you all. I sometimes feels as though I must fly to you — at the same time I am perfectly contented & happy here. Will you not sometime come & see how happily we live here?" (letter to Herman and Flora Gold Vaill, 29 March [1832]). In this way, her letters display a constant negotiation between her longing to participate in the female community she remembers from before her marriage and her assertion of the rightness of her decision to absent herself from that community:

I have thought much of my Father's family of late, & especially my [dear] Sisters. I suppose you sometimes get together. Le[t] Harriett be remembered, though absent, I sometimes very much wish to compose one of your circle again. I do not mean, that I could be placed <u>back</u> among you; (<u>that</u> I could <u>never</u> submit <u>to</u>, unless providence made it as plainly my duty as it did to leave you) but that I could sit with you as I am; with the Husband of my choice. (letter to Herman and Flora Gold Vaill, 7 January 1831)

By juxtaposing submission with choice, Harriett reveals exactly what was at stake in her marriage. Choosing her husband was an act of self-assertion, expressed though it was in the language of Christian obedience, which contradicted the expected female trait of submission. She chose her life's course rather than accepting the one set out for her by tradition, cultural expectation, and family example. And though she experiences the costs of that decision—the rupture in the sisterly circle because of distance, Abbey's continuing resentment, and her own longing for her mother—she never admits to regretting it.

There is no hint anywhere in the letters that the affection Harriett expresses for Elias is anything but true and is returned in kind. Though one must remain attuned to the rhetorical situation of her letters, which repeatedly attempt to reassure her perhaps skeptical relatives of her happiness, Elias and Harriett seemed to have experienced, according to the evidence produced by the letters, the companionate marriage of mutuality that had emerged as an ideal in the late eighteenth century (Norton, *Liberty's Daughters* 234–35). Soon after her marriage, she writes to her mother with a newlywed's enthusiasm, "My mother will remember what my opinion was with regard to my dear husband before I left Cornwall. Indeed he is all that I could wish him to be. . . . [M]y sisters need not think it is saying anything against their husbands to say I have excelled them all. I know they are all good <u>positively</u>, but mine <u>superlatively</u>" (qtd. in Church 14). It seems difficult for Harriett to describe Elias without the use of superlatives; even six years later, she describes him as the man who "not only professes, but is truly worthy of my warmest affections—m[y t]enderest love" (letter to Herman and Flora Gold Vaill, 7 January 1831). This love was no longer an innocent or untried entity as it was when she announced her engagement; it was tempered by experience and pain, yet it endured nonetheless. On the occasion of her wedding anniversary, she reflects,

> I think it is this day 6. years since I received the hand of Mr. Boudi-nott & gave my own in the covenent of marriage. I now look back to that day with pleasure, & with gratitude. Yes I am thankful. I remember the trials I had to encounter—the thorny path I had to tread, the bitter cup I had to drink—but a consciousness of <u>doing</u> <u>right</u>—a <u>kind affectionate devoted</u> Husband, together with <u>many</u> <u>other</u> blessings, have made amends for <u>all</u>. Surely I have, ere this, entered upon the "<u>sober</u> realities of a married life" & if any tears have been shed for me on that account—I can now pronounce them <u>useless tears</u>. (letter to Herman and Flora Gold Vaill, 29 March [1832])

She betrays a consciousness that her husband might still suffer slights tinged with racial prejudice; when Elias was snubbed by the Everests while on a trip north without her, she writes: "I cannot [endure,] at least I am not <u>willing</u> to endure the thought that my worthy companion should be treated with coolness or neglect by any of my friends. I have been pleased to hear of the reception he has thus far met with among our family connexions in N. York & in Boston. He is worthy of it all—but my heart is warm & I cannot express half what I feel" (letter to Herman and Flora Gold Vaill, 29 March [1832]). Her comment indicates her repudiation of any hierarchies of race that would place her husband in a subordinate position.

Harriett's letters only hint at the acculturation to Cherokee life that she must have been experiencing, to whatever degree. She never mentions the challenges of language translation anywhere in the letters collected here, though a descendant records an anecdote described in an unrecovered letter about how Harriett asked one of Elias's sisters to translate a comment his father had made (Church 15). Yet it is significant that in her letter announcing the birth of her fourth child, she gives the girl a Cherokee name written in the Cherokee syllabary with no English equivalent or translation appended. More often, though, the letters depict her playing the role of a model white woman who is conveying "civilized" values through her domestic role; as mentioned earlier, she hosts a quilting bee and sews bonnets for Cherokee women, and she presumably instructs Elias's sisters and other missionary students in domestic skills.

In a muted way, however, the letters do reveal a shift in Harriett's attitudes toward the Cherokees and her place among them. During her engagement, she viewed her marriage as a means of carrying out Christian missionary work among the heathens:

> May we be more watchful & prayerful—live as strangers & pilgrims —knowing that this is not our continuing city. May duty ever be plain to each of us, & may it ever be the greatest desire of our hearts to know the will of God and do it. When I realize the parting with my dear Father, dear Mother, dear sisters, & dear brothers & friends—the thought pierces my very heart, it is trying beyond description—still it is my desire to go. I cannot but rejoice in prospect of spending my days among those ~~illegible~~ despised people & as the time draws nearer I long to begin my work. I think I may reasonably expect many trials, hardships, & privations. May I never be disposed to seek my own ease any farther than is consistent with the greatest usefulness. (letter to Herman and Flora Gold Vaill, 2 January 1826)

Her use here of the language of Christian "duty" and benevolence emphasizes her elevation over the Cherokees in her characterization of them as a "despised people," which serves to mark her as the superior personage in the exercise of charity (Ryan 19). This sort of sentiment largely disappears after Harriett takes up residence in the Cherokee Nation. It is replaced with more overtly political, rather than religious, commentary on the situation of the Cherokees. She writes to Herman Vaill:

> I will only say, I am astonished at the apathy which prevails in the States in regard to the Cherokees. The friends of the Indians seem sleeping while their enemies are diligently pursuing their work & the sufferings of the poor Cherokee are daily increased beneath the oppressor's rod. You say there are a few "Ancient Lords of the soil"

still left in your town. Now Dr Brother do you treat them as ~~such~~ though they once were such? Do you with the most untiring diligence endeavor to instruct and enlighten them. I am sure if I were there I should be willing to be shut out from all other society that I might manifest my friendship to them—if by so doing I could be beneficial to their interests. I am not enthusiastic on this subject. How are the American people ever to atone for the injuries done the original inhabitants of this Country? With shame for my native State, I notice the proceedings of the late Connecticut legislature towards a remnant of the Mohegan Tribe of Indians. Could they not do a little? I know not how to stop or write of any thing else, so greatly are my feelings interested & sympathies excited for the suffering Indians. (letter to Herman and Flora Gold Vaill, 1 July 1831)

While Harriett here writes of the importance of "instruct[ing] and enlighten[ing]" Native Americans, thus still showing some adherence to the idea of "civilizing" them, she introduces another, more egalitarian possibility, that of "friendship." Crucially, she states that she would offer her "friendship" only if it "could be beneficial to their interests." There is no missionary rhetoric here, no argument about the need to remove them from a state of savagery. Though Susan Ryan has explained that much of antebellum benevolence was aimed at remaking the recipient of charity in the benefactor's own image (19), Harriett's primary concern as expressed in this letter is not to create Christian Indians. Instead, there is a suggestion that she has come to see "instruct[ion] and enlighten[ment]" as tactical strategies. This view is closer to the Cherokee view, according to which the Cherokees selectively adapted the instruction missionaries offered (Perdue, *Cherokee Women* 181). Harriett's views now differ significantly from those of the pious Christians in her native Cornwall who saw education primarily as a means to conversion and who focused their charity on the "heathens" far away rather than in their own backyard.

Cherokee Politics
With the passage of time spanned by the couple's letters, Cherokee politics became more and more volatile. Emboldened by south-

erner Andrew Jackson's election as president in 1828, Georgia moved to extend its jurisdiction over the Cherokee Nation, an act Jackson did nothing to prohibit. Along with this extension of jurisdiction, the state deprived Cherokees of their civil rights, governing systems, and the presence of supporters. The state refused to acknowledge the Cherokee's Supreme Court victory in 1832, which upheld Cherokee sovereignty, and instituted a land lottery that reassigned Cherokee lands to white settlers, propelling large numbers of white Georgians onto Cherokee lands and into direct conflict with Cherokees. The political upheaval of these years occupies increasing space in the couple's letters; Harriett writes presciently in 1831, "We know not what is illegible before us. Sometimes I fear the Cherokees will see evil days" (letter to Herman and Flora Gold Vaill, 7 January 1831). Elias, in the same letter, writes, "I think the matter is coming to a crisis, and I am glad it is. Very soon the virtue of the Republic will be put to the test." This test has been well documented by historians who have examined the large-scale effects of Andrew Jackson's election as president, the passage of the Indian Removal Act, and the state of Georgia's and settlers' increasingly aggressive attempts to gain Cherokee land.[36] The letters of Harriett and Elias record the personal effects of these circumstances on individuals living in the Cherokee Nation who identified their interests with the Cherokees.

In the *Cherokee Phoenix*, Elias frequently documented the murders, assault, and thefts white Georgians committed against Cherokees, abuses from which Elias and Harriett would not have had special immunity. Indeed, by virtue of the prominence of his public position, they would have been justified in fearing being singled out. In 1831, they watched authorities jail their close friend and neighbor, missionary Samuel A. Worcester, for his refusal to take the oath of allegiance to Georgia and witnessed the suffering his wife, Ann, and children endured as they awaited his release for a period of two years.[37] Elias himself was twice taken in 1831, questioned, and threatened with violence by the commander of the Georgia Guard; because they came directly to his house to take him, Harriett almost surely witnessed the frightening encounters. Elias comments rather wryly on these events: "[W]e have been in hot water ever since our last to you, that is the masculine portion of us. We have hardly known which ~~illegible~~ way to turn. Trouble upon trouble, vexation upon vexation" (letter to Herman and Flora Gold Vaill, 1 July 1831). He described in the *Cherokee Phoenix* why he persevered in the face of such danger:

> I believe I should feel as keenly as any other man the indignity offered to my person, if my back were indeed subjected to the lash; but yet that would be but a trifling consideration in my mind when compared with the dictates of my conscience, and what I consider to be the line of honesty. I could not abandon these on account of threats. . . . And why should I care about a threat if I really thought I was doing my duty, and felt not the workings of a guilty conscience? I should be unworthy of the confidence of my countrymen and friends, if, for fear of a personal chastisement, I should be guilty of a dereliction of duty. (qtd. in Perdue, *Cherokee Editor* 135)

His letters to white northern relatives become somewhat pointed; he writes plaintively, "Why do our friends at the north appear to be so careless? Do they not know that a piece of great wickedness is in a course of perpetuation?" (letter to Herman and Flora Gold Vaill, 1 July 1831).

If Harriett's views evolved, so too did Elias's, though in a way that has marked him as one of the most controversial figures in Cherokee history.[38] As editor of the *Cherokee Phoenix*, Elias had consistently articulated a wide-ranging argument resisting removal. He celebrated the Supreme Court ruling on *Worcester v. Georgia*, describing it as "glorious news" (Dale and Litton 5). In a letter to his brother, he writes:

> The laws of the State are declared by the highest judicial tribunal in the Country null and void. It is a great triumph on the part of the Cherokees so far as the question of their rights were concerned. The question is for ever settled as to who is right and who is wrong, and the controversy is exactly where it ought to be, and where we have all along been desirous it should be. It is not now before the great state of Georgia and the poor Cherokees, but between the U.S. and the State of Georgia, or between the friends of the judiciary and the enemies of the judiciary. We can only look and see whoever prevails in this momentous crisis. (Dale and Litton 5)

It was after Elias realized that the U.S. government, under Jackson's lead, would not intervene to prevent Georgia's abuses that he began to have doubts about the continued possibilities for coexistence between Americans and Cherokees in the Southeast. By late 1832, Elias began to advocate removal, believing that the Cherokees needed to secure through treaty making whatever advantages they could to palliate the harsh effects of a removal that he now saw as inevitable. Principal Chief John Ross continued to resist removal adamantly and retained the support of most of the conservative Cherokees, while Elias became a leader, along with his uncle Major Ridge and his cousin John Ridge, of a party rival to Ross's leadership called the Ridge Party or the Treaty Party. In an undated fragment of a letter, Harriett distinguished between the parties of Ross and her husband as "lovers of the land, and lovers of the people" (Harriett Boudinot, letter, n.d.). Though Elias hoped to initiate an open discussion of the issue in the pages of the *Cherokee Phoenix*, the National Council wanted the paper to voice only antiremoval views, and he resigned as editor in 1832. Harriett voices the uncertainty of this period in the undated letter fragment: "Our situation is becoming truly desperate. . . . For my own part, I look upon this pleasant land, this delightful climate as no longer a home for ourselves or our children. Even should the Nation choose to remain, and meet the consequences, we have no idea that we shall do so." In 1834–35, Elias, Harriett, and their children took a trip that Harriett had long anticipated to New England to visit her family. While in the North, Elias also took part in treaty negotiations with the U.S. government.

After returning to the Cherokee Nation, Elias signed his name in December 1835 to the Treaty of New Echota, which ceded the Cherokees' land to Georgia. The signing of this infamous treaty took place in Elias and Harriett's own house. In an 1837 letter, Elias described the factors that led him to sign the treaty. After reciting a litany of the abuses—including multiple murders—that the Cherokees had suffered at the hands of white Georgians, he writes:

> I see here nothing but certain death, and at the West a probable way of escape. I cannot hesitate. Whether it is right and justifiable on the part of the United States that the Cherokees should remove,

is not now the question. That it is right for the Cherokees to save themselves from destruction, bears no question in my opinion; and such is the dictate of wisdom and sound reason.

But whether or not it will be of any advantage to the Cherokees to remove, that they will have to go, is a proposition that bears no reasonable dispute, and of which the Cherokees ought long since to have been fully satisfied. But for want of proper information they have not been, and those who have been satisfied, comprising a portion of the intelligence of the Country, have pursued, what I conceive to be a very destructive policy, to remain here at all events until they are forced away, as though that would add credit to their character, and disgrace and infamy to the oppressors. This is a mistaken policy.

It was in view of all these matters, to which I have referred in the foregoing paragraphs, that I was induced to sanction the Treaty of 1835. I was fully satisfied that it was the best that could be done for the Cherokees, and that it was far preferable that they should go, however reluctantly, with the advantages of that Treaty, than that they should be driven away degraded and impoverished. (letter to David Green, 1 August 1837)[39]

His role in the making of the treaty led to his being considered a traitor by the very people to whom he had dedicated his life's work, the consequences of which he bore in his life and in the reputation history has assigned him. Generations of historians have puzzled over the apparently contradictory impulses that drove Elias to take the course he did. Most recently, Perdue emphasizes that Elias viewed himself as working conscientiously to preserve the Cherokee Nation. Yet despite the sincerity of his motives, Perdue argues that Elias's high level of assimilation to white culture rendered him out of touch with the vast majority of Cherokees who were traditionalists, rejected "civilization" to one degree or another, and resisted removal. Indeed, Perdue contends that the "Nation" of Cherokees — "civilized" and Christian — that Elias worked so hard to preserve did not, in fact, exist. It was a colonialist vision to which he too readily acceded (*Cherokee Editor* 33).[40]

In the last letter written by Harriett collected here, she writes, "Indeed I wish you could see us in our family, in our neighbourhood, and our Nation. . . . I wish you to see how Indians can live—how families, & how a nation of Indians can live" (letter to Herman and Flora Gold Vaill, 29 March [1832]). Her underlining of the word "live" rather than "can," a word that would suggest an argument about how Indians can be "civilized," perhaps functions as a repudiation of the vanishing Indian myth and a validation of the vigor of the Cherokee Nation; her emphasis on "nation" suggests not just a pride in her own family's "civilized" existence but an extension of that pride across the entire population, traditionalist and assimilationist alike.

Posthumous Reconstructions

After bearing her sixth child, Harriett suffered an unspecified illness and died three months later in August 1836 at the age of thirty-one. Elias, whom a friend described in 1836 as "of the finest sensibilities—very domestic in his feelings and habits" (Sophia Sawyer to David Greene, 21 September 1836), was overwhelmed with "extreme anguish" at Harriett's death and took to his bed in "very low spirits" (letters to Benjamin and Eleanor Gold, 16 August 1836 and 22 March 1837). He found that his customary eloquence with the written word deserted him in his grief: "You cannot imagine the extent of my bereavement. I cannot express it—it is beyond the power of language to express. When I think of that dear individual—for ten years my endeared companion—one who was willing in youth to leave her paternal home & her friends for me—now no more—whose face I am never to see in this illegible world. Oh it is more than human nature can bear" (letter to Herman and Flora Gold Vaill, 28 August 1836). The memory of what had occurred years before in Cornwall still rankled. Elias defends Harriett's memory from those who called her "criminal" years earlier, challenging "any in her native country, in her native village, who can bring aught against her" to come forward and "allege their charges" in the Cherokee Nation, where "she spent the best ten of her years" (letter to Job Swift Gold, 26 October 1836). In the same letter, he describes her as "emphatically the favorite of this Country," "honored in the recollection of all who knew her," and one who "commanded such universal respect" from the "highest to the lowest."

Even white Georgians, who despite being "carried away with over-wrought passions and prejudices against our race, such as personally knew her, or had heard of her from report have testified to her worth and unsullied character." Elias thus begins to construct a posthumous version of Harriett's life in which he defends her in death against the slurs he could not prevent in life because of his own marginalization.

An obituary printed in the *New York Observer* soon after her death also constructed a posthumous image of Harriett, one well suited to the gendered norms of the day. The bulk of the article is a reprinting of Elias's letter dated 16 August 1836 to Harriett's parents describing her death, but the letter is bracketed by the comments of an anonymous author who provides the context, background, and commentary on Elias's letter.[41] The writer memorializes Harriett as the pattern of female benevolence and charity, a person who "sacrificed a thousand earthly comforts and sought a place where she might better exercise her benevolence," one whose "highest happiness consisted in the ability to minister to others." Ever "forgetful of self," she dedicated her life to "acts of good to others," seeking out "the bed of sickness and cottage of the poor." "She has left us a bright example for imitation," the article states ("Last Hours" 102–3).

The article concludes with a tantalizing suggestion that a biography of Harriett's life was being contemplated, though it was evidently never written. The writer then makes a revealing comparison of Harriett's life to that of Harriet Newell, subject of the biography *Memoirs of the Life of Mrs. Harriet Newell* (1815), popular in missionary circles. Newell married a missionary at the age of eighteen, departed with him to India, and died within a year. Harriett and her family were familiar with the book; in a letter before her marriage, Herman Vaill recommends it to her as "a good Pattern for the female missionary" (letter to Benjamin Gold, 5 September 1825), and according to Elias's description, Harriett compared the circumstances of her last illness to those of Newell. Indeed, there were significant similarities between the two women's lives. Newell also believed that her marriage was a response to a call from God to enter the missionary life, and she, too, faced opposition from family members and accusations that love for her intended husband was actually motivating her. Both women found their removal from mother and siblings very painful and died soon after delivering a child. Even the news of Newell's death is delivered to her mother in a letter written by her husband in a very similar form to the one Elias sends Harriett's parents after her death, suggesting the conventionality of such letters and the etiquette of nineteenth-century grief.

Scott Casper has examined the increasing number of women's biographies published during this period, many of which emerged from religious movements. According to Casper, biographies like Harriet Newell's or that of Harriett Gold Boudinot, as it is presented in brief form in her obituary, illustrated "the public, active roles that women could play within the boundaries of evangelical Christianity and without losing their femininity" (113). The writer does emphasize Harriett's fulfillment of her gendered role in a statement that a lengthened version of Harriett's biography would "be entertaining and useful presenting an elevated character in the domestic relations as well as in that of a missionary sent forth by her divine Master, to speak salvation to those in darkness" ("Last Hours" 107). The writer also presents, however, an opportunity to read Harriett's life as one of political engagement. Though Casper characterizes such missionary women as participating in "evangelical empire" (113), the obituary positions Harriett outside and in opposition to the United States' efforts to colonize the Cherokees: "[A]n eye witness of Indian wrongs," according to the article, "[s]he was devoted heart and soul to the welfare of that race, into which she was adopted; and while laboring in their behalf, and mourning over their deplorable condition, she delighted in being one of them and in sharing with the oppressed, rather than with the oppressor" ("Last Hours" 102–3). Though the image of Harriett "mourning over their deplorable condition" could be interpreted as referring to her sorrow over their unconverted state, the phrasing is ambiguous enough to suggest that Harriett grieves over their political situation, caused by the "oppressor" Georgians and U.S. government. In the obituary, then, Harriett's idealized feminine nature stands in tension with the political meanings her life signified.

After her death, Elias placed his children with relatives and missionaries until he could make a plan for the future. Though he considered taking the children to Connecticut, he instead married Delight Sargent, a missionary teacher, in 1837, thereby providing a woman, as he explained to Harriett's parents, who was "universally acknowledged to be like your dear daughter Harriet" as a mother for his six children (letter to Benjamin and Eleanor Gold, 20 May 1837). The family removed to Arkansas in 1838 ahead of the large-scale exodus known as the Trail of Tears.[42] Assassins killed Elias in 1839. Elias's old friend, missionary Daniel Butrick, described the event soon after it happened:

> Mr. Boudinot was killed near his own residence. A Cherokee went to his house, appeared friendly, and perhaps requested him to go to his new house not yet finished. While there, three Cherokees came up, and asked him for medicine. He started with them to the house, but had proceeded but a few steps, when he was thrown down, and stabbed in the back; but as the knife broke, a tomahawk was taken to kill him. His face was cut, and his head very much bruised. (letter to John Howard Payne)

Elias's killers probably saw themselves fulfilling one of two laws. Ten years earlier, the National Council had enacted a law that promised death to anyone who signed away Cherokee lands. The tradition of blood vengeance also called for retribution against anyone who caused a death, and Elias's signing of the Treaty of New Echota made him responsible in the minds of many for the deaths along the Trail of Tears, which historians number around four thousand (Perdue, *Cherokee Editor* 30–31). Major Ridge, Elias's uncle, and John Ridge, his cousin, both of whom had also signed the Treaty of New Echota, were killed on the same day.[43] Longtime friend and collaborator Samuel Worcester wrote after Elias's death, "I would that my beloved friend Mr. Boudinot, had had no part in that transaction; yet I have no doubt of the sincerity of his own conviction that he was doing right, and hazarding his life for the good of his people. He was a great and good man — a man who, in an uncommon degree, exhibited the spirit of the gospel" (letter to Daniel Brinsmade, 26 June 1839). He was also a man, as Perdue emphasizes, whose "historical reputation is, at best, tarnished" and who might be "condemn[ed] . . . not only for his part in negotiating Cherokee removal but also for his narrow view of culture and society" (*Cherokee Editor* 31). In the aftermath of his death, Delight Sargent Boudinot returned to Vermont, her state of origin, with some of the children and placed others of them with Harriett's sister Mary Brinsmade in Connecticut.[44] The Cherokees in Arkansas and Oklahoma, meanwhile, existed in a state of civil division for decades afterward.[45]

A newspaper article printed at the time of Elias's death set out the main contours of the romanticized version of Elias and Harriett's marriage that has passed down through family lore and local histories. Titled "The Cherokee and His Beautiful Bride," the article recounts Elias's education at the Foreign Mission School, where he was successful in "acquiring the arts and accomplishments of civilisation, and with these added to the manly figure and noble bearing of one of the most majestic of the youthful sons of the forest." There he "succeeded in captivating and securing the affections of a beautiful and accomplished young lady" whose family "remonstrated long and resolutely against her encouraging a passion so strange and unnatural." She overcame their resistance, however, and "the beautiful, the lovely and accomplished young girl became the INDIAN'S BRIDE!" "The delicate bride" with her husband "pushed far off to her wigwam home in the lone forests on the Cherokee land." In the conclusion of the article, Harriett lives on while Elias, predictably, seems to have vanished, for when visitors from New England see her, the article concludes, they find Harriett "contented and happy with her lot, in the midst of her little family of half-papoose, half-Yankee urchins, which were the fruits of the Cherokee's marriage with his lovely and beautiful Connecticut bride."[46] Hollowed out of individuality and specificity, this version of Elias and Harriett's marriage masks the complexities and nuances of a very human story filled with conflict and division, joy and loss, love and betrayal. By revealing the epistolary negotiations carried out by the actors in this remarkable narrative, the letters in this volume restore richness and vitality to a family story played out on the larger stage of two nations' histories.

NOTES

1. Eunice Taylor, a distant relative, told this story to her daughter many years after the events she describes (Starr 154). She seems to have underestimated the difference in Harriett's and Stephen's ages—they were actually almost four years apart rather than eighteen months—in order to emphasize their closeness.

2. The title of this volume is inspired by family members' frequent repetitions of the phrase "to marry an Indian"; see Herman Vaill to Harriett Gold, 29 June 1825; Catharine Gold to Herman and Flora Gold Vaill, 18 July [1825]; Flora Gold Vaill to Herman Vaill, [19] September 1825.

3. On missionary efforts to Christianize American Indians generally, see Berkhofer, Salvation, and Satz, and Cherokees specifically, see McLoughlin, Cherokees and Missionaries. See Berkhofer, White Man's Indian, and Pearce for classic studies of white attitudes toward and perceptions of American Indians during this period. For background on the ABCFM, see Andrew and Strong. Houghton Library, Harvard University, Cambridge, Massachusetts, holds the organization's voluminous records.

4. For information on the Foreign Mission School, see Starr 136–57; Gold 29–31 and 341–51; Gabriel 33–42 and 49–56; Andrew; Paul Chamberlain; French; Wilkins 119–52; and Parins 9–11.

5. In the interests of gender equity and because of the many individuals in this study bearing the surnames Gold, Boudinot, Brinsmade, and Vaill, I refer to central players, male and female, by their first names, using last names when needed for clarity's sake. Though there is variation in the spelling of her first name throughout the letters, Harriett usually uses two t's, and I follow her lead; in contrast, although Elias and Harriett both sometimes spell Boudinot as Boudinott, I follow the convention established by most publications in using only one t.

6. See Herman Vaill to Harriett Gold, 29 June 1825, and Bennet Roberts to Herman Vaill, 1 August [1825]. While in Cornwall, English visitor Adam Hodgson lodged with the Gold family, whom he does not name in his Remarks but does mention (Hodgson 247; Starr 142).

7. On transformations in Cherokee culture, see Malone, Cherokees; McLoughlin, Cherokee Renascence; Young; and Theda Perdue's works. Sheidley presents a provocative reading of the shift in late eighteenth-century Cherokee notions of masculinity that would have affected Elias and others of his generation. See Prucha, American Indian Policy; Satz; and Sheehan for background on civilization programs.

8. In what follows, I rely heavily for biographical information on Theda Perdue's introduction to Cherokee Editor, the most recent and complex biographical work on Elias Boudinot. For additional considerations of his life, see Church;

Delly; Foreman, "Murder"; Gabriel; Starr 276–79; Robert Walker 152–53, 155–56; and Wilkins. A word about the pronunciation of Elias's surname: Descendants pronounce the name Bŏŏ-dĭ-nŏt. This pronunciation accords with two additional pieces of evidence: 1) Elias sometimes spelled the name Boudinott, in a seeming desire to distinguish his identity from his benefactor, Elias Stockton Boudinot, and, perhaps, to emphasize the pronunciation of the final t; 2) In a letter to Elias, a correspondent with rudimentary spelling skills rendered his name "Budinote," perhaps a phonetic spelling (Dale and Litton 14).

9. According to Eunice Taylor's reminiscence decades later, the Foreign Mission School students "were never allowed to go beyond a certain limit from the school, never into people's dwellings without an invitation, or sent for an errand from headquarters. When they embraced Christ as their Saviour, they had a written permit to go two or three miles as the permit stated, and talk with people, and tell them what Christ had done for them. We always laid aside all our work when the scholars came" (qtd. in Starr 155).

10. For the story of the Ridge family, see Wilkins. John Ridge's marriage to Sarah Northrop produced the author John Rollin Ridge as one offspring; see Parins for his biography and Cheryl Walker 111–38 and Powell 52–73 for readings of his dime novel, *The Life and Adventures of Joaquin Murieta* (1854).

11. Bunce and other critics of the Foreign Mission School could be considered as taking part in what Ryan describes as an "antisentimental strain of antebellum benevolence" that questioned the costs, both literal and figurative, of the exercise of benevolence. Ryan explains that this critique of benevolence resulted in a "bureaucratizing movement" and elaborate organizational procedures to authenticate the proper uses of charitable contributions (19). Indeed, administrators of the Foreign Mission School printed in the public papers a record of the donations they received and denied reports that the scholars were being dressed or fed too well for their station, as in the report of January 1825 ("Foreign Mission School").

12. For discussions of the relationship between race and gender identities during this period, see Wiegman, Sorisio, and Stepan. On black-white interracial relationships, see Hodes and Lemire. For consideration of colonization's impact on Native American marriage practices, see Plane.

13. For the complete text of "To the Indians of Cornwall," see Gold 31–32; for "The Indian Song, Sarah and John," see Gold 32–34 or Gabriel 182–86. Of course, more-accomplished writers than these two poets—including such well-known figures as James Fenimore Cooper, Catharine Sedgwick, and Lydia Maria Child—also displayed fascination with the theme of interracial intimacy during this period. A partial list of the extensive criticism of such literary depictions includes work by Burnham, Castiglia, Faery, Lemire, Nelson, and Tilton. For dis-

cussions of the function of the figure of the American Indian in American literature more generally, see Bergland, Maddox, and Scheckel.

14. Burnham; Castiglia; Derounian-Stodola and Levernier; Faery; and Namias have participated in the recent attention turned on the genre of the captivity narrative.

15. For descriptions of the change in thinking about race that occurred during the first half of the nineteenth century, see Bieder, Horsman, and William Stanton.

16. For details on these incidents, see Harriett Gold to Herman and Flora Gold Vaill and Catharine Gold, 25 June 1825; Daniel Brinsmade to Herman and Flora Gold Vaill, 29 June 1825; and Catharine Gold to Herman and Flora Gold Vaill, 18 July [1825].

17. See Daniel Brinsmade's letter to Herman and Flora Gold Vaill and Catharine Gold, 14 July 1825.

18. See Godbeer and Perdue, *Cherokee Women* 81–83. It is interesting to note that Elias's father's maternal grandfather was a Scottish frontiersman (Wilkins 4). Thus Elias, like many other Cherokees of the early nineteenth century, was biracial.

19. For treatments of the epistolary novel, see Cook, Favret, Gilroy and Verhoeven, Goldsmith, Kauffman, and MacArthur. For considerations of letter writing, see Barton and Hall, Earle, and How. My work here is heavily indebted to Decker, who offers the most comprehensive consideration of letter writing as a genre and practice in the United States.

20. Though Gabriel quotes from large sections of letters in his book, he does not provide the complete texts, nor does his editing of the letters, which resulted in the regularization of many aspects, conform to accepted documentary editing procedures today. Some of these letters have also been more briefly quoted or cited as sources in various articles on Elias Boudinot or Cherokee history; see Church; Gannett and Gannett; Luebke, *Elias Boudinot*; and Wilkins. This volume is the first to present the complete texts edited according to current scholarly methods. For discussions of the evolution of editing procedures for correspondence, see Kline and Decker 27–37.

21. Sidonie Smith distinguishes between the public act of writing autobiography and the private act of writing autobiographically in letters or diaries (44), which she situates within the domestic sphere (42). Other critics have problematized this distinction; collections on women's autobiography edited by Domna Stanton and by Broughton and Anderson, for example, prominently include essays on letters.

22. Janet Altman, for example, argues that "the paradox of epistolarity is that the very consistency of epistolary meaning is the interplay within a specific set of

polar inconsistencies" (190). Earle discusses how scholars tend to divide into two camps when considering the generic status of the letter. Some scholars emphasize its consistent formal features, whereas others assert its "shapelessness" (8).

23. For a general discussion of these developments, see Decker. For more-detailed discussions, see Fuller on the development of the postal system, Hall on innovations in the material aspects of letter writing, and Schultz on the relationship between letter writing and schooling in the nineteenth century. Dierks describes how letter writing became a marker of social refinement and middle-class status during the late eighteenth century.

24. Decker has questioned whether the differences between manuscript holograph and published text are so great that they actually comprise separate genres (21).

25. An exception to the general neglect of the issue of how the material circumstances of letters' composition affects their content is Sharon M. Harris's discussion of the "interruptive discourse" of women's private writings (24). She argues that the interruptible nature of women's domestic labor also shaped the production, content, and style of their writings, and that some writers transformed what could be seen as a negative factor into an "intellectual and philosophical aesthetic" (22). Decker also considers the materiality of letters (37–56).

26. These wax seals have become the source of much of the disintegration of the letters, which are otherwise in good condition. The color and oil of the wax sometimes has bled through the page, obscuring the words on the other side, and very commonly, the person who opened the letter created a small hole when pulling the wax seal away from the paper, with a resulting eradication of the words under the seal.

27. With the reference to blackness, Daniel Brinsmade takes part in a long tradition of characterizing American Indians as black and linking them with evil. See Norton, *In the Devil's Snare* 58–59.

28. The only documentable factual errors in the narrative are the characterization of Harriett as the youngest child (she was the youngest daughter; she had two younger brothers); the length of time between engagement and marriage (nine instead of six months); and the mention of Sarah Northrop Ridge's effigy being burned (in Harriett's letter of 25 June 1825 to Herman and Flora Gold Vaill and Catharine Gold, she describes the figures as representing herself, Mrs. Northrop, and "an Indian," presumably Elias). Harriett did have two sisters, Flora and Abbey, who married ministers, but whether Sarah's or Catharine's husbands were lawyers or judges is unknown. Taylor's description of Stephen rushing in and saying, "How do you do, Flora?" "How do you do, Boudinot?" may seem confusing to the reader, since Harriett was married to Elias; Starr, for example, calls it either "a slip of memory or a purposed error by Stephen Gold"

(157). I account for the apparent discrepancy by noting that in the previous sentence, Taylor explains that a sister and her husband (probably Flora and Herman Vaill) were visiting. When Stephen greeted his sister Flora, then, he also acknowledged Elias for the first time. The statements Taylor attributes to Harriett are not authenticated by any other documents. The story is repeated with some variations in Robert Walker 161–63.

29. For further discussion of these changes, see Malone, *Cherokees*; McLoughlin, *Cherokee Renascence*; Young; and Perdue, *Cherokee Women*. For the earliest biography of Sequoya, inventor of the Cherokee syllabary, see the 13 August 1828 *Cherokee Phoenix*. In the 1835 census, 43 percent of households in the Cherokee Nation had readers literate in Cherokee, 18 percent had English readers, and 39 percent had no readers in either language (Perdue, *Cherokee Editor* 63 n. 38).

30. The two collaborated on the translation of *Cherokee Hymns Compiled from Several Authors and Revised* (1829), *The Gospel according to Matthew* (1829), *The Acts of the Apostles* (1833), *The Gospel of Jesus Christ according to John* (1838), *The Gospel according to Luke* (1840), *The Epistles of John* (1840), *The Epistles of Paul to Timothy* (1844), and *The Epistles of Peter* (1848). Elias also translated *Poor Sarah, or, the Indian Woman* (1833), the authorship of which is sometimes mistakenly attributed to him.

31. Other native writers from this period include William Apess, Black Hawk, and Betsey Chamberlain. Seaver's account of Mary Jemison's life is one of the rare first-person accounts of racial intermarriage during this period.

32. See Price and Smith for considerations of the status of periodical literature during the nineteenth century. On Elias's role as editor of the *Cherokee Phoenix*, see Luebke; Malone, "*Cherokee Phoenix*"; Martin; Murphy and Murphy; and Perdue, *Cherokee Editor* and "Rising." For critiques of the quest for authenticity in native writing, see Konkle, Warrior, and Angus.

33. Reminiscent of the way he declared himself free from the Foreign Mission School's control at the time of his marriage, Elias consistently asserted his and the paper's independence from missionary influence, emphasizing that the press and types were bought with funds appropriated by the Cherokee Council, not the U.S. government or missionary organizations (Perdue, *Cherokee Editor* 146), and denying reports, including one circulated by his own printer, that the *Cherokee Phoenix* was actually edited by Samuel Worcester.

34. Once a year, those in the employ of the ABCFM submitted lists of needed supplies, and one of Elias and Harriett's gives fascinating insight into the needs and material conditions of their household. "Do." appears to mean "ditto" in what follows:

Mr. Boudinot wishes
50 Reams Super Royal Printing Paper

4 do. Retre Cartridge Paper

2 Canisters Printing Ink

4 lb. Twine

2 lb. Full-faced Brevier Capt. Type

2 lb. do. Long Primer do.

½ lb. small pica letter

½ do. do. do.

16 Bevil Column Rules [such as are (apparently) used in printing the
    N.Y. Observer.]

1 ream Letter Paper

1 Sand box

1 Paper Sand

½ doz. Pencils

2 oz. Wafers

2 Papers Ink Powder

½ doz. cakes Windsor Soap

½ lb. Chalk

2 oz. Ep. Tansey

1 bottle Opodeldoc

1 box Lee's Pills

1 lb. Cream Tartar

2 oz. Paregoric

4 good Bed Cords

1 blue cloth Frock Coat

1 pr. do. Pantaloons

1 do. do. best

1 pr. lasting Pantaloons

1 silk Vest. [Mr. Boudinott is 5 ft. 7 in. in height, and 2 ft. 8 in. around
    the waist. He would like loose pantaloons.]

2 Handkerchiefs

2 prs. woolen Socks

2 prs. cotton do.

2 prs. dark cotton Stockings

2 pieces dark Am. Gingham

9 yds. Calico for little girls

7 yds. English buff gingham, double width

1 pr. good Boots right & left No. 5 ½

1 pr. Morrocco pumps No. 5

2 pr. Women's Shoes calf good thick No. 5

½ lb. white cotton thread

½ lb. assortment do.

½ lb. Sewing Silk

7 yds. British Shirting

15 yds. unbleached Cotton Shirting no. 16

1 large Hair Comb

2 Side Combs

3 fine Darning Needles

3 common do.

1 paper Needles No. 5 Sharps

1 do. do. No. 4 Betweens

1 do. do. No. 6 Sharps

1 do. do. No 7 Sharps

6 yds. red Flannel

8 lb. black Tea

2 lb. green Tea

1 oz. Nutmeg

4 sheets Tin Plate

2 long flat Tins

2 10 qt. Milk Pans

1 doz. Cups & Saucers

1 block-tin Teapot largest size

1 pr. Iron Candlesticks

1 pr. Steel Snuffers

Garden Seeds [the same as for the Mission] [ed. note: The Mission had
    requested cabbage, lettuce, cucumber, radish, onion, parsnip, and
    carrot seeds (Bass 62).]

1 5 pail Brass Kettle-bailed

2 rose Blankets

1 roll Paper Hangings

1 bottle Cayenne Pepper

1 dressing comb

1 ivory Comb

1 cheap Dressing Glass 8 in. by 10.

1 pair Fire dogs 12 lb. or 15 lb.

1 flute, & directions for playing [cost not to exceed $6] (brackets in
    original except for those labeled editor's note; qtd. in Bass 63–64)

Four days later, the family added to their list:

Mr. Boudinott wishes added

1 lb Redwood

1 pair mantuamaker's Shears

1 doz. good common knives & forks

Mr. Wheeler's teakettle, already mentioned, to contain 6 quarts

"I shall be enabled to oblige some of my neighbors if you send me

    1 doz. Webster's Spelling Book" (quotation marks in original;

    qtd. in Bass 66)

35. Perdue describes the efforts by Cherokee women, for example, to spin and weave so as to carve out a niche for themselves in the market economy in which the Cherokees were now participating (*Cherokee Women* 115–34).

36. See Prucha, *American Indian Policy*; Satz; and Sheehan for the U.S. government's policies toward Native Americans during this period.

37. See Bass for Worcester's biography.

38. See Perdue, *Cherokee Editor* 25–30, for a concise outline of Elias's actions in the years 1831–39.

39. For Elias's criticisms of John Ross's leadership, see his *Letters and Other Papers Relating to Cherokee Affairs* (1837).

40. Susan Ryan has argued that in his advocacy of removal, Elias adopted the "benevolent paternalism" of white reformers and signed the treaty "for his people's good but against their will" (22). To some degree, however, Elias's turn to removal can be read as signifying a continued distancing of himself from missionary views following in the tradition of his denial of the authority of agents of the Foreign Mission School over his life choices and his defense of the *Cherokee Phoenix* from imputations of missionary control. It is too simplistic to view Elias's assimilationist tendencies as always allying him with white interests in opposition to Cherokee; the mapping of political allegiances is rarely neatly categorized according to racial identity. Indeed, as historians have pointed out, multiple and overlapping factions existed among the Cherokees (Young 504), and there was also significant disagreement among white Americans concerning removal. Indeed, Elias's support for removal placed him at odds with some white interests, such as those represented by the ABCFM (Young 522). Missionaries who were close friends with Elias, including Samuel Worcester and Daniel Butrick, believed the Treaty of New Echota to be false and Elias's signing of it to be misguided at best. Worcester described the treaty as a "fraudulent and wicked transaction," though he continued to "believe that Mr. Boudinot was, in the ordinary sense of the term, conscientious in the part he acted" (qtd. in Gabriel 176); Butrick wrote a letter to Elias in 1839 pleading for him to acknowledge and apologize for the impropriety of his actions (letter to Elias Boudinot, 9 June 1839). Elias's action set him in opposition to missionaries and to the desires of most

Cherokees, though, ironically, it aligned him with the interests of the U.S. government he had opposed for so long.

41. I have included the full text of the writer's commentary in the notes to Elias Boudinot's letter to Benjamin and Eleanor Gold, 16 August 1836.

42. On the Trail of Tears, see William Anderson; Ehle; Filler and Gutman; Foreman, *Indian Removal*; and Wallace.

43. Reportedly, a large group of assassins took John Ridge from his bed at dawn, dragged him out into his yard, stabbed him twenty-five times, cut his jugular vein, and stamped one by one on his body as they walked across it. His killers restrained his wife, Sarah Northrop Ridge, in her struggles to reach him, according to their oldest son, John Rollin Ridge (called Rollin by the family). She ran to his side in time to witness his last breath. Rollin describes the images that haunted him throughout his life:

> Then succeeded a scene of agony. . . . In a room prepared for the
> purpose lay pale in death the man whose voice had been listened to
> with awe and admiration in the councils of his Nation, and whose
> fame had passed to the remotest of the United States, the blood
> oozing through his winding sheet and falling drop by drop on the
> floor. By his side sat my mother, with hands clasped and in speechless
> agony—she who had given him her heart in the days of her youth and
> beauty, left the home of her parents and followed the husband of her
> choice to a wild and distant land. (qtd. in Wilkins 322–23)

Later in the day, Major Ridge was shot and killed instantly while crossing a creek on horseback along the Arkansas border. Stand Watie, Elias's brother, was also believed to have been targeted but escaped unharmed.

After her husband's death, Sarah Northrop Ridge and her eight children settled in Fayetteville, Arkansas. Because of difficulties in settling his will occasioned by Cherokee politics, the family experienced reduced financial circumstances. Rollin harbored revenge fantasies toward his father's killers for most of his life. He attended school for two years in Massachusetts, near his Northrop grandparents, before returning to Arkansas and eventually settling in California, where he began his writing career. See Wilkins and Parins for descriptions of the murders and the effect of their aftermath on the family.

44. Dale and Litton reprint letters written by Harriett and Elias's children Eleanor Susan, Mary Harriett, William Penn, and Elias Cornelius in *Cherokee Cavaliers*, and the Cornwall and Torrington Historical Societies also hold letters written by Mary and William. The letters express the children's longing for their deceased parents, reunion with each other, and a return to their "old home at

the West" (Dale and Litton 62) and their "Indian friends" (Dale and Litton 63). After her sister Sarah's death, Mary wrote in an 1845 letter to her grandparents, "Ours is indeed a broken family. Three have already entered that unseen world from whence there is no return, while the remainder are left in different places to mourn their early departure. We do not lament them for their sakes, knowing that they are far better than they could have been on Earth; but we mourn our own loss which is great indeed" (letter to Benjamin Gold, 24 September 1845). As Eleanor wrote eight years after Elias's death, "God saw fit to take Pa and others away. . . . [T]here is some good reason unknown to us why Pa was snatched from us, and at the time too it seemed when he was most needed by his family; but we have found friends and very near ones too, yet how many times have I thought if I only had a father and mother I would be happier but it is wrong to murmur and I will try and not indulge myself in such murmurings" (Dale and Litton 61). Eleanor Susan (b. 1827) married Henry Church in 1848, had one child, and died in 1856. Mary Harriett (b. 1828) attended Mt. Holyoke from 1846 to 1848 (Dale and Litton 55), married Lyman Case in 1849, and died in 1853. William Penn (b. 1830) worked briefly as an engraver in Philadelphia before returning to Arkansas. He there commenced a long career as a newspaperman and public servant (Dale and Litton 63, 73). He fathered a child with Eleanor Reese, married Caroline Fields in 1853, and had eight children with her. He disappeared in 1898; family members speculate that he was murdered or committed suicide. Sarah Parkhill (b. 1832) died in 1845 at the age of thirteen. Elias Cornelius (b. 1834) studied civil engineering and worked briefly in Ohio before returning to Arkansas and beginning a career in law (Dale and Litton 84). He later acted as an officer in the Confederacy during the Civil War and, after the war, served the Cherokees in a number of prominent public roles. He married Clara Minear in 1885 and died in 1890. See Adams for further information on his life. Unlike his brothers, Frank Brinsmade (b. 1836) remained in the North and became an actor. He married a woman named Annie and had one child, dying in 1864 during the Civil War while serving on the Union side (Dale and Litton 170).

45. For the period after removal, see Dale and Litton and McLoughlin, *After the Trail of Tears*.

46. For discussion of the myth of the "vanishing" Indian, see Dippie.

PART I

Connecticut Letters, 1823–1826

[Addressed to:] Miss Harriet R. Gold, / Cornwall / Connecticut

Rutland N.Y. August 22. 1823.

Dear Sister Harriet,

As I shall have an opp. to send to Ct next week, I can hardly refrain from dropping you a line.

The general incidents of my journey & labours, you have doubtless learnt from my weekly epistles to Flora;[1] ergo, I shall in this letter make some desultory remarks upon topicks perhaps especially interesting to you. You know that I used to love to keep school; & teach young ideas how to shoot. By the by, how many & how various were the ideas that I learned ^taught^ to shoot, when I kept school in Cornwall. (Some ideas that begun to shoot that winter, have continued to grow ever since. Ask Flora if it isn't so.)

I love to visit schools still; I have visited 3 the present week; & several others before. In this region, I find that, generally the teachers are not thoroughly qualified to teach even Webster's spelling Book;[2] & his "Easy Standard of Pronunciation," is very far from being strictly followed. For instance, in Diaphragm Table, the teacher puts out words thus, "definite," "perquisite" &c, & the same inconsistencies go thro every table in the Book. In the method of instruction, there is no pains taken to make children understand the reason of things. Everything is done by rote, and children learn their a, b, c, from top to bottom, and from bottom to top, without knowing perhaps a single letter, but round o and crooked s.[3] They are not learnt to pronounce their [abc?] —nor to keep their own place—& in short their whole system, (Parents, & Teachers, & children) seems to be going wrong. Still there may be some exceptions—but I have found only one that I tho't come anywhere near the right way. In the schools which I have visited, but one teacher professes religion. She is a Baptist; but does not pray in her school; nor is such a thing as a catechism, nor indeed any kind of religious instruction, known. I trust you would change the face of things, were you here. This subject I conclude must be somewhat familiar, if not interesting to you—but from it, I will turn to one which I suppose, by this time, to be more familiar, if not more interesting; Both I guess.

Poor Harriet, I am sorry that you are so attractive, that every old bachelor who owns land near you, & every old widower that comes along in search of minerals, should fix their eyes, on you. They come up, I suppose, & stare at you, just as if you were a Guide Board; & I dare say they think they can read on you, the road they would choose to walk in. The Col⁰ reads, The Direct & nearest road to a State of Second Youth, & the name of Dada—while Mr H_ reads, The nearest road to "Mine Mountain," & I suppose he thinks there is Gold there. The latter object of remark it is said is poor; I believe he has lost his property; But Poverty, honestly come by, is no disgrace; if it were your brother Vaill would be disgraced to the uttermost. He [end of page 1] wished for Gold to mend his fortunes, or to aid him in bearing his mis-fortunes & perhaps Mr H. wants it for the same reason; & you know any man would rejoice if while he was looking out for minerals in the earth, he should discover a solid junk⁴ of Gold above ground. & dear sister, I do not know but thee will make him a good wife. Dost thou affection him, verilie & trulie? marry him, & let others talk. You have intrinsic, & extrinsic worth & he has "great larnin." He can make Almanacks, and your children can peddle them.

You see I do not urge you to "Forbear"—choose who you please, white, or black, or red. Give by all means, my best, & warmest love to your sister Flora, & accept the sincere, & fraternal regard of your friend

Herman L. Vaill

* * *

Dear Flora, I should write to you by Judge B. but he may go thro' Goshen, & I choose to send to you direct, by mail,. I hope to hear from you next Monday night. You may expect one from me per mail of Wednesday after next. Should he call, either way—thank you to send me one pair of Drawers by him, without fail. I am well as usual; love my wife as usual, or rather more; wish to see her as usual, or rather more; & hope to see her before long, as usual. Your affectionate husband— Herman L.V.

[LM 1] I took a severe cold last night and today am almost sick.

[RM 1] Saturday—P.M. Dear wife—Upon second thoughts I would thank you to send one of my flannel wrappers, as well as a pair of Drawers by Mr Bronson. I shall want both on my journey. If convenient, you can perhaps leave them done up at Mr Harveys—unless you see Mr B. on his way down.

1. Flora Gold Vaill (1799–1883), Harriett's older sister, married Rev. Herman Landon Vaill (1794–1870) in January 1823. Herman courted Flora while acting as a teacher and assistant to the principal at the Foreign Mission School.

2. Noah Webster's *The American Spelling Book: Containing an Easy Standard of Pronunciation*, first published in 1783 and reprinted frequently thereafter, was a widely used textbook in American schoolrooms in the early nineteenth century.

3. The *o* and *s* in the preceding sentence were written in a decidedly darker and wider stroke. I have used italics to replicate this emphasis.

4. The *Oxford English Dictionary* gives a British meaning for "junk" of "lump or chunk."

STEPHEN GOLD TO HERMAN AND FLORA GOLD VAILL
AND CATHARINE GOLD, 11 JUNE 1825
HLVC, m.

[Return address:] Cornwall Ct. / June 13th [Addressed to:]
Rev. Herman L. Vaill / East Hadam / Millington Soci [Postage:] 10

Cornwall June 11th 1825

My verry dear Brother & Sisters[1]

The dye is cast, Harriet is gone, we have reason to fear. Yes. She has told Mr Harvy[2] that she was engaged to that Indian E.[3] and that she is determined to marry him. O!! dear!!!

Last Tuesday, Mr Brinsmade[4] made his suspisions know to the Board,[5] and it made them (as he expressed it,) "as white as sheets." Mr Stone[6] rose up and said it was a lie, but upon hearing Mr B reasons, his mouth was stop'd. Mr. Harvey was over yesterday, purpose-ly to talk with Father and Mama and H— left a letter, that in full expressed her determinations. Mr H. is going to preach hear to morow, & is going to hand H— a letter, which she is to answer by the next Thirsday—on that day, the commity meet for no other purpose, than to publish to the world what they know, & their surprise! or should H— give up her purpose, to enjoin secrecy.

Words cannot, no. let imagination only express, the feelings of my heart.

Your brother
Stephen J. Gold

[LM] (Now if you can help do)

1. Stephen Johnson Gold (1801–80), Harriett's older brother, wrote this letter to their sister Flora and her husband, Herman Vaill, as well as to their sister Catharine (1803–1888), who was visiting the Vaills in Millington when the news of Harriett and Elias's engagement became public.

2. The Reverend Joseph Harvey, minister in Goshen, Connecticut, and an agent of the Foreign Mission School in Cornwall.

3. Elias Boudinot studied at the Foreign Mission School from 1818 to 1822. Born in 1804, Elias had been educated from the age of six at missionary schools in the Cherokee Nation and was viewed as one of the most promising scholars at Cornwall. He had hopes of going on to study at the Andover Theological Seminary in Massachusetts, but ill health forced him to return to the Cherokee Nation in 1822. Elias and Harriett's courtship progressed entirely through correspondence.

4. Harriett's brother-in-law, General Daniel Brinsmade (1768–1862). The husband of Gold's older sister Mary (1794–?), he was an agent of the Foreign Mission School. A family history describes him as "a tall slender man of nervous, active temperament" (Brinsmade 20).

5. Members of the Board of Agents for the Foreign Mission School were appointed by the American Board of Commissioners for Foreign Missions (ABCFM), an organization comprised mainly of Congregationalists and Presbyterians, to oversee the operation of the school. Lyman Beecher, father of Harriet Beecher Stowe, was one of the agents.

6. Timothy Stone (1774–1852), the minister of Cornwall's Congregational Church.

[Return address:] Goshen Ct. / June 27 [Addressed to:]
Rev. Herman L. Vaill / East Haddam / Millington Society
[Postage:] 11

Saturday P.M. June 25, 1825

Dear Brother & Sisters,

I expected to spend a principal part of the day in writing to you but
have been so much troubled with the toothache that I have not been
able to do much. In the first place I thank you for your letter & friendship thus far. I am truly rejoiced to learn that you are so pleasantly
situated. May a kind providence ever smile upon you & make you happy
and useful. Now what shall I make the subject of my letter? A painful
one to you no doubt but you will not be so much surprised as I hear you
have been to Windham.[1] Yes it is so—the time has come when your
Sister Harriett is already published to an <u>Indian</u>. If you have seen Mr
Stone quarterly report you have seen our names and intentions.[2] Pen
cannot describe nor language express the numerous & trying scenes
through which I have passed since you left us. But I trust I have had
that support through them all, which the world could not give. Never
before did I so much realize the worth of religion & so much pity
those, who, in time of trouble were without this inestimable treasure.
I have seen the time when I could close my eyes upon every earthly
object & look up to God as my only supporter, my only hope—when
I could say with emotions I never felt before, to my heavenly Father,
"other refuge have I none, So I helpless hang on thee"[3] I still have the
consolation of feeling that I have not acted contrary to duty & that
what I have done as respects forming a connexion is not adverse to
divine approbation. I know that I appear at present to stand alone, the
publick, "good people & bad," are against me. I cannot say that all are
against me—there are many who are still my friends, but the excitement at present is such that they dare not have it known that they are
on my side. You can have no idea of the scenes we have witnessed the

week past. Yes, in this Christian land. The members of the M.S. many of them said [end of page 1] it was more than they ever knew among the heathen & I should not wonder if people said that such could not be [termed?]. But it was not done merely by the wicked world—professed Christians attended & gave their approbation. I will give you a brief description. Mr. Brinsmade gave information to the Agents that another Indian wedding[4] was in contemplation—consequently I soon received a long letter from Mr. Harvey which after prayerful consideration I answered & the result was known far & wide as speedily as the wings of the wind could spread it & wednesday last was appointed for the day when great things were to be and [illegible] were effected. It being thought unsafe for me to stay at home I left the night before & was kept in a chamber at Capt. Clarks where I had a full prospect of the solemn transactions in our Valley. In the evening our respectable young people Ladies & Gentlemen convened on the plain to witness and approve the scene & express their indignation. A painting had before been prepared representing a beautiful young Lady & an Indian; also on the same, a woman, as an instigator of Indian marriages.[5] Evening came on. The church Bell began to toll one would conclude, speaking the departure of a soul. Mr. John C. Lewis and Mr. Rufus Payne[6] carried the corpses & Brother Stephen set fire to the barrel of Tar or rather the funeral pile—the flames rose high, & the smoke ascended—some said as it were it reminded them of the smoke of their torment which they feared would ascend forever. My heart truly sung with anguish at the dreadful scene The Bell continued to toll till 10. or 11 O'c This much is accomplished. The transactions were a few rods east of the Mission School-house. In that very season the members of the school were assembled in their Academy praying & I trust earnestly & sincerely for their enemies. Brother Roberts[7] has since told me, he never knew a more quiet & peaceable time in school than now. Within a few days & since this tumult began between 2 & 3 thousand dollars have been given to build the new Academy. But it is true we are in many respects in gloomy circumstances There is a great division of feeling among many but especially in our family. It appears as though a house divided against itself could not stand.[8] Ma[9] is almost worn out she feels as [end of page 2] though her children had no tenderness for her & instead of comforting her were ready to fill up her cup of affliction till it is more than running over.[10] (Sabbath eve.) I attended meeting to-day as usual. As I had been requested to leave the singers seat that I need not disgrace the rest of the girls I took our pew. Church Communion is put off on account of some difficulty occasioned by the Report. I fear the Agents will be in trouble, but I feel it my solemn duty publickly to contradict what they have there stated I do know it to be false. Whatever you, or others may think I do know that no individual whoever has in any way influenced me in forming a connexion. Mr & Mrs. Northrop do suffer most cruelly & unjustly. They feel grieved to the heart. Mrs. N & her family have left Cornwall for the present—it being unsafe for her to be here.[11] Many of the good people of this place do feel greatly [wounded?] by the proceedings of last Wednesday eve. I fear Brother Stephen has, to prevent scandal brought a real scandal upon himself which cannot easily be wiped off. Even the most unprincipled say, they never heard of any thing so low even among the heathen as that of burning a Sister in effigy. Tomorrow eve. is appointed for another meeting what will be done I know not. The Lord reigns & I often repeat these comforting words

> Through waves & clouds & storms, He gently clears the way,
> Wa[it]
> [th]ou his time—so shall this night, Soon end in joyous day[12]

Could I see you I could say many things to you. I cannot by one letter give you any idea of my feelings or circumstances. Brother Vaill you doubtless well remember the morning of my birthday when I was 18.[13] We walked in the garden. A thick, dubious cloud o'ercast the sky. Do you not recollect our conversation? The time has come & I see a thick cloud & although you then said you would sympathise with me, as you so little expected such things—I do not expect that sympathy. The few friends I now have are dearer to me than ever—many delight in showing disrespect, others take uncommon pains to notice & respect me. I feel as though I had wronged no one. I have done nothing but what I had a perfect & lawful right to do. I need say nothing of going to Millington—after reading this—you will not desire it. Ma says Catharine must do as she pleases about coming home. Our wool is safe in the garrett & if C. is not intending to come home soon we wish to know it so that we [can?] let the wool to some body. As to the carpet nothing is done. To tell the truth it is out of the question to do much work of any kind [end of page 3] while under our present circumstances. Angelina does what she can I hope we shall be able to send the other load of your furniture before long. But Stephen says not till after haying. Pa has bought the table at Mr. Kelloggs. The bedticks are brought home & I hope we shall be able to make them & have them filled before long—but it must depend upon circumstances. You can have no idea of our situation. I am glad you are out the way of our trouble. Maria sends love to you all—wishes me to tell you that Elvira is well & grows—but does not learn to talk much. I trust I shall never forget Maria's friendship. I hope I am thankful that I have a few precious friends. I have not been to Brother H's[14] since you left. I understand little Sarah is quite unwell. Ma has been to Br H's but does not feel as though she could ever go again untill she is treated differently. Swift[15] still is troubled with sick turns, looks very poor & pale & I fear will not live long if he does not get help soon. H.R.G.

* * *

My health is pretty good. If you please kiss little Catharine[16] for me. I should like to see the sweet little girl, but perhaps never shall. I hope dear brother & Sister you will be happy & useful as long as you live & may heaven be your home at last. The Lord only knows whether we ever meet again on earth. But if we are the children of our heavenly Father, our separation will be short. Permit me unworthy as I am to subscribe myself once more your affectionate

Sister Harriett R. Gold

Mrs. Prentice has been called to part with her dear little Lucius. Her afflictions are great. I hope you will write to her. May the Lord spare you your little one.

[LM 1] I am reluctant to send you a letter containing what I know will be so un welcome to you. If I had time I would like to say many things. I shall always be glad to hear from you, & hear of your prosperity. I love my friends as well as ever, & think I can also say I love my enemies & hope I can pray for them.[17]

Harriett.

[LM 2] Mrs. Stone[18] advised the singers all to dress in white to-day & wear a piece of black crepe on the left arm—but they did not.

[LM 3] Tabbietha Lewis will go to H. with Esq. Clark tomorrow—is go [missing] the Milliner's trade.

1. Windham, Connecticut, was the home of Gold's sister Abbey (1798–?) and her husband, Rev. Cornelius Everest (?–1869?).

2. In the report, the agents condemned the match, writing, "[W]e feel ourselves bound to say, that after the unequivocal disapprobation of such connexions, expressed by the Agents, and by the christian public universally; we regard the conduct of those who have been engaged in or accessary to this transaction, as criminal; as offering an insult to the known feelings of the christian community" ("Foreign Mission School," 17 June 1825, 6).

3. The first two lines of the second verse of a hymn titled "Jesus, Lover of My Soul," published in John Wesley and Charles Wesley's hymnbook *Hymns and Sacred Poems*, are: "Other refuge have I none, / Hangs my helpless soul on thee" (216–17).

4. A year earlier, John Ridge, another Cherokee student at the Foreign Mission School and Boudinot's first cousin, had married Sarah Northrop, daughter of the school's steward.

5. This woman, "the instigator of Indian marriages," represents Mrs. Northrop, whose daughter Sarah had married Ridge. Many in the community suspected that she had encouraged her daughter's match because of Ridge's wealth and speculated about her role in Gold and Boudinot's engagement.

6. John C. Lewis and Rufus Payne played prominent roles in an organization called the Bachelors of "Cornwall Valley," formed in 1824 in the wake of the controversy surrounding the Northrop-Ridge marriage. The group of young men, led by Lewis and Payne, submitted an editorial to the *American Eagle* disputing earlier newspaper accounts that "young ladies of this place show an undue partiality toward the members of the Foreign Mission School" and asserting that "we spurn at the intimation that we have been cast into the shade, by our rivals, white or tawny" (qtd. in Gabriel 63–64).

7. Bennet Roberts, a former student, was assistant to the principal of the Foreign Mission School and a concerned friend of Harriett's. See his letter to Herman Vaill, 1 August [1825].

8. Matthew 12:25, Mark 3:25, Luke 11:17.

9. Eleanor Johnson Gold (1764–1858) was sixty years old at this time and the mother of fourteen children.

10. A combining of two biblical verses: "cup of affliction" (Obadiah 1:16) and "my cup runneth over" (Psalms 23:5).

11. The agents' report had displaced responsibility for the match from the school onto Mrs. Northrop, describing her as the "single individual, to whose misguided and extraordinary conduct, all our troubles on this subject are justly to be ascribed" ("Foreign Mission School," 17 June 1825, 6). They were, in part, responding to earlier accusations published in a local newspaper that intermarriages were the "fruit of the missionary spirit, and caused by the conduct of the clergymen at that place and its vicinity" (qtd. in Gabriel 61). Isaiah Bunce's editorial went on to directly name the agents of the school as "mediately or immediately the cause of the unnatural connection" (qtd. in Gabriel 62). Elias and Sarah Northrop Ridge corroborated Harriett's sentiment that Mrs. Northrop was "unjustly" treated. Evarts reported in February 1826 that Elias "exonerates M. Northrop entirely from having enacted any agency in promoting the match, so far as he is concerned. Neither she, nor her daughter, advised him in the matter. He commenced the courtship of his own motion. In the course of it, he inclosed two letters to M. Northrop, intended for Harriet" (letter to Henry Hill). Sarah Northrop Ridge's "story perfectly agreed with that of Boudinot, in regard to the fact that the proposal of marriage originated with him & that neither she nor her mother had any thing to do with it—that, on the contrary, her mother dissuaded Harriet from it on the ground that her daughter's marriage had made so much difficulty in Cornwall," wrote Evarts in April 1826 (letter to Henry Hill).

12. Words from the hymn "Give to the Wind thy Fears," written by Paul Gerhardt in 1685 and translated into English by John Wesley.

13. Harriett had just turned twenty at the time of writing this letter.

14. Samuel Hopkins (?–1834), husband of Harriett's sister Sarah (Sally) (1788–?). "Little Sarah" refers to the Hopkins's one-year-old daughter.

15. Harriett's youngest brother, Job Swift Gold (1810–44).

16. The Vaills' seven-month-old daughter.

17. Based on Matthew 5:43–44.

18. Mary Merwin Stone, wife of the Reverend Timothy Stone.

[Return address:] Washington Co / June 30 [Addressed to:] Rev^d.
Herman L Vail / East Haddam / Millington Society [Postage:] 10

Washington June 29th 1825

D^r B^r & Sister,

You have doubtless ere this heard that the Cornwall business is all
before the publick the agents have published the thing to the world
The excitement is very great in Cornwall. the young men burnt them
in effigy and toll^d the bell nearly the whole night. Mary has this morning gone to Cornwall with Lewis will return to day to ascertain their
situation. Mrs. N_ has left Cornwall she went off in the night and has
not as yet return^d as I have heard Our trials are great but we must submit. I shall do all in my power to prevent her getting away but expect
it will be in vain. I shall know more particulars when Mary returns and
will write hope you will let us hear from you often.

June 30th—Mary has return^d and I am now more distress^d than
ever our parents have long since given their written consent to the
union. thro Harrietts craftiness by making them believe that she
should die if she did not have her Indian last winter. [end of page 1] I
have not words to express my indignation at the whole proceeding—
the whole family are to be sacrificed to gratify if I may so express it the
animal feeling of one—of its members—and lo! The whole is clothed
under the garb of religion they could not fight against God—is the
reply. I think the brothers & sisters are in duty bound to address their
parents on this subject with suitable but decided disapprobation of
the transaction. They at first gave a decided negative to it but for fear
H would die in love for the Indian they wrote again and said yes—and
behold—the last letter reached him first. I wish I could see you for one
blessed minute I could tell you more than I can convey in two letters.
They have business enough in Cornwall—this marriage (O forbid it),
has already brought about difficulty. Col. Gold feels much injured by
the report of the agents—and two letters has pass^d between him &

M^r. Stone the communion is put off and I know not when it will end.
[end of page 2]

Cornwall is in great turmoil and if the disturbers of the peace could be disposed of and had in safe keeping—it would rejoice the Christian publick

> In haste I subscribe myself
> Your friend and B^r
> D. B. Brinsmade

Give my best love to Sister C—and let her consider this as address^d to her as well as you she appears more & more endear^d to me since this thing has transpired—Eleanor has rec^d an invite to become a [widowers?] lady [missing] the instrumentality of Capt Clarks—[he] lives on the shore of lake Erie in the town of Vermillion—so we go—White & black[1]

1. As he does in his later letter of 14 July 1825, Brinsmade seems to refer here to Elias as black, a not uncommon description of Native Americans in the colonial period. See Norton, *In the Devil's Snare* 58–59.

HERMAN VAILL TO HARRIETT GOLD, 29 JUNE 1825
HLVC, m.

[Return address:] Et Haddam [illegible] / July 1 [addressed to:] Miss Harriett R. Gold / Cornwall / Con [Postage:] Paid 20

East Haddam, Millington Society June 29. 1825.
Dear Sister Harriett,

Intelligence, such as we never expected, has reached us, concerning you; & it is this that induces me, with the affectionate regard of a friend, & a brother, to address you, at this time. You have heretofore expressed your willingness, always to receive advice from your friends. I know I am your friend; & am confident you will be willing to read, & reflect upon, what I shall write.

I am aware that the subject of matrimonial connexions is a delicate one; & that advice to one who is herself interested in the subject, ought to be cautiously given. But the present is such a plain case, &

one that has such important bearings, & is likely to produce such lasting consequences, that I must at least give you my candid opinion & advice, with regard to it. And, my dear Sister, I do hope that, on account of your present personal interest in this subject, & the danger lest you should read with a spirit of prepossession in favour of your own scheme; I do hope you will here stop, & resolve to read & consider my advice, & my reasons for such advice, with a mind open to conviction, & prepared to decide according to evidence of right or wrong.

I know you have long had a desire to become a missionary helper in the cause of Christ among the heathen; & that you were ready to say, whenever the Providence of God should open the door for your entrance upon the work, "Here am I; send me."[1] And, had the Great Head of the [Church], & of Missions, seen fit to prepare the way, by the manifest leadings of his Providence, for you thus to go, & become a labourer in the work, your Christian friends, your Christian relatives, much as they love you, could still, in such circumstances, have cheerfully given you the parting Blessing & the Farewell.

But there is a wide difference between going among the heathen, by the call, & the leadings of Providence; & going among them merely because we will go. There is a wide difference between going, because we love the cause of Christ, & have a single eye to his glory; &, going because we love another object; & have a selfish inducement.

In one case there is obedience to the call of God; in the other there is nothing but rash presumption, & disobedience. And there are manifest rules by which we can decide concerning between the call of Providence, & the way of our own will. Providence calls, when the way is prepared by Providence; When obstacles are removed; & the rational prospect becomes such that we can hope & expect to be made the occasion of more benefit to the cause we profess to love, by going, than in any other way. But where there are obstacles in the way which as yet are not removed; where there is the manifest danger of showing a spirit, & a determination, inconsistent with a Christian profession; & where there is the apparent prospect of doing more injury to the cause by going, than by remaining, then the Christian may be satisfied that Providence, as yet, has not called him. [end of page 1] In such a case, the Christian ought to be satisfied; & the Christian, with a proper spirit, will be satisfied, to submit; & however his own feelings may have led him to hope; to still he will be resigned to the will of God, as the Being, who, if he has work for his people to do, in any particular sphere, will order circumstances, & overrule obstacles, so that the way shall be made plain, & strength be given them to perform their duty.

I suppose you are not in doubt as to the nature of the intelligence that has reached us concerning you. And after having given the subject in question, a deliberate, & I trust, a prayerful consideration; after having looked at in all its probable bearings, & viewed it in connexion with what I deem its inevitable consequences; I am prepared to advise; & my dear Sister, I do, most affectionately advise, that you give up all present intentions, & all thoughts, of becoming united in marriage with an Indian.

I do not give you this advice because I feel no interest in the welfare of the Indians. I trust I love the cause which is operating to raise them from their degraded condition. I rejoice that success has so far attended the efforts of Christians in their behalf; & one of the great reasons why I advise you to abandon your intention of marrying among them, is, that under existing circumstance, such a step will probably do far more to hinder than to promote, the measures which are in operation for their welfare.

Nor do I advise you thus, because I view such a connexion, as unlawful, in itself. On this point my opinion has always been, That there is nothing in the nature of such a connexion, merely, that can stamp it with criminality.

Nor do I give you this advice because I have any personal objections against [the] man. I have always respected him for his talents, for his diligence in [study?] & the proficiency he made in learning, while at the F.M. School; & for his hopeful piety. I know nothing personally against him as to his disposition; & I would even hope that he may not be one of those who return to their former sins, but that he may prove himself faithful to Christ, & grateful to his Christian benefactors; & of great good to his Nation. But to become thus useful, & to prove himself thus grateful to his friends, & faithful to Christ, it is not necessary that he should marry a white woman. He has the good example of David Brown[2] before him, & if he would not show ingratitude to the school where he was taught, & to the Christian community by whom he was supported; if he would not show that ingratitude which <u>Indians are said to be incapable of committing</u>, one would think that he would choose to select a wife from among the daughters of his people.

But as it respects <u>yourself</u>, Harriett, I give you this advice, because, as I view the subject, you cannot fulfil your designs of marriage with the person in question, without an evident disregard to the interests of the School, & the cause of missions; & a total inconsistency as it respects your Christian profession. A thing which may be right in itself, ~~may~~ still, in given circumstances, be very wrong. For instance, <u>in itself</u>, your Father has a perfect right to kindle a fire on his own land; but if his neighbor comes & expresses his fears that that fire so kindled, will be driven by the wind into his fields, & if there is indeed manifest reason to fear that such fire will injure his [end of page 2] neighbour's property, then, though it be <u>on his own ground</u>, your Father cannot kindle such a fire without doing that which, in such circumstances, becomes absolutely wrong; & <u>he</u> must answer for its consequences.

On such principles we are to reason in the present case. And are you told by others, since you have concluded to marry an Indian, that there is <u>danger</u>? Do they point it out; & tell you what will be the conseq<u>ce</u> if you take such a step? <u>Before you kindle the fire</u>, which if once kindled may burn, we know not how far, nor how long, O Harriett, before you kindle the fire, <u>remember</u> that so far as there is danger, so far it will be <u>wrong</u>; & that <u>God will hold you accountable to Him, for all the injury which His cause may thus receive.</u> You <u>are warned</u> that there is danger; that there is reason to fear that such a step will greatly injure the cause of Christ, both in its relation to the Mission School, & to the interests of missions from our churches to the heathen.

You cannot but know that the friends of the School do feel opposed to such connexions, as wholly inexpedient, on account of their <u>tendency</u> to injure the school, & the interests of the great cause which the school was designed to promote. This is the <u>fully expressed</u> opinion of the best friends & most liberal patrons of the Institution. You know this to be the case. The experiment has been tried; & it was an experiment which nearly cost the school its life. Besides, that experiment was tried under the most peculiarly favouring circumstances. & yet how often were the committee, & the friends of the school, who knew these circumstances, obliged to repeat them from their lips, & from the press, that the Christian public abroad might be satisfied that there was no danger of the recurrence of a similar event.

That the former marriage did have a tendency to injure the school, Let facts decide. Some of these facts you know. Yes, you know, & so do the friends of the school all know, that with all the favourable circumstances attending that marriage, it still required all the wisdom, & all the exertion, of the agents & instructors, to prevent the school from actually going down. And even now, go where you will, the best friends of the cause, will quote the Indian Marriage, as evidence that some thing relative to the former management of that school, must have been wrong; or the marriage would not have taken place. And if those who suspect this, knew as much with regard to former management, there, & about there, as you know, they would have reason to think that something had been wrong. You perhaps know also, that the present Instructor has declined for the present, being inaugurated as its Principal; & he expressed to me, last summer, his fears that the school would suffer for a long time to come; & his full belief, that though it might ultimately recover its former standing, on account of the favourable, & peculiar circumstances under which that marriage took place, still, another such event would annihilate the Institution.

You see then the situation of the School, at present; but you will not plead that because its situation is critical, your proposed marriage will not be the cause of its ruin. If it must gradually go down, still, such a step would hasten its fall, & prevent the good which it may yet accomplish. But if [end of page 3] another such event does not occur, we believe that it will not go down, but that it will rise in time, to become the occasion of all that good to the heathens, which its friends have hoped. But if it stands, it must stand in the confidence, & the support of the Christian public.

And are you aware how such another event would serve to lessen the confidence of the Christian community, in the managers of that school? Are you aware how it would weaken the hands of the Instructors, & give license to others of the scholars, to think they might follow the example of Ridge & Boudinott? But this was not the object for which the school was established. The object of it was to civilize, & to Christianize the heathen; to prepare them to become, like Thomas Hopoo, the sober, chaste, kind husbands of wives from among their own people;[3] & to qualify them to become the enlightened, converted, & obedient subjects of the kingdom of Christ.

But besides, that which would tend to the injury of the school, would also tend to injure the interests of missions, in our churches generally. The Mission School has always been identified with the missionary cause; & all the labours of the Churches, in behalf of the School as a branch; in missionary operations or in behalf of any particular mission, as another branch, have been labours to which Christians have been prompted by the same Spirit. It is a diffusive, prevailing Spirit of Missions; & yet if confidence in one department of its operations, be so withdrawn by Christians, that they cease to pray, & to give in behalf of that, it will naturally follow that their confidence, & their prayers, & their exertions, will be diminished as it respects other branches of missionary operations. Less of a missionary spirit will prevail; fewer Missionary sermons will be preached; Less money will be contributed; & if God does not save the souls of heathen except by that Grace which he causes to attend the means which Christians use in their behalf, then more of the heathen will be lost. And who would dare to assume a situation connected with such responsibilities, & drawing after it such widely felt, & lasting consequences. And yet if you fulfil your purpose, this situation alarming as it is, will be yours. But perhaps you will say as others have said before, that if the Mission School be of God, it will stand; but if it be of men, it ought to fall; & no matter how soon. Beware how you say it, or even think it. Beware how you try the experiment to ascertain the nature of the Institution. Men have established the school, so far as the means are concerned, it is true; but God has evidently directed them & owned their labours. He has poured out his Holy Spirit on the School, & we have the past evidence of his special favour, that it is an Institution of God. This you will acknowledge; & will you therefore argue that because it has borne evidence of the favour of God, it must stand? If this arguing be just, then no matter what you do. On these principles, you may go & set fire to the Missionary Rooms at Boston;[4] & as you see the flames begin to spread, & hear the alarm of Fire, still you may say, "If these Rooms are used to aid [end of page 4] in the extension of the Gospel, they are of God; & He will keep them from being consumed." Now you do not doubt but that the American Board do devote these Rooms to the cause of Missions, & that God owns the labours that are there performed; nor do you doubt but that, although they are of God, still the Torch of the incendiary might lay them in ashes. Beware then how you suffer yourself to hope that God will defend the Mission School, while you take measures to overthrow it. He can defend it if he pleases; but He works by means; & we are to take heed what we do to render these means unavailing. The church is safe; & the people of Christ, wherever they are, shall come to Him. Should you become the instrument of the School's extinction, God will cause the heathen to hear his word thro' some other channel; "Deliverance will arise to them from another place;" but, remember the word, "but thou, & thy father's house, shall be destroyed." (Esther 4:14.)[5]

And now, are you prepared for such a work as this? I entreat you, Harriett, to read again the Narrative of the Sandwich Island Youths;[6] read again the Life of the lamented Obookiah;[7] call to mind the time when the best friends the heathen ever had, met at Cornwall. That was a memorable day.[8] Young as you then was, you joined on that day, in the Praises of God. In the Name of their God, they set up their Banners; & they hoped to see these banners wave as long as they lived; yes, & that future unborn generations would see them wave, till the ends of the earth should look unto Christ, & be saved. And yet, in the life time of its founders, shall this school go down? Will you, who saw the Banners set up in the Name of Christ, will you put forth your hand, & pluck the Banners down?[9] Before you say you will, go, my dear Sister, once more, & read the inscription over Obookiah's grave.[10] Think of his redeemed Spirit, falling down before the Throne, & blessing God for a Christian education, & for all the good which the School will bring to poor Owhyhee. Think of the good it has already done; Think of the youth now at Cornwall, preparing to go, either to heaven, to unite with Kirkpatrick, & Patoo, & Backus, & Brainerd,[11] in singing Redemption thro' the blood of Jesus; or first to their native lands, to preach a Saviour, & then to heaven, in company with those unto whom they may be made the instruments of salvation. And will you become the voluntary agent in undoing all that the people of God have thus sought to accomplish. Will you be that individual, who, having borne, for these few years, the honoured appellation of a daughter of Christ, having seen the good accomplished, knowing the hopes that are directed to the School, & warned of danger by a past event; will you; O can you be left, to become that one female enemy, who shall quench the Light which the Mission School may yet shed upon the heathen world? If so, "Thou alone must bear it."[12] [end of page 5] And what will you say to justify yourself. Here you take direct measures to ruin the School, & to do away much of the interest wh. the churches now feel in the cause of Missions. But farther than this, you put the means of triumph into the hands of the enemy. While Christians weep, the enemy will rejoice. I know the enemies of the cause are not worth our notice, as it respects their opposition, nor as it respects the hope that they will help us in the work. Still a step like this may be the means of hardening them the more, & of preventing their ever being bro't to love the cause; & especially it will give them occasion of rejoicing in the calamity which you bring upon the cause. Already have the wicked prophesied ill of the cause of Missions. They have prophesied ill concerning you; & when this event takes place; & the calamities which I have mentioned are seen to follow; then they will exult, saying "Aha, aha, so would we have it." And thus you must take into the account, not only the injury done to the cause at large, but also, all the tears of the people of God, & all the dishonour thrown upon his cause, & his friends, by the occasion which you thus give the enemy to blaspheme. But infinitely more than all this, you will bring dishonour upon the Saviour. His church & his cause are dear to Him as the apple of his eye. & if you wound them, you will by the same stroke open his wounds afresh. You profess to be his disciple. He expects to see his disciples engaged supremely in the interests of his Kingdom. For this Kingdom He has bled; & O Harriett, He has already bled enough; & should you go on, well might the Redeemer say, in view of the wound which you would thus give him. "They are those with which I was wounded in the house of my friends." (Zech.13:6)

And in view of all this, are you still able to find a plea for going forwards? Do you reason for so doing because others have done so? You may have fondly hoped that there was a similarity between your case, & the former one. But I ask, where is the resemblance?

In the other case, neither of the parties professed to have any regard for the interests of religion; nor have we any reason to suppose that either of them entered the marriage state with one solitary desire of promoting the welfare of the Mission School, or the interests of the Church. How often was it stated, as an apology, that they were not pious. That they, in such circumstances, & with their hearts set on their own pleasure, should disregard the interests of the cause which Christians love, we need not wonder. The Bible has declared before, that such "seek their own; not the things that are Jesus Christs." [13] But shall the friends of Christ thus imitate the conduct of the world.

Besides, as to the means by which that marriage was thought about, I ask where is the resemblance in the present case? Where are the palliating circumstance? John Ridge had been an inmate in the same family, & on account of illness, ~~illegible~~ confined for a long time, in the same room; so that [end of page 6] there was full opportunity to form that attachment, & those engagements which led to the marriage. We find no such circumstances here. The truth is, & if things go on, it is a truth which must come out; the Christian public must know the whole of it; & shall I say it, so must the unbelieving world know it all; The truth is, That you never had any conversation on this subject, with the person to whom you are engaged, previously to his leaving the Mission School, nor any communication with him on the subject, till since the consummation of the other marriage. Since that marriage took place, you have said to some of your friends, "No Indian ever said [a word?] to me on such a subject."

Here then, if you have not grossly falsified, by your own declaration, The subject has been proposed, & listened to, & settled, since the other party went off; & directly in the face of the public opinion; & the feelings of your fathers & mothers, & brethren & sisters, in the church at Cornwall. Nor must it be doubted but that all this has been going on with the knowledge, & at least, the silent secret aid, & approbation of your Parents; & this too, in the very face of your Mother's repeated protestations of ignorance, & of your Father's public affidavit;[14] which all who have read will now turn against him, as evidence that he has knowingly disguised the truth. This must follow, even if the business has been begun since the other marriage. But this the Christian community will never believe.

No; glaring as such deception, & inconsistent as such conduct, would appear in Christian professors; such deception, & inconsistency will be small when set in the light with which Christians will view the real case. They will consider it so absurd in you [to] enter on such a project, after what has been said; that they will fix the time of the proposal, & the engagement, prior to the other marriage.

And then when they remember what you have said, & what your Parents have said, O how must you all appear. How must your Father, an elder in the very church of God, appear; How must your Mother appear; & How will you appear. "This is she that wishes to be a Missionary," (they will say,) "& is she fit to be a missionary, who, for a husband, has deceived her Pastor; & deceived her Christian friends; & bro't injury to the cause of Christ.

Where then is the resemblance in your case, & that which has taken place. In truth there is none that appears to your credit; none to your justification; none so much as to palliate your design; none, at all, except that in both cases, there was by some means or others, an engagement existing between a white woman, & an Indian, & a full determination to carry the engagement into effect, in spite of consequences.

On this ground you stand; & O Harriett, How are you to go away with the infamy upon you, not of marrying an Indian, but of, like Judas, betraying the interests of that cause into which you had entered, in covenant with Christ, & his church. So, to do good, & to enjoy Gospel ordinances; & you will need a letter from the church at Cornwall. But how can you ask, or they give, a letter of Recommendation, when the steps by which your removal from among them has been effected are steps marked by gross deception, & even falsehood, on your part towards some of them. [end of page 7]

Do you hesitate? Do you fear that because you have gone so far, you cannot turn back? Yes, you can. True you have wandered; & yet you will never get right in that way. The only way is to turn back; & if you turn there will be more evidence in it that you are a Christian, than you ever gave before. Do not go away like Cain, & Judas; but come back like Peter. Your friends invite, the cause of the Redeemer demands; the vows you have made to Christ require; The Providence of God has shut the door against your going; & be afraid, O my Sister, be afraid to burst it open. For if you do, all the evils which may result, thro' your life, & thro' Eternity, will stand charged against you. You may return yet & returning because Christ[ian d]uty call, you may be happy hereafter [reflecting] that your [intended?] way was not the best way; & that [illegible] in mercy set you right.

* * *

I will not mention our own feelings [illegible] brothers, & sisters. If you stay, we shall rejoice over you, & love you more than ever. But if you go, still we can bear it. We shall love each [illegible] still. When we are permitted to meet we shall still rejoice; But then, in the fraternal Thanksgiving circle, we shall see that "One is not," & that one will feel that she is not. Still we can bear it.

We shall feel for our aged Parents; for their sun is near his setting; & we fear that if you go, the sun of their Christian reputation is already set. We feel for your Aged Father, (You know his worldly troubles;) & you may visit the Home of your childhood yet, ah, & so may we, & find its once happy inhabitants all gone.

But, Oh the Bar of Judgment. He that doeth evil; or becomes the voluntary cause of evil, of Him will the final Judge take account. Will you go? if you are a hypocrite, & designed for a reprobate, doubtless you will. But if you are a Christian, it must be you will listen, & regard the advice of friends, & the call of God, & his church. As ever, your affectionate brother

H.L.Vaill

[LM 3] Your sisters would have written you an expression of their feelings, but they cannot just now. They both wish to be remembered to the family, & to you in particular with affectionate regard, & they feel as tho' their dear sister H. had not confided in them as she ought. They feel as if you had deceived them.

[M 4–5] The ignorance in which your brothers & sisters have been kept with regard to this mysterious affair, has been very trying to them; & will continue to be so, when, (should you go on) the world shall know it. But, we must vindicate ourselves from all charges of knowledge or participation in it, & if it does go on, I shall publish this letter of wh. I have kept a copy. But I do hope that will not be necessary.

[LM 8] I should have given you this advice long ago had I anticipated such a trying event; & should have written assoon as I heard the certainty of your designs, had I not expected brother Stephen here last week with our goods. Poor Stephen, I don't know what he will DO. You know his former love for you, & his fears expressed long ago. But we never believed it.

Perhaps ere this reaches [you] the business will have become public; & you w[ill] feel [th]at it is too late to listen to advice. No. Sister, C[hr]istian[s w]ill forgive her that does right, even tho' sh[e] may [h]ave before done wrong. Still your Brother, with [illegible] unaltered Love, H.L.V.

1. Isaiah 6:8.
2. Like Elias, David Brown (1804?–29) was educated at mission schools and converted to Christianity, as did his sister Catharine, who was well-known in evangelical circles for her piety and was the subject of Rufus Anderson's *Memoir of Catharine Brown* (1824). After completing his studies at the Foreign Mission School, David studied briefly at Andover Theological Institute before returning to the Cherokee Nation. He married a Cherokee woman named Lydia Lowery in 1825 (Starr 280).
3. Thomas Hopu was a student at Cornwall before returning to Hawaii, where he acted as an interpreter. He married Henrieta Halekii in "the first Christian marriage in the islands" (Starr 146; see also Gold 344).
4. Headquarters of the ABCFM.
5. In the King James version of the Bible, the relevant passage of Esther 4:14 reads "then shall there enlargement and deliverance arise to the Jews from another place; but thou and thy father's house shall be destroyed."
6. *Narrative of Five Youth from the Sandwich Islands* (1816).
7. Edwin Welles Dwight's *Memoirs of Henry Obookiah* (1819).
8. The date was 6 May 1818, when Herman Daggett was inaugurated as principal of the Foreign Mission School.

9. Vaill refers to the sermon preached at Daggett's inauguration by Joseph Harvey, titled *The Banner of Christ Set Up*. The sermon extensively uses the metaphor upon which Herman draws, as in the passage, "We are now assembled to set up a banner in the name of our God—a banner, which indicates a new breach upon the adversary, and the approach of a fresh triumph to the cause of Christ" (4). The sermon ends with this warning to those who, as Herman accuses Harriett, betray the values the banner represents:

> But we have called you together to point out to you the Standard of JESUS CHRIST, and to call you to the rallying point. This banner, remember, must be supported. Cowards and traitors only, forsake the standard of their King.
>
> Is this the banner of Christ? has he committed its keeping to our instrumentality? Then if we neglect it, we neglect our Master; if we desert it, we desert the Captain of our Salvation; if we betray it, we betray the interests of Zion. (29–30)

10. The inscription over Obookiah's grave reads:

> In
> memory of
> HENRY OBOOKIAH,
> a native of
> OWYHEE.

> His arrival in this country gave rise to the Foreign Mission School, of which he was a worthy member. He was once an Idolater, and was designed for a Pagan Priest; but by the grace of god, and by the prayers and instruction of pious friends, he became a Christian.
>
> He was eminent for piety and missionary zeal. When almost prepared to return to his native Isle, to preach the Gospel, God took him to himself. In his last sickness he wept and prayed for Owyhee, but was submissive. He died without fear, with a heavenly smile on his countenance and glory in his soul,
>
> Feb. 17, 1818,
>
> Aged 26. (Gold 29)

Relatives of Obookiah, more properly rendered Opukahaia, removed his body from its burial place in Cornwall in 1993 and returned it to Hawaii. A plaque and the original gravestone remain in the Cornwall cemetery, and tributes of seashells and leis mark the site to this day.

11. Cherokee William Kirkpatrick died in 1823, Thomas Patoo of the Mar-

quesas Islands died in 1822, and Hawaiians Charles Backus probably died in 1823 and David Brainerd in 1825 (Starr 146–47, 151).

12. From John Bunyan's *A Holy Life, the Beauty of Christianity, or, An Exhortation to Christians to Be Holy* (1684).

13. Philippians 2:21.

14. Refers to a letter, signed by Benjamin Gold and seven other Cornwall men, in which they denied "frequent assertions . . . that there is a kind of intercourse subsisting between the families in the 'valley of Cornwall,' and the 'foreign scholars' which is highly improper." The signers of the letter claimed that "[w]ith the best opportunity to know the truth in this case, we fully believe that such assertions as have appeared in your paper upon this subject are not *facts*; we deny that they are facts; and, in our turn, assert that they are *base fabrication*" (qtd. in Gabriel 65). The *Connecticut Journal*, printed in New Haven, published the letter on 10 August 1824.

CORNELIUS EVEREST TO STEPHEN GOLD, 2 JULY 1825
CornHS, pm.

Saturday Eve^{g} July 2$^{\underline{d}}$ 1825.

Dear Brother Stephen,

Already have we seen in the public prints an extract from the communication of the Agents of the Mission School. A paper has been brought in to us. The question has begun to be asked, what does it mean?

The same excitement is again produced as in the case of the other wedding. But O it is a different case. It comes home to us. We weep; we sigh; our feelings are indescribable. Why must we all be so cruelly tormented?

Why must the school, & the cause of Christ suffer so much?

Ah, it is all to be summed up in this—our sister loves an Indian!

Shame on such love. Sad was the day when the mission school was planted in Cornwall. What wild enthusiasm has been cherished by some in that place! And how much wickedness has been committed under the cloak of religion & of a missionary spirit. But can [end of page 1] this unnatural—this foolish—this wicked & mischievous connection be permitted to take place? O the thought is too much to bear. Our parents & Harriet may depend upon it that we shall plead & remonstrate, & plead again & remonstrate to the last extremity. No we cannot give up. This contemplated marriage must not take place. And what a Jezebel of a woman has employed her art, her intrigue, her selfishness, & her deviltry in bringing the whole family connections into this distressed state, & in ruining Harriet. Our hearts are full. Do all you can to prevent the completion of this business. And write to us; do write immediately.

With weeping I bid you an affectionate adieu.

C.B. Everest.

Tuesday morning. The fire spreads. People are talking; many questions are asked. We are sick of answering. This business [end of page 2] which looked awfully bad to us at first, looks worse & worse. The best people here, & neighboring clergymen say that they would oppose it to the last moments, & that if she was a friend of theirs they would much rather follow her to the grave. We are not alone in our feelings. Nineteen twentieths of New Endland view the subject just as we do. Our parents ought to have done two things—one is directly & absolutely forbid it, & another is, they ought to have frankly told us all about it. I see not how any justifiable reason can be given why we should be so treated. The business concerns us all. I hope no efforts will be relaxed. We wish we had a cave in which we could hide away from the sight of man. It is cruel, irrational, & ungodly business. CB.E.

Do write first mail.

MARY GOLD BRINSMADE TO HERMAN AND FLORA GOLD VAILL AND CATHARINE GOLD, 14 JULY 1825
HLVC, m.

[Return address:] Washington Ct / July 14 [Addressed to:] Rev[d] Herman L. Vaill / East Haddam / Millington Society / Con

Washington July 14th 1825.

Dear Brother & Sisters,[1]

I have been calculating to write you this week by mail, & have just found that to day instead of tomorrow I must put my letter in the office

& though I have but a short time in which to express to you my feelings of "the subject," I am unwilling to remain silent another week. I have had a multitude of conflicting emotions concerning our sister Harriet since we last saw each other, but my mind has at length become more calm. I have conversed with H. read her communications to her friends, Mr Harvey's letter to her, & her answer. Harriet never appeared more interesting than she does at present. It is a time of great commotion in C. still Harriet is meek, though firm as the hills. She has, for a long time past, been seriously weighing the subject, endeavoring to know her duty, & I believe she has earnestly sought divine direction & she now thinks that we shall at a future time see that she has done right. I opposed the thing till conscience repeatedly smote me, & now, I must acknowledge that I feel it my duty to be still— my feelings are in unison with the multitude of my christian friends who tell me to comfort Harriet. Some of the most conscientious & best informed christians in Washington think that some great good is to be brought about in these latter days by means of this event. Mr Mason & several other clergymen in this region say, decidedly, that they think no one ~~illegible~~ [end of page 1] ought to oppose & distress H. now. Mr Talcott was here last evening—he said he thought no one had any right to call H. "criminal" in this thing. He said, he wished to have the agents govern the mission school, but he could not see that they have any thing to do with Elias, or Harriet. We complain of the tendency of this thing but let us not forget that we are shortsighted, beings of a day. We have a great trial, & may we be enabled to exercise the spirit of Christ & be actuated by the benevolence of the gospel. Let not pride have any hand in distressing us. I anxiously wish to see you all that we may bring up in conversation a thousand things which I cannot write. Mothers conduct which in some instances appeared strange, can now, I think, be satisfactorily explained. When H. had come to a conclusion in her own mind—she brought the subject before her parents—for she had no idea of acting without their consent. They had previously felt that marriages of this kind were not sinful & now they had a severe trial in the case of their beloved daughter— merely to part with her, was like breaking their heartstrings & they brought up every argument which has since been brought forward to dissuade her & prevent the connection—this was done last fall, a few weeks before H. sickness—when their oppo-[end of page 2]sition was expressed in a letter to Boudinot. Our parents felt, afterwards, that they might be found fighting against God—& sometime during H.'s sickness they told her they should oppose her no longer, she must do what she thought best. Another letter was accordingly sent on to B. which he afterwards acknowledged with gratitude as having reached him sooner than the one in which their opposition & refusal were expressed though their refusal was sent on several weeks first. Our parents thought it not best to tell the rest of the family at that time—as, in their opinion our opposi[tion would] do no good & H. was in a delicate state of health. [Missing] thought she could not bear it. Another reason why they d[id] not tell us was, if this thing should ever take place it would not soon—perhaps in the providence of God, never. They did what they thought was their duty & if any of us think they were in an error, still we are bound to treat them tenderly & affectionately— still we are bound to honor them & to comfort them in their declining years. A thousand false reports are abroad, envious & unprincipled people are watching opportunity to afflict—the lying tongue is heard with approbation: but it will all soon be over—yes, our accounts will be sealed up soon. Oh! how changed will all things appear in the light of eternity [end of page 3]

Permit me to tell you, my dear brother, that I was sorry to see some expressions which I saw in the latter part of the letter which H. received from you last week. Our parents thought you said very hard things & very unjustly—but I endeavored to make allowance for it, in the warmth of your feelings when you first saw the agents report [&c. &c. ?]

A letter was also received from brother E. & Abbey & which I think was dictated by an improper spirit. I trust they will think so upon sober reflection.

* * *

I wrote to brother E. & Abbey & Catharine last week—supposing C. was, by this time in W. but I saw by your letter she was still with you. So I illegible address this letter to you all, hoping & expecting you will all answer it immediately, & do tell us all your concerns as far as possible. Kiss little Catharine, Harriet, for her aunt Mary. Eleanor sends much love, but thinks she cannot write at present & she says tell C. I hope I shall see her before I ~~illegible~~ go off—which, by the way, may happen soon. Your ever affectionate sister

Mary

1. In the left margins of pages 1 and 2 and the margin between 2 and 3, lines of script are heavily crossed out so as to be rendered illegible.

According to a family history, Mary Gold Brinsmade was "conservative and dignified, strict in her principles" (Brinsmade 19). Characterized as "a responsive, warm-hearted woman, never failing in sympathy and kindliness to family or friend," Mary "moved about quietly and more slowly [than her husband], and was invariably a little late" (Brinsmade 20).

DANIEL BRINSMADE TO HERMAN AND FLORA GOLD VAILL
AND CATHARINE GOLD, 14 JULY 1825
HLVC, m.

[Return address:] Washington Ct / July 14th [Addressed to:] Revd Herman L. Vaill / East Haddam / Millington [Postage:] 10

Washington July 14th 1825

D^r B^r & Sisters,

Mary has written a letter to you to which I beg leave to dissent—and have written two or three small notes on the margin at which she seems to be wrathy and will probably scratch them out before she sends it.[1] I would however inform you that my opposition to the marriage is fix^d and unalterable—and to suppose that I should be fighting against God, to oppose it, is as idle as to suppose the same by putting on shingles on my house or erecting a lightening rod—she has been drawn in to this vortex by the opinion of friends who have endeav^d to soothe our feelings and she catches at it as a drowning man does at straws. I hope you will write her a lengthy letter and express your feeling fully The good people in this place do oppose such connections and all who have express^d an opinion favorable to them would revolt in a moment if it was brought home to their own firesides. There is high times in C. and I expect nothing but that Father's property will— [2] you know his situation—the Church has become the seat of trouble & Col. G. & wife—think M^r and Mrs S.[3] the cause of all their calamity and their poor innocent Indian girl has don nothing to [end of page 1] cause such a [rumpus?]. O the Delusion of that family. Bunce[4] has come out with a particular notice of the respectability of the family and all the <u>Indians</u> brothers in law are mentioned except Br Everest. I think he must consider himself slighted.

how does Millington people like the idea of having a clergyman who is brother to an Indian

So we go. I wish to see you. your letter you sent to Cornwall made them <u>mad</u>. Mother said you had sent up one of your old sermons but she was glad you had paid the postage for it was not worth reading & yet no evil results from Indian marriages—all the blame lies on our side we dont see and feel how good and how pleasant a thing it is to be kiss^d by an Indian—to have black young ones & a train of evils. O I am sick—at heart—do come up and contrive what shall be done to prevent this [sore?] calamity

In haste & with great love to all I
subscribe myself yours &c.
D B Brinsmade

Rev^d HL Vaill

1. Refers to the crossed-out marginal insertions in the previous letter.

2. This dash is elongated in the manuscript, as if to suggest a word should be inserted in its place (e.g., "Father's property will plummet" or "Father's property will crash").

3. Timothy Stone, Cornwall minister, and his wife, Mary Merwin Stone.

4. Isaiah Bunce, editor of the *American Eagle*, printed in Litchfield, wrote a series of inflammatory editorials about the Cornwall intermarriages.

[Return address:] Goshen Ct. / July 18th [Addressed to:] Mr
Herman L. Vaill / East Haddam / Millington Society [Postage:] 11

Sabbath Morn July [1825]

Dear Brother & Sister,

I do not feel able to write much to you, but I will try to write a little
because I know you will be anxious to hear. Thursday night I watched
with Eunice Birdsey Friday morning I came home feeling about as well
as usual, but before noon I began to have a severe pain in my head &
cold spells & at night, I had quite a high fever—ma sweat me Fryday
night, yesterday I sat up but little, but to day I feel almost well, & I
think if I am careful I shall be quite well soon. They have had a distressed house to Mr. Birdseys Eunice & Ketchel, have been very sick
with the Billous intermitant fever, the night before I came home no
one that saw Eunice, expected that she would live the night out—the
next day she was very low, but since that day, she has appeared to be
some better, & it is thought that she will recover. E. could talk but little
while I was with her, what she said was about Harriett, she said that
she used to think that she had rather a friend would die, than to marry
an Indian; but she did not feel so now, she found that it was a [great?]
thing to die—she said, we have condemned Harriett for doing as she
has—but perhaps our Saviour loves her better than he does any of us.
There are many that feel very different from what they did at first. After
hearing Mr. Clark say what he did—you will not be surprised, if I tell
you, that there were some things in your letter that were not well received, by Pa & ma & H. [end of page 1]

It is as much as ma can bear to be contradicted & it is more than
she will bear, to be charged of telling a falsehood; especially by her
children. Pa was very much offended, he was outrageous—he could
hardly speak peacibly about you. They began as soon as I came home.
I told them your reasons for writing as you did & endeavored to make
them feel better towards you—but pa said you should have waited untill you had found out the truth, before you wrote & not be so ready to

condemn, without knowing the circumstances. Pa & ma both say, that they do not desire to see you, as long as you are of the same mind as when you wrote the letter. Notwithstanding we thought we had every reason to believe, that it was, as you stated in your letter—yet I do think myself—it would have been better, had that part been omitted: but I did not think so then. One reason for my coming was—to find out how it had gone on, in what way & how far they had deceived us & after hearing their statements, I was convinced that they had not told falsehoods. True they have deceived us, they meant to deceive us— they kept us in ignorance, but we were wilfuly ignorant. How often ma used to tell Flora & me that she believed that Harriett loved Elias & that she could not say, that she did not think it possible but that she might marry him—we thought that ma was criminal in saying as she did, & used to tell her so, we thought that it would give people occasion to talk—we were always offended when she introduced the subject be- cause she did tell us she did not know, (ma says now that she always thought it was uncertain, because she knew that her ^{H's} brothers & sisters would prevent it if they could) but we heard & saw enough to convince us of the fact, had we not been determined, not to believe it. Tabitha Lewis, told me when I was in Hartford, that Harriet had been engaged to Elias nearly 3 years, but was not espoused to him till last winter. She was mistaken. Harriett [end of page 2] in her statement to her friends mentioned (to show that Mrs Northrop had not influenced her in the least) that her mind had been made up for more than two years. Flora will recollect that H. received a letter the day that Mr Gai- lord was ordained: that was the third letter that she received from him, & H says that there were some things in that letter, that convinced her that she must stop short—or continue to correspond, & be ready to meet the consequences She says that she asked a good many Christian people, if they thought it could be any injury to the school, or do any hurt, in any way, if any one of th[e] scholars ^{Cherokee youth} should re- turn and marry one of our gir[ls &] they all said, no!—you was then of that mind. H. was then ready to make up her mind, she was convinced of his attachment to her, & she knew that she should be unhappy if she stopped there—she made up her mind to marry him, should he propose it, & she did not doubt but that he would. Proposals were accordingly made, about 5. months after Ridge was married H. was then ready to answer him & did Soon after, pa was asked to give his consent, [he said] no, the letter was sent, a few weeks after [chang]ed his mind, & wrote again, that he was w[illing] that H. should do as she pleased, he should n[ot] oppose—the last letter reached him first. H. says that he was then prepared to receive the other Mr Reuben Talor came up here a few days since he said on purpose to tell pa & ma that they had very many sympathizing friends, he said he had been to visit brother Mason & he told Mr M. that he thought it was a good plan, he approved of it, Mr Mason told him, he was glad to find some one of his mind, Mr Talcott, & Mr Starr are of the same mind, & Mr. Smith says he is ready to marry another couple, whenever he shall be called upon.[1] Mary is turned clear about before she came up she sent a letter, & asked their forgiveness, & then [end of page 3] came up to comfort them, Sally seems to be quite submissive. Stephen is the same, He has not been to meeting, for several Sabbaths, I hope he will be remembered by you in your prayers I do not wonder that he feels bad, but he has no right to threaten, I hope he does not mean all that he says. As for Catharine she feels much as she did when she left you, respecting the expediency of such connections, With respect to their deceiving of us, I do not feel as I did. I want to tell you a thousand things but I have not time, I am not well enough to write more.

As ever y[our] affectionate sister
Catharine

* * *

[LM 1] Sabbath Evening I hope you will excuse the very bad manner in which this letter is written, I tru[st yo]u will. Your goods will be sent on as soon as next week, Pa [says?] he don't care whether you have any thing or not

[LM 2] Boudinot will come to Cornwall for H. Harriet says she don't wish for her friends to flatter themselves that she is not going, she says she shall go if they both live. H. sends her love to you both. She was pleased with measures that you took after receiving the report. I hope you will send that bible to H. by S. if you [conclude?] to send it. The first work that [illegible] will be your carpet. Give my love to the girls, you know who, I cant mention their names. Mrs C.H. has many friends in C. I can't name them Catharine

[LM 3] Harriett has not heard from the South since February, She feels bad, She is jealous that ~~illegible~~ letters are sent, but are taken out of some office before they reach Cornwall, Every letter that she ever had from, Elias or Sarah,[2] has been taken from Mr Northrops, she has not seen them for more than 2 months, the one that has got them has had sufficient time to read them, & I think he ought to return them

1. Walter Smith, pastor of the Second Congregational Church in Cornwall (Wilkins 145).
2. Sarah Northrop Ridge, now residing in the Cherokee Nation.

CATHARINE GOLD TO HERMAN AND
FLORA GOLD VAILL, 30 JULY 1825
HLVC, m.

[Return address:] Cornwall Ct / Aug. 1st [Addressed to:] Mr
Herman L. Vaill / East Haddam / Millington Society [Postage:] 11

Sabbath Evening July 30th 1825
Dear Brother & sister,

I wrote you last week, but as Mr. Clark went an hour sooner than usual I missed the opportunity of sending it, I was so foolish as to destroy the letter, & now as I have but little time, I must write short. How do you do? & how have you been since I left you? I long to hear from you. How does the dear little Catharine d[o]? [K]iss[1] her for me. I hope her cough is better I want to see her, & you all. I suppose you would be glad to hear something about the letter you wrote to Harriett. I have not seen Lewis, to speak with him, since I came home, untill to knight after meeting; then I had no opportunity to speak to him about the letter. (Lewis has taken his fathers stand, & is going to keep tavern) I believe it is not thought best by any one that has seen your letter, that you should publish it. Mary says unless you wish to disgrace yourself; you must not publish it. I think there was but one sentence in your letter that I really did not like at the time you wrote it—that is "if you are a hypocrite & destined for a reprobate, doubtless you will go forward," Harriett's feelings were very much wounded by this expression. She said she thought your letter was a prretty candid one, till nearly the close [missing] but she cannot put up with this. H. has [missing] letter from Boudinott. The time is now set when she is to go. I know not when it is, if I did I would tell you. I suspect not this summer. If you visit us in the fall you will see her again. I want you should see her, & hear, what she has to say for herself. It is now quite still times here to what it has been, Sally appears very friendly, to her parents, & to Harriet. She does not think it worth a while, to forsake her parents, because they differ in opinion from her I do not intend forsake them. I love them as well as I ever did. I believe they have acted conscientiously. Whether they have been in an error, or not, is not for me to say, I do not feel disposed to condemn their motives, nor do I Harriett's. Strange that she can love an Indian but it is so. And she will get him if she can. [end of page 1]

I cannot now tell you, how soon I can go to Millington. I shall wish to come. & I shall as soon as I can. We are now spinning the carpet, Ma says it may be Flora's if she behaves well, if she treats ma ill, she [ant] to have it, so you must look out how you do. How do you get along with Mrs_ & _ Mrs_ write & tell me. Remember what Mrs. Stone said to you—"Prudence, Prudence, Prudence." I hope, & pray, that your labours in Millington may be blessed. Be faithful; be prudent. I must close. I shan't write again, till I have received a letter from you. Give my love to Mrs. Cone, Mrs W. Cane & B. to [Allis], Miss Arnold, Miss Griffins, & others that take the trouble to enquire, if there be any. Your affectionate

Sister Catharine

* * *

[LM 1] I thought when I wrote you that your things woul[d] have been sent you before this, but our people are busy—they will be sent as possible. Yo[u m]ust both be very careful what you write to Harriet. if you write, Pa came very near saying you should not have another article sent you, & it would take but little now to make him say it. Pa & m[a say t]hat you must make some acknowledgment

[LM 2] Kamo[2] is dead. he was buried to day. Why is it that most all of the most promising [Owyheeans], do not live to return home Mysterious Providence

Kamo died a happy death—was very much as Brainard[3] was, It is quite sickly here, our family are all as well as usual[4]

1. The letter k is omitted on this word.
2. Hawaiian John Iris Kamo died of tuberculosis in 1825 (Starr 146).
3. Hawaiian David Brainerd died in 1825 (Starr 146).
4. These sentences continue the marginal insertion horizontally below the end of the letter.

BENNET ROBERTS TO HERMAN VAILL, 1 AUGUST [1825]
HLVC, m.

[Return address:] Goshen Ct / Augt. 1 [Addressed to:]
Rev. Herman L Vaill / Millington Ct. [Postage:] 1

Goshen [1825 Aug 1][1]

Much Respected brother,

Pardon me for my boldness in addressing you at this time & on this occasion. You have doubtless often called to mind the substance of a conversation I once had with you, on the unpleasant situation of your sister Harriett. You then doubted what you now know to be true. I often regretted that I mentioned the fact to you because it proved a matter of so much censure that fell on me, while it appeared to be the means of doing no good. I lost the confidence of H whom I had long considered one of my best friends, & also the confidence many others had formerly placed in me. I had the mortification to feel that you supposed my motives to be selfish, & entirely unmanly, improper & unchristian. I could not then feel this & I cannot now. I think it was the regard I had for the wellfare of H & her family & connections which led me to say & do what I did. Your friends have censured me for not divulging what I knew to them. I could make no apology only that I did make know the fact to the most suitable person, & one I supposed would take the best course. I have thought best to make this statement to you because I am aware you will hear, of the matter when you see your friends. Friends & others have conducted entirely unreasonable, & could almost say they have gone beyond the bounds of decency. They have used H in such a manner that instead of influencing her to give up the subject she would feel it a great relief to find shelter from their unnatural society, even among the <u>wild</u> men of the wood. I have had frequent interviews with Harriet of late. She is disposed to go forward in case Boudinot wishes it. She has thought she would have to leave the country & meet him in some place agreed on. I have reasoned with her on the subject till I believe she will conclude to be married in Cornwall like other folks. I cannot bear to have any ambush work about it. I regret that it must take place; but if it must I wish it to be done in as honorable way as possible. We ought not to abandon a friend & make them wretched for life merely because they do not please us. We should make the [end of page 1] best we can of the affair. Stephen is outrageous & for his own comfort, for the comfort of H & the whole family, I wish something might be done to bring his feelings down where they ought to be. The only hope that now remains that the connection will not be realized arises from what we hope may be done by laying the subject before him & urging proper motives to induce him to relinquish. Esq Evarts[2] will be here soon. He will probably write. Harriet is really respected & will be if she stays here: But no more of this subject. If you still feel that I did wrong in saying what I did, I can only ask your forgiveness. I regret on some accounts that I said it. But I presume that if it had been the means of putting an end to the negociation we should all have acknowledged it to have been a good course.

Now for other news. Mrs Goodyear is very low & will probably not get up again. Mrs Everest & Widow Patterson are also very low—Mr Judd—Mrs. Barns—Eunice & Kitchel Birdseye are quite sick. I now live in Goshen & read ~~illegible~~ on the medical system with Medicus Gold.[3]

It is a general time of health here, & there is something of a revival of religion. There are more than 20 who are willing to come to the anxious meetings. The good work goes on in Litchfield.

I have nothing of importance to write further Remember me affectionately to Mrs Vaill Also to ~~Mr~~ [Dea?] Harvey & family when you seen

them. I should be glad to see you & hope I may have the pleasure before many weeks. I have heard nothing from Br— Prentice for a long
time. The last I heard he had lost his child.

In health, peace & prosperity, I subscribe myself

Yours truly & forever—in the bonds of the Gospel

Bennet Roberts

[LM 1] I should be happy to receive [missing] from you if you can afford time and will take the trouble to write it.

Rev. Herman L Vaill

    1. The date and brackets are written in pencil in what looks to be twentieth-
century handwriting. Bennet Roberts had been a student at the Foreign Mission
School before becoming assistant principal.

    2. Jeremiah Evarts (1781–1831), corresponding secretary of the ABCFM.
Evarts did not oppose intermarriages, and he chastised Rev. Timothy Stone and
the school's agents for their condemnation of the match (Andrew 338–39).

    3. Dr. Samuel W. Gold (1794–1869), cousin of Harriett, practiced medicine
for twenty-five years in Goshen (Gold 296).

HERMAN VAILL TO MARY GOLD BRINSMADE, 2 AUGUST 1825
HLVC, m.

[Addressed to:] Mrs. Mary W. Brinsmade / Washington / Con

East Haddam, Millington Society, August 2. 1825.

Dear Sister Mary,

I wrote a brief & hurried reply to your letter of July 14th, the day I
received it; & now, with a little more leisure, I will write again.

In this, I shall express my mind freely, & I hope candidly, upon that
which not only is, but will, I fear, long continue to be—"The subject."

I would be the last to say, or to do, any thing unjustly, or needlessly
to injure the feelings of either Harriett or her Parents; or, as I would
dutifully & affectionately call them, our Parents. Still, if they act conscientiously, I do not see why they should feel unwilling to have others
look into the subject; nor can I see how a candid view of the business,
as it appears to us, either in its tendency, or its management, should

give reasonable offence to any one. If, in my letter to H. I drew some closing inferences that were severe, I did it because I tho't they grew out of "the subject." If I was too severe; & especially if the true case did not render them just, I am sincerely sorry that I wrote them. But when sister H. entered upon this affair, she certainly assumed the responsibility that is attached to it. She has voluntarily taken her stand, & we have an undoubted right to look at her & "the subject," just as they present themselves. If those who look at the outside appearance are disposed to say all is well, let them say so; as far as they have a knowledge of facts, & ground of forming honest judgment, they may judge correctly. But if you, or myself, or any other person, have had opportunities to peep behind the curtain, & have thus been able to see some of the secret springs of the machine, we have a right to form our opinion as the affair appears to us; & to express our opinion on the ground of knowledge thus obtained.

For myself, I do assure you I have no objections that sister H. should marry the man of her choice, be he white, or black, or even red, if that is the colour she prefers; Provided, she can do it without endangering the interests of the Great Cause which she ought to love; & without a sacrifice of the Xtian consistency of character which, as a professed Xtian, she is under obligations to maintain.

If the bare act of marrying were all, I could reasonably have nothing to say; & show me, dear Sister, that this is all; show me that this is a common case, (apart from dissimilarity of complexion, for that I care nothing about,) & I shall cease to object. Let Harriett herself make it appear that this proposed connexion can have no natural tendency to injure the F.M. School, & the general interests of the Church, & of American Missions; & above all, let her make it appear that this match has been proposed, & the negociations carried on, in a proper manner, & without the use of inconsistent & unchristian duplicity on her part, & I shall feel it my duty to be "still," as well as you.

But if, with all the palliating circumstances that attended the former marriage, that had a tendency to injure the School, & to damp the ardour of some of the friends of Missions; what must be the greater tendency here. The public mind has not been prepared to expect another marriage. It was officially, & publicly stated that such cir-

cumstances as led to that marriage, could not be likely, from their nature, ever to exist again; & of course, the Xtian public were prepared to
expect, & did expect, that [end of page 1] no such event would ever re-
cur. And certainly they had a right to expect that the friends of school,
& the members of the church, in Cornwall, would be united in their
exertions to prevent another occasion tending to so much evil. And it
is true, that in the present case, those circumstances wh. led to the
other marriage have been wanting; but aside from them all, (except it
be the Love for an indian,) & under circumstances, which, so far as I
can see, admit of no palliation, another, & we have reason to fear, a
fatal stroke, is given to the School for the Heathen, & for Christ.

But I will here say nothing farther of its tendency to injure the
School; I will say nothing of its tendency to make Xtians weep, & the
foe exult, these points I considered at length in my letter to H. & I
could wish she would yet stop, & consider them as fully herself.

Here I wish to take up "the subject" as it has been managed; that
we may judge of its merits or demerits, according to knowledge of
facts relative to the manner in which it has been carried on.

You will recollect that long before the other marriage took place,
brother Stephen frequently expressed his fears that sister H. would,
some time or other, marry one of the Indians. The rest of us then had
no such apprehensions. But after that marriage took place, & rumours
were abroad that H. had similar intentions, you know that we all became somewhat suspicious. And it is a fact with which I am well acquainted that H. did endeavor to allay all such suspicions in the minds
of her relatives & friends. She manifested a degree of obstinacy, it is
true; & would not tell us every thing that we wished; but her back-
wardness to speak decidedly, & to our entire satisfaction, we then tho't
arose from her inherent disposition in part; & in part, from a sense
of personal injury from the suspicions that had bee[n] raised against
her. Still she said enough to satisfy her brot[hers] & sisters who were
most conversant with her, that she had no design of forming such a
connexion. More than once or twice she declared that people had no
occasion to say what they did with regard to her; That no indian had
ever said a word on such a subject to her; & That she herself had never
thought of such a thing. In Feby of that winter, she rode to Washing-

ton, with Flora & myself; & on the way, she told us that her Parents had seen, or heard all the letters she had received from Boudinott; & that she would by no means carry on a correspondence without their knowledge & approbation. (I may be mistaken as to the time; perhaps, it was before our ride to W. — but the fact that she said this is still the same.) Besides, when on our Way to W. while talking concerning her correspondence with Boudinott, & the suspicions that had risen from it, with regard to her, she said if she could have foreseen that her correspondence would have led to all this, she should not have written as she had; & when I put the direct question, just before we arrived at your house, whether she thought she should ever marry an indian; she gave a direct reply, 'I don't think I ever shall."

I had before heard her Mother repeatedly say that if H. had any such designs, she knew nothing of it; & her asserted ignorance [end of page 2] of any such intentions, joined to the fact that she had seen the correspondence, or heard it read, when added to Harriett's own repeated declarations that she had never thought of such a thing, were enough to remove all suspicions from my mind. They did remove my suspicions; The numerous incidental expressions which Harriett continued to drop during the summer; & her positive denial to Flora & Catharine, this last spring, with regard to her intentions of purchasing some articles noted in a memorandum, all conspired to remove suspicions from my mind; so that I would not believe, I could not believe, till the tidings reached me here, in black & white, that she had declared her absolute engagement & her determination.

Now, how do her recent declarations coincide with the expressions & assertions to which I have alluded, made by her since the marriage of Sarah Northrop? I understand that in her statement recently made to her friends, she tells them, in substance, that her mind has been made up on this subject, for more than two years; & that she has also said that in a letter she received from Boudinott, the June before the other marriage took place, there were some expressions which convinced her that she must stop short, or continue to correspond, & be ready to meet the consequences of a proposal from him; That she then asked a good many of her Xtian friends whether they thought the marriage of one of the scholars, or one of the Cherokee youth, with any of the Cornwall girls, would be likely to injure the school; That they all said no; & that she then made up her mind to marry him, should he propose it, & she did not doubt but that he would. Here, Sister Mary, I wish you to lay your hand on your heart, & ask how these two facts, as she declares them, can be consistent with each other. She declares in Feby 1824. that she never thought of such a thing; & in July of 1825. she declares that she has had her mind made up on this very thing, for more than two years.

I will not add on this point; You see the declarations which she has made. Those which she made in Feby 1824. have the memory & can have the mouth of more than one witness to establish them. You can look at these seeming contradictions for yourself; & as for me, they must be reconciled with each other, before I can admit that she has done that which she could do without a sacrifice of her consistency & sincerity as a professed friend of truth, & righteousness. Harriett writes to us that she still has the consolation of feeling that she "has not acted contrary to duty," & that what she has "done as it respects forming a connexion, is not adverse to divine approbation." She has however told two stories, & they are to my mind wholly inconsistent with each other. If one was true, what was the [n]ature of the other? & it must be a strangely infatuated mind that lo[oks] for divine approbation in positive contradictions.

You say that she "never appeared more interesting than now." Did you look at her, apart from the facts that I have related? If so ^{not}, I do not see what there could be so very interesting in her present situation. For certainly to look at her in this situation, & then to look at the steps which have bro't her into it, I should say that her meekness was feigned; & her firmness, as you call it, nothing but obstinacy. [end of page 3] But perhaps you were not acquainted with all the devices that she had practiced. I am persuaded that those who express approbation, do not know, all that may be known. I fear, sister Mary, that you do not know all. Indeed, the half that I know, I have not been able to tell; & I believe the hundredth part of the secrets of the affair, have never yet come to the light. If Mr Mason, & Mr Talcott, & other conscientious people knew facts, even as far as I have here stated them, they would no longer approve. There may be nothing "criminal" in the marriage itself. The Report of the Agents did not call H. "Criminal," on account of the simple design of forming the connexion; but solely in allusion to the way in which the business had been carried on; by covered correspondence, & contrary to the fully expressed feelings of the Xtian public. And so long as plain Gospel sincerity is one thing, & deep & subtle artifice another, their criminations of those concerned in this affair will rest on ground which is solid & safe.

But you say it is tho't "that some great good is to be bro't about by means of this event." That is all conjecture. The evident tendency, & the certain tendency, if not overruled, will be the bringing about of great evil. Besides, who has a right to do evil that good may come? Once a man said "hail, Master, & kissed him," [1] & betrayed him; & great good, eternal good grew out of the treachery; but the traitor went to his own place. This reasoning is wholly fallacious; it is the irrationality that masks a bad cause, voluntarily engaged in.

* * *

And if she goes forward, sister Mary, can you find any motive that leads her but love. What other motive can she have? She may hope in vain to carry with her a heart that feels for the heathen, & for Zion. Her heart is engrossed with other feelings. And how shall she become the reprover of deception among the heathen, when the fact is known to them, as it will be, that she stooped to deception, & lower still, the character for her common virtues; but if she goes we may say of her, & her virtues;

"Poor virtues that she boasted so, This test unable to endure;

"Let home, & friends, & Missions go, To make an Indian husband sure."

In view of "the subject" as it appears to us who know the real nature of it, we feel as tho' we ought, all, brothers, & sisters, to unite in faithful, friendly, & decided opposition, To treat H. kindly as a still beloved sister, is my wish; & to treat our dear Parents with all affection & respect, shall be my aim. & would we not knock away the props of their declining years, & leave them to go down to the grave in sorrow, I do feel that we ought not to encourage the thing; but to represent the true reasons of our disapprobation, & beseech them to use one more effort to stop the business where it is. They may yet do it; & if H.

must die for an Indian or have him, I do say she had as well die, as become the cause of so much lasting evil as the marriage will occasion; better to die on the side of Xtian honour & Gospel sincerity than to pine away with satisfied love, & its consequences, on the bed of Love. Do you consider the case, as it is, & I am persuaded you will do right. Your affectionate Brother

H.L.V.

[LM 1] Dr Brother

We are all brothers of one mind I hope. I was sorry that Sister Mary had so [enco]uraged H. as to express approbation. I hope they will not make you into a turn over, & I hope that Mary will turn back again. Brother Everest [and Sister?] Abbey are as yet "Cakes not turned;" & we must all show that when John Randall spoke of Yankee "dough faces,"[2] he did not mean us. Do write to us immediately, & tell when you will visit us.

[LM 2] We expected Stephen last week with a load; he has not come but we shall look for him the last of this week. Our love to all the family. Tell Cousin Eleanor, she had better wait a while; White is going out of fashion. Some think "red becomes their complexion best, & red it shall be," if the milk dont spill.

[M 2–3] As to health we are all well. This subject has been painful to us; we wish to visit Cl in Sept, but can't, because they say they don't wish to see us, as long as we feel so. How shall we feel diff^{tly}? I love all there as well as ever; & I am using the [missing] of honest open love in what I write to them, & to you.

1. Matthew 26:49.

2. Refers to the comments made by John Randolph (1773–1833), describing northerners who supported southern interests in the Missouri Compromise of 1820.

[Return address:] Windham Ct / August 11th [Addressed to:]
Rev. Herman L. Vaill / East Haddam / Millington Society
[Postage:] 6

Windham Aug. 10th. 1825.

Dear Brother & Sister,

We have just rec^d your kind letter. I lose no time in answering.
Depend upon it we are steadfast, unmoveable & almost continually
abounding in our efforts to break up the Indian wedding. I wrote as
I promised as soon as I returned home, to Potter,[1] a letter that I am
sure will make him feel; another to E.B. which will be a damper if not
a death blow to this business. I have written to Brother Brinsmade;
another to brother Hopkins — another to sister Katharine in answer
to one just like the one she wrote to you. I wrote a letter, mild & respectful but high charged. I have written to Uncles Thos R. & Thomas
Golds;[2] & have an answer from Uncle Ruggles stating that in comply-
ance of my request he had written to his brother Benjⁿ "pretty fully to
endeavor to recal him, ~~back~~ from his devious course back to the sentiments of his friends & [conn]ections." I knew all you have stated about
sister [Ma]ry &c &c. But we are firm, & shall remain so whether the
wind blows high or low. I cannot believe that the wedding will take
place. I hope not. Fighting agt. God — I cannot endure such stuff. But
it has proved with Kath [n?] just as I predicted when I was at your house.
I feared the consequences of her return to Cornwall. O that we had
all written jointly week ago to E.B. & this business would have been
stopped — I do believe. If it be not too late I wish you would write to
him with out delay. I requested Brother B to write. Perhaps he has not.
Stand firm. You need not fear about us. You may ever know where to
find us. We are well. We shall come & see you when we can. Affectionately Yours

CB. Everest.

[LM top half] Uncle Ruggles stated moreover that he should be in Cornwall early in Oct. Do write to us. I will answer you.

[LM bottom half] Poor Stephen! We pity him, but he [is] on the <u>right</u> side, & I hope will not <u>turn over</u>

1. William Potter (1796–1891), a missionary working in the Cherokee Nation under the auspices of the ABCFM.

2. Thomas Gold (1759–1827) and Thomas Ruggles Gold (1767–1827) were brothers of Benjamin Gold. Both were graduates of Yale University and practiced law; Thomas Ruggles was elected to the New York Senate and the United States Congress. In addition to public service, he also contributed to the *North American Review* and other publications (Gold 291, 294–95).

CATHARINE GOLD TO HERMAN VAILL, 10 AUGUST 1825
HLVC, m.

[Return address:] Goshen Ct / August 11 [Addressed to:] Mr Herman L. Vaill / East Haddam / Millington Society / Conn [Postage:] 11

Wednesday Evening August 10<u>th</u> 1825

Dear Brother,

I have just received your letter. I thank you for it. I am glad to hear of your good health, & of the good health of your wife, & Catharine, You dont know how much I want to see you all—but brother, I have <u>heavy tidings</u> for you. You wrote, "tell all the news, but little do you expect to hear such, as I shall write you—surprising indeed will it be to you. In a very sudden & unexpected manner has Col. Pierce been called from time into eternity, yes, he is gone—he sleeps in death.[1] This morning he arose in healh, & his prospects for living then were as good as ours, but before 10 this morning, God was pleased, in a very striking manner, to take him hence—he was killed instantly—For the purpose of taking his cart out of the barn, he chained his Oxen to the hind end of the cart, the Oxen were frightened, & run the cart did not go the same way that the Oxen did (it is said that he stood with his back toward the cart, so that he did not perceive the danger that he was in) the cart came against him, and through down upon a stone wall, & the wheel run over him & crushed him to death instantly. O how [end of page 1] uncertain is life. Truly we know not what a day nor an hour may bring forth. O may this solumn event of God's providence, be sanctified to this people. It seems as if this death (like others) would not soon be forgotten by us. How strange it is that we should be so stupid so much taken up with the vanities of this world, that we should think so much of the honors & distinction of this vain world. When life is so uncertain

"How vain are all things here below
How false & yet how fair—
Each pleasure hath its poisons too—
And every sweet a snare—²

I think some times that I feel this, that I have a desire to have my affections entirely weaned from all transitory things, & placed above where I profess to have my treasure, but O my wicked heart—prove to lead me astray. How unfaithful & unprofitable I have been I feel that I have almost, if not quite lived in vain. Life is not desirable unless it is spent in doing good—pray for me, that I may live more as I ought. Pray for this church that God may pour out his Spirit upon it, & revive His work here At present all things look dark—but I hope we shall soon see different times.³ [end of page 2]

Sabbath evening

I did expect that H. would write some in this sheet to you, but she's sick and cannot. She has a billious complaint⁴ about her, The Doctor has been to see her to day—he says he thinks she is not going to be very sick, I hope she an't. H has not been very well for two or three [da]ys, she went to Litchfield with pa yesterday, & I suspect the ride was too much for her Mr & Mrs Northrop are now in Litch'd with their family, but they do not expect to stay there much longer. They dont know yet where they shall live. yet I think it was cruel that they were obliged to leave [Corn]wall as they did. The Chocktaws⁵ were expelled fr[om] school, for writing letters & for giving Mrs Northrup a writing that she had not in any ~~degree~~ way influenced them. This she wished to show to her friends, because they had heard many false reports. It is said that Carter was expelled from the same but if the truth was k[nown] they had some other reasons. No doubt they thought when they dismissed him he would go directly to Cherokee nation so that H. could not have a chance to see him he has not gone — he is at his unkle's in Goshen & [end of page 3] expects to stay there several months. They think much of Carter, & wish to have him stay with them [6] Alun [7] left Cornwall immediately after the affair was settled, he did not wait to see the agents, for fear of being expelled He has gone to England. Chew [8] has gone to New York to study divinity. The school is red[uce]d pretty low 15 scholars. The agents need [illegible] of wisdom. [There] are a great m[any] ✫ ✫ ✫

good p[eople] that feel very much wounded on account of what the agents have done The agents knew not what to do. I have no doubt they meant to do that they thought best, but they have dismissed some of the best of the scholars & they have never told David Carter [end of page 4]

[LM 1] why he was expelled. His friends ask him, & he is obliged to tell them, he never has had any reason given him, Mr Harvy is going to leave Goshen, is going [Han]over. It will be [a] great loss to this part of the country. I cannot tell you how soon I shall to Millington My love to the folks there I should be glad to see them I am as ever

your affectionate sister Catharine

[LM 2] I don't know what you will do for a [bureau?]. Ours is not fit on account of the brasses I wish pa would get some kind of one for you The carpet gets along slowly We don't any of us feel much like driving business. My love wife & Catharine does she grow any?

[M 2–3] I cannot tell you when your things will be sent — but I believe me I shall try my best to have them sent this month if possible Pa is determined not to go to Litchfield, for any thing. He has bought Mrs N dining table — it is a very nice one

1. "Col. Pierce" was John Hart Pierce (1777–1825). His sister, Maria, was married to Benjamin Franklin Gold, Harriett's older brother.

2. The first verse of Hymn 48 of Isaac Watts's *Hymns and Spiritual Songs* (146–47). Though its placement in the letter suggests the verse is a commentary on Pierce's death, the full lyrics of the song indicate that Catharine is obliquely commenting on Harriett's engagement. The third and fourth verses read:

> Our dearest joys and nearest friends,
> The partners of our blood,
> How they divide our wav'ring minds,
> And leave but half for God!
>
> The fondness of a creature's love,
> How strong it strikes the sense!
> Thither the warm affections move,
> Nor can we call them thence.

3. Here Catharine inserts a lengthy dash stretching to the right margin.

4. An ailment related to indigestion.

5. Miles Mackey and James Terrell (Starr 148).

6. David Carter's father had been taken captive by American Indians as a boy, remained with his captors, and married a Cherokee woman (Starr 148). David thus had relatives on his father's side residing in Connecticut. See Gold 254–58 for details of this captivity narrative. On the dismissal of Mackey, Terrell, and Carter, Evarts wrote in February 1826: "The Cherokees are at a loss to conceive why Terrell and Mackay, and David Carter should have been expelled from the school; and the two former sent off, with five dollars each, to find their way home a distance of 1400 miles: and this, after they had been brought to the school at the expense of the Board, & were entirely dependant upon the Board. You will remember, that we at Boston knew nothing of this bussiness, till after Terrell & Mackay had reached the Cherokee nation. It is presumed that they begged such things as they needed all the way home, and told the story of their disaster to all that who befriended them" (letter to Henry Hill).

7. Alun could be a misspelling of one of two Chinese students' names, William Alum or Henry Martyn A'lan. Both left the school in 1825, with Alum reportedly being dismissed for misconduct (Starr 145).

8. Tuscarora Guy Chew sometimes preached at meetings and "drew large houses; won sympathy; moved people to tears; and once . . . had to address the crowd out of doors" (qtd. in Starr 150).

[Addressed to:] Revd Herman L. Vaill / East Haddam

Cornwall Sept—1—1825

Mr H. L. Vaill—Sir,

After a length of time we send you & Flory things we have promised
—the sickness has been so great here that we could not send sooner—
if you are thankful for them well—if not you will be unthankful—I saw
the long letter you wrote Hariott—in which you throu out many things
against her & me & my wife—about the Indian connection—which are
altogether uncandid—unjust—[untr]ue—where you charge us with
deception—si[gnin]g affidavett in violation of truth &c &c &c—to all
which I do not see fitt to make any lengthy reply at present. It is
through pride & prejudice—that all this clamour has been raised
against Indians, And the least that can be said & done against Christian connections of any coular I belive to be best—our whol family
which have been together this summer have become very harmonious
on this subject—together with Sally Hopkins—Mary Brinsmade—&
many other good people around us & & throughout the country—as
you may yourself perceive—in very great hast I subscribe myself your
Father & Friend

Benjn Gold

[LM 1] Sister Vaill, we have been so sick much, & have had so much to
do, that I have not had time to see to your things so much as I should
wish Ma refuses[1] to give you any more linnen at present I have cut
[short] a little my peace for the sake of you[r] having enough for one
pair of linnen pillowcases [you] recollect [end of page 1] that your
piece was six yards long You can put one yard of it with mine to make
out the pair I want to see you I hope you will visit us soon It will not be
possible for me to go to Millington at present I wish you to send my
cloak by Stephen or bring it when you come yourselves Be so good as
to send the Journal that contains the piece signed by the old men of
this vally,[2] There seems to be a considerable differing of opinion respecting it, I think the truth ought to be known.

Your affectionate sister Catharine

* * *

[RM 2] H. has just ~~mentioned~~ requested me to mention that she well recollects your invetation to have E. Boudinot & herself visit you while on their way to Cherockee She wishes you to be making preperations as fast as possible

[LM 2] She can then learn Flora to make "Indian puding" if she wishes to have her[3]

1. At this point, Catharine continues writing below her father's signature.
2. The 10 August 1824 issue of the *Connecticut Journal* containing the letter signed by Benjamin Gold and seven other Cornwall men claiming that no inappropriate interactions were occurring between Foreign Mission School students and local young women.
3. Indian pudding was a colonial dish that relied on cornmeal and used molasses as sweetener.

HERMAN VAILL TO BENJAMIN GOLD, 5 SEPTEMBER 1825
CornHS, pm.

[Addressed to:] Col. Benjamin Gold / Cornwall

East Haddam, Millington Society, Sept. 5. 1825

Respected Father,

Sedgwick arrived here on Saturday with the furniture you had the goodness to send. The tables received some injury on the road, but on the whole the load came pretty safe, & the things were very acceptable to us both. The high post bedstead, & the one that was bro't the first load, were both of them 6 or 8 inches too wide. Flora gave directions to make them about 6 inches wider than the green bedstead; (that is,) about the width of Mrs Northrop's, but by some mistake Mr Barnes made them more than 6 inches wider than he was directed. But we got a man this morning to come, & cut off the end pieces, so that they do now very well.

I cannot concieve why you should think that we might be <u>unthankful</u> for your favors. We needed the furniture, & as it was bestowed by the kindness of Parents whom we hon[or] & love, I can assure you we have no disposition to feel [un]thankful, or ungrateful. We do sincerely thank you for all your kindness; & hope we may never cease to regard both our Parents with the filial & respectful feelings of dutiful children. I am very sorry to find that there should have been any expressions in my letter to Harriett, which you tho't "uncandid, unjust, & untrue." I meant to be candid, & honest in what I wrote, & if I failed to preserve candour in my letter, I can only say that the error was unintentional. In looking over a copy of it, I can see nothing which ought to be interpreted, as tho' I meant to implicate the character of either you or Mother. I did not mean to implicate your conduct in respect to the indian connexion, but I did fear that the public would think that on account of all that had been said against such connexions, & on account of what the people in the Vally who are friends to the school, had said, & certified, to quiet the fears lest another marriage would take [end of page 1] place, On these accounts I did fear that blame would fall on you. And my sole object in that part of my letter was to show Harriett that there was reason to fear that if she went forward under such circumstances, her own Christian character would suffer, & that there was also danger lest her Parents should be implicated, on the presumption that they had known & approved the project. I warned Harriett of these consequences, not to cast blame on the conduct of her Parents myself, but to persuade her not to do that, which might lead others to blame you. I don't know what Ground Mr Brinsmade, & Mr Everest have taken in their opposition. You speak of pride & prejudice, perhaps they may have it; but as to there being prejudice in my mind against indians, or indian matches, I certainly have none. Harriett knows I have none. She has my own declaration in black & white that I do not think a red connexion to be sinful in-itself. She knows I have no particular objection to the man;

And if H. had married Boudinott in precise[ly the] same circumstances in which Sarah Northrop mar[ried] Ridge, (that is,) before the tendency of the thing upon the school & upon missions had been proved; likely as not I should have said, "Let 'em mix." But the experiment has been tried, & it has been so hazardous that under almost any circumstances, it does now appear to be inexpedient. Still I harbour no ill will against those who think otherwise. I have no doubt but that you designed to do the thing that was right, & as I have no prejudice against Indian matches, when they are formed as they ought to be, I shall be wholly reconciled in this case, if it can be made to appear that the matter has been managed by Harriett, with a consistent regard to her character as a Christian, & a Missionary. The difficulty with me lies here. I do not see how she could have said so much, after Ridge's marriage; such as that she never thought of marrying an Indian, & other expressions of a similar nature, (which she certainly used,) when, as she has since declared, her mind was made up on the subject, the summer before Ridge was married; & she had then resolved to [end of page 2] continue the correspondence with Boudinott, & had resolved to marry him if he should propose it, as she had no doubt he would. There is a kink here which I wish to have somebody else unravel, for I cannot do it.

But I still love Harriett as a sister, & hope that if she goes, she will go to do good. I hope she has taken, & will continue to take, such a course in going among the heathen as any good missionary would take. I hope she has taken a course which Paul would approve; & the Saviour bless. Harriett Newell is a good Pattern for the female missionary.[1] Harriett Gold has the same professed object; I hope, & trust, she will take as fair a course. I do hope she has done nothing, & will do nothing, in her endeavors to attain her object, which would lessen her usefulness, or take away the respect of the indians, & of her future husband, if they should hear of it.

If she can't go, & go as one who has pursued an honest Christian course, to get there, a course which will insure her the respect of the indians, & the approbations of God; you & I, dear Sir, will both agree that she had better not go at all.

But I fear I shall trespass again, upon your patience at least. I here wish you & mother, & the family to remember that if I write freely it is because I have been accustomed, during my long residence in your family, to speak freely; & if I have seemed to you, to meddle, it is my apology that I feel an ~~illegible~~ interest in all things that concern the family, that prompts me to speak, as readily as if I were arguing my own case. My home is now here; & my attachments are forming among my people; but still my tho'ts are often with you. No family circle will ever be more pleasant to me than that in which I have spent so many happy hours, & where I found my good wife. There are none whome I more honour & love than her Parents. None whom I should more rejoice to see, & welcome here than they.

Flora wishes to go home, & make a 2 or 3 weeks visit. I cannot be gone so long, but I shall carry her to Hartf^d next Monday, & I wish to have Esq. Clark informed of it, that he may fix a good soft seat for her & the babe. She loves her old home & her Parents as much as ever. My love to all. I hope errors will be excused. I have written in great haste — your dutiful son

Herman L. Vaill

1. Like Harriett Gold, Harriet Atwood Newell (1793–1812) faced opposition from her family when she announced her plans to marry and accompany her husband to India as a missionary. Unlike Harriett Gold, her betrothed was a white man. Her letters and diaries were published in Leonard Woods's *Memoirs of the Life of Mrs. Harriet Newell* (1815).

ABBEY GOLD EVEREST TO HERMAN AND
FLORA GOLD VAILL, 5 SEPTEMBER 1825
HLVC, m.

[Addressed to:] Rev. Herman L. Vaill / East Haddam

Sept 5 1825

Dear brother & sister

I am very sorry it is not in our power to visit you this week. The Association of this County meet to-morrow, Mr Everest thinks it necessary for him to attend. I Think that we must defer our visit to Millington a few weeks. I wish very much to see you Mr Everrest expects to go to Cornwall some time in the course of the month He will make a very short visit. He will go on purpose to see his poor widowed mother. I presume there will be no hard feelings if he should visit no other family. I think of my dear friends in Cornwall almost constantly, not with pleasure as I have always been accustomed to do, but with pain

inexpressible. O that their eyes might be opened to see the right way
I have no hard feelings against my Parents & sister but I do think that
they are greatly in an error. We feel more & more opposed to the intended connection. I hope that it may be consistent [will] to prevent
it. [end of page 1]

I shall visit you soon after you return from Cornwall, I do not know
when I shall visit there. I have no disposition to go ~~as long as long~~
while things remain as they are. Mr. E. would write a line but he has
the headache severely.

Do write soon. from your sister A Everest

We are all very well. It is a time of health with us for which ~~illegible~~
we ought to be very thankful.

CORNELIUS EVEREST TO HERMAN VAILL, 14 SEPTEMBER 1825
HLVC, m.

[Return address:] Windham Ct / Sept 15$\underline{^{th}}$ [Addressed to:]
Rev. Herman L. Vaill / Millington Society / East Haddam.
[Postage:] 10

Windham Sept. 14. 1825.

Dear Brother,

I have this day rec$\underline{^d}$ the letter wh. you mailed for me at Hartford.
You wish to know whether I am going to Corn$\underline{^{ll}}$. It is uncertain when,
but I cannot go soon. On week after next is ordination at Lebanon wh.
I am invited to attend in council; week after that is our Consociational
meeting; week after that is the first annual meeting of our auxiliary
F.M. Society at wh. I am expected to preach. These are a part of my
calls besides all my duties to my family, & to the people of my charge.

The poisonous close in the Col.^{s} letter has not killed me or my
wife. The pie crust was pretty short—very different from what a par-
ent ought to send to Children.

The amount of it is, we may keep away from his house, if we please.

We are neither frightened nor angry. Perhaps your wife will be made
a turn-over before she comes back. [end of page 1] I have many, very

many things to say but have not time. We remain as we have done, opposed to the connection contemplated. And, brother, what will become of that family! What are the prospects of the unmarried & unsettled children? Kath^e has no idea of coming to Windham. My predictions are fulfilled. We mean to come & visit you as soon as you will let us know that sister F. has returned home. The blessing of God be upon you & yours. In great haste

Affectionately your brother CB.E.

FLORA GOLD VAILL TO HERMAN VAILL, [19] SEPTEMBER 1825
HLVC, ts.

[postmark: Sept. 19] [1]

Cornwall Sept—1825
Sabbath P.M.

My dear husband,

I will now devote a few leisure moments to you to inform you how & where I have been since I left you. We came to Griswold the first night. Next morning rode soon after sunrise to the Village & breakfasted, arrived at Cornwall about 2 of the clock safe, & sound, but some what fatigued. I lay down at Mr Smiths 2 or three hours & brother Ruggles [2] came for me & carried the babe down to Fathers in his arms & walked, sent for my things in the evening. Now you will wish to know what reception I met with. When I came, all rushed to the door, Catherine first, Harriet next & we saluted each other as usual. All were rejoiced to see our Catherine father & mother in particular. Mother says she has not wanted to see anyone since we left, but our babe. She bore her journey well & is as playful as ever. The letter that you sent prepared the way for me & father is kind as ever. I hope you will come as you proposed, every one asked when you were coming & I am convinced that you had better come & talk the matter over. As to my becoming a turn-over, I feel the same unwillingness to have Harriet go as ever. But I am satisfied & reconciled to whatever she may have said & I am confident you would be, if you could talk the matter over. I am perfectly reconciled to our parents, that they have taken an upright course & do not let us afflict them. Every one of the family say that they should rejoice to have it otherwise, & opposed as long as they tho't it would do any good. Stephen feels strenuously opposed to indian connections, but has given it up & sings with Harriet as usual, rides & walks with her & is as chirk as ever. He has just told me that he is not troubled on account of pride in the least. I asked what he intended to do when E. B. came. He said he should be gone at that time, I do not think he intends violence at all. It is a harmonious time as father wrote, because they are all convinced it will do no good to say anything. Come to read over your letter of 2 sheets to H. I think it is hard to bear, H. says it cuts the hardest of anything she has ever received from anyone, but she is willing to forgive. I know you would not have written so if you knew the circumstances as I do now. Much of what Mr Harvey told us is ascertained to be absolute falsehood. Father & mother have sustained good character in this place too long to be overthrown by the agents or any other one. It is not good policy for us to disgrace them, they have done nothing worthy of it. The letter which mother received from the agents is a most insulting one. She has never had a moments conversation with one of the school in <u>private</u> nor has she ever requested it. Mackey & Terrill never in <u>one instance</u> said that Mrs N. <u>ever so much as hinted</u> about writing letters. What Clark told about Harriet's walking with Pluma Loomis is entirely without foundation, made out of whole cloth, Deacon Loomis & Mrs Stone I expect have given information to the agents & I expect they have all got themselves into hot water. Some people are quite disappointed because they find it is not going to destroy the family & cannot bear to think that father & mother have acted an honest part. <u>Curtis Carter</u> says that people do very wrong to countenance our family & says he shall not visit here at all & avoids even a compliment. <u>We shall all feel very bad.</u> I must tell you the rest when I see you.

Cousin Elish Swift was married 2 weeks since Catherine & H. attended by special invitation Stephen could not go on account of ill health. When the ceremonies were over Mr Osborne asked what has become of the girl that expected to marry an Indian, & after cousin had hawed & hitched a little he told him that the lady was present, upon which Mr O. apologized, & requested an introduction. He invited H. home with him, & she was highly gratified with her visit, & treated by all with great respect. By the by there hapened to be a gentleman there cousin to Elisha's wife, that took quite a fancy to our sister C & waited on her home, came over to training since, & is coming over again next tuesday, perhaps for the last time. Upon first being introduced they were both quite struck with each others appearance, he is a widower with three children, son of Capt. Lovell of Sharon, goes to meeting at Mr Perry's, Harriet says she saw their situation, it was most delightful. He has been one of the kindest of husbands, has always sustained a good character but is not professedly pious. what C. will do I do not know. Harriet says now she will have her trial. I believe it will go, for I believe they both fell in love at first sight. Stephen likes him, & every one that has seen him. His father signed 12,00 dollars for the canal, is a man of wealth. "so they go" My love to my husband first, then to his house-keeper, & all my neighbours. I am well, have attended meeting all day. H. went up gallery in the afternoon. Every one of the young men left the seat, in the morning for fear, & Stephen sung alone all day. I have not heard better singing in a year.

This morning a letter has been received by Mr Northrop from Rev'd Mr Butrick contradicting all the reports about Ridge's conduct & speaks highly of every one of the scholars. & says he is grieved to see the report of the agents concerning Boudinot & H. for their proposed connection speaks in the highest terms of his character. Mr N. is going to send a copy to be printed, you will probably see it. Mr Northrop wept like a child when it was read.[3]

In haste I am your affectionate wife,
Flora Gold Vaill

Father said Aunt Hubbard was not very much pleased about the news, but after talking the matter over said, well, I do not believe that any indian ever got such a lump of gold before.

Sister Flora's hand trembles so much that she wishes me to fill the margin, and tell you that she wishes you to write immediately to Br. E.

& request him by all means to bring Sister A. with him to C. She says that Abbey will feel much better satisfied & relieved if she will but come home and learn the truth, though she has said she wished no more to come under this roof, yet I hope she will for I am confident should she come & be candid she would not long retain the impressions she now has of her parents & Sister. I also wish much to have a talk with my Br. Vaill. My heart is often grieved. A wounded spirit who can bear! H.R.G.

H. says she don't want to exchange complections with Catherine. He has black eyes, black hair, & a black skin.

1. The typescript of this letter in the Herman Landon Vaill Collection is the only source text remaining; the manuscript is not present in the collection. The typescript gives no information about what appeared in the address area other than the date of the postmark, nor does it record the placement of marginal insertions or postscripts.

2. An older brother, Thomas Ruggles Gold (1787–1829).

3. Rev. Daniel Sabin Butrick (1789–?) was an ABCFM missionary stationed in the Cherokee Nation. In this letter, which was later published in the *Religious Intelligencer*, he denied rumors of "Mr. Ridge's abusing his wife" and claimed that John Ridge was "a gentleman" and that Sarah Northrop Ridge "dresses richer, and appears more like a lady, than when at Cornwall" and "appeared cheerful and contented" ("Cherokee Mission" 280). Butrick went on to deny the report that the Cornwall-educated Cherokees "have nearly all turned back to their heathen ways." He notes that his "feelings have been much hurt" (281) in learning of the "public censure and reproach" (281) directed at Elias and Harriett's proposed marriage, commenting of Elias: "if virtue, piety, and sound knowledge can recommend a youth, he would evidently adorn your distinguished circles in Connecticut" (280). In April 1826, Evarts also described Sarah's Northrop Ridge's situation: "As to the inquiry whether young M^{rs}. Ridge is contented & happy, it is certain that she often says she is; and surely she ought to know. I should think most persons believe her; but some are incredulous" (letter to Henry Hill).

[Return address:] Cornwall Ct / Jany 9th [Addressed to:]
Rev. Herman L. Vaill / East Haddam / Millington Society / Conn.
[Postage:] 10

Tuesday morn Cornwall Jan 2nd. 1826

Dear Brother & Sister,

With pleasure I hasten to answer the letter we received from you yesterday. I have been for sometime wishing to write & shall probably have time to write more than one girls letter—but as to Sister Catharine, in vain do you wish for another girls letter from her. I am now left an only daughter & Sedgwick is the only brother I have left at home. Catharine is now in Sharon. She was married Christmas morning before meeting. The day was rainy, but the wedding very pleasant. We had two Mr. Chafy's from Sharon—Brother H. & wife—[Ann?] & Eleanor,[1] & Sarah Calhoun besides our family at home. Should have had a few more had it been pleasant weather. The day after wedding— Catharine left us, we expect her back this week to spend only a few days & then pack up what she can get & bid farewell to ~~home~~ a fathers house. Father is going to Litchfield to day to purchase some chairs— Table &c for C. I expect to accompany her when she removes & spend one week. You cannot imagine how much I do wish to visit you; & know how you are situated before I leave my ^{native} land—but it is not probable that I shall enjoy so great a privilege. Just as I had written this—I heard the sound of sleigh bells & who but Brother & Sister Lovell with their daughter Elizabeth—a sweet little girl she is too. She appeared very fond of her Ma & Catharine appears quite like a Mother.[2] [end of page 1]

As Sister C— has returned I shall not say much about her but leave her to speak for herself. Brother Lovell wishes me to give his respects to you both & also to Swift. He says he hopes & intends to visit you if there should be sufficient sleighing & will bring the carpet—but that Catharine shall not weave it. Catharine's carpet is now in the Loom,

& we shall try among us all to weave it. As soon as hers is out of the Loom Mrs. Brown will get in yours & I have long since by my own contrivance paid Cousin Laura Swift for the weaving of yours. If we have an opp—we shall send you some Cheese & Sausages & perhaps some small presents for the wonderful Grandchild.

Now what to tell you about myself I hardly know. I appear to remain illegible stationary—nothing new since Swift left us—but I hope to hear from my far distant friend before long & know how soon I shall go. My Box is made & I am trying to fill it with something—have some presents from friends for all which I am very grateful. The week before Thanksgiving Sister C. & myself went to N.H—traded a little. We returned by W.[3] & I spent a week there very agreably. Sister Mary comes home very often & we have precious family visits. You have probably heard of Br. Everests visit to Cornwall. Many remarks are made. Some will say— "Is this a minister of the gospel"? others— "why I think ministers are worse than other folks"— "It appears to me such conduct is not becoming a minister" & also some few such as Joshua Pierce are pleased, & say, "it's just right." As for our part we are sorry Br. E has given occasion for so many remarks. We th fear he can does not feel so a christian ought to feel & we do sincerely [end of page 2] pity Sister Abbey. Does she not remember the pleasant interviews she has enjoyed in the family circle? Can she not call to mind any kindnesses she has received from home, which were tokens of regard for her? Is she ready to believe every false report & know nothing of the truth. It seems it is so & perhaps she still continues to say, she wishes no more to come under the parental roof. We believe Abbey to be a christian & for this reason we feel confident that her present state of feelings will not always remain. I think she must be unhappy & I am sorry for her. You cannot think what precious interviews we four Sisters, (who are at present situated near each other),[4] do enjoy. We shall have but few more opportunities of praying and singing together here—but we part with the blessed hope & expectation of meeting in that happiest world where we shall reunite in perfect songs of praise which will never cease. O how comforting—how comforting. May we not any of us be deceived. May we be more watchful & prayerful—live as strangers &

pilgrims—knowing that this is not our continuing city.[5] May duty ever be plain to each of us, & may it ever be the greatest desire of our hearts to know the will of God & do it. When I realize the parting with my dear Father, dear Mother, dear sisters, & dear brothers & friends—the thought pierces my very heart, it is trying beyond description—still it is my desire to go. I cannot but rejoice in prospect of spending my days among those ~~illegible~~ despised people & as the time draws nearer I long to begin my work. I think I may reasonably expect many trials, hardships, & privations. May I never be disposed to seek my own ease any farther than is consistent with the greatest usefulness. Dear Brother & Sister how I wish to see you once more in the flesh. I think as the prospect now is I should not leave home at least this winter—but we know not how to calculate as our lives & all the things of this life are uncertain. It is quite sickly [end of page 3] in C. & deaths are frequent. Widow Joseph Judson died last week after fourteen days illness. The fever which she died with & which many are now sick with is the same as prevailed & swept off so many several years ago. The Bell has just been tolling for Mr. Shepherds youngest son, about 20 years of age. Widow David Patterson is almost gone with the consumption. I have written in haste with a miserable pen—but trust you will excuse all. Write again before long. I am as ever your affectionate Sister

Harriett R. Gold

The family send love to you & Swift
My respects to Miss Diantha
H.

* * *

[LM 1] If you see Brother & Sister E. please give my love to them, I wish them prosperity—but if we are not reconciled to each other here, how can we meet in Heaven? Sister C. wishes you to find out whether they would be glad to see her & her husband in W.[6] They wait only for sleighing to visit you

[M 2–3] Write to me & give me all the good advice you can. Harriett

1. Samuel and Sarah (Sally) Gold Hopkins, who had daughters named Ann and Eleanor.

2. Elizabeth was John Lovell's daughter from his first marriage.

3. Given the reference in the next line to "Sister Mary," "W." probably refers to Washington, Connecticut, home of the Brinsmades.

4. The four sisters are Harriett, Catharine Gold Lovell, Mary Gold Brinsmade, and Sarah Gold Hopkins.

5. The previous sentences are filled with scriptural allusions: from the King James Version, "blessed hope," Titus 2:13; "heed that ye be not deceived," Luke 21:8; "take ye heed, watch and pray," Mark 13:33; "strangers and pilgrims," Hebrews 11:13 and 1 Peter 2:11; "continuing city," Hebrews 13:14.

6. This "W." probably refers to Windham, Connecticut, home of the Everests.

HERMAN VAILL TO HARRIETT GOLD, 5 MARCH 1826
HLVC, m.

[Addressed to:] Miss Harriett R. Gold / Cornwall

Sabbath Evening. East Haddam, Millington Society,
March 5. 1826.

Dear Sister Harriett R. Gold, whose Gold will shortly become dim, & to whom, I write now, with this appellation, probably for the last time; I have long intended to write you, a sort of Adieu; or Farewell Letter; but ill health, & various calls & labours have hitherto prevented. I suppose you will be going far away before long; My best wishes & my Prayers attend you.

You know, dear Sister, you know I always loved you; & that difference of opinion with regard to the propriety & expediency of your contemplated connexion, (for you are aware that I did not think just as you did,) has not abated my desire to see you happy & useful. I have the same affectionate, fraternal regard for you as ever; & hope that you will be the instrument of accomplishing much in behalf of that People whom I suppose you now consider as your Nation.

As to the Principle you know that I have maintained it as correct, & scriptural that such connexions should be formed. [I] have always, in this respect, been an advocate for intermarriages &c. The present expediency, all circumstances considered, is another thing. But as you & I talked the matter over when I saw you last, & parted amicably, I am willing it should there rest. Go dear Sister, & if you have erred, beseech God to forgive you; go, & in His cause, & in His strength, do all the good you can. And must we thus part? Am I never to see you more? Are you never more to see your dear Sister, & my dear wife, never to see our dear little Catharine Harriet? It may be so; but—my health is at present feeble; I may be obliged to visit a milder climate again; I may go to Georgia; yes, & to your Nation, & see you there. My sister, we shall remember you; we shall remember you at the Throne of Grace;[1] & you will there remember us. Our request is that you would always write to us—once in 3 mo^t & we will answer you as often. My kind regards & best wishes, to Brother Boudinott; when he becomes your husband. Affectionately yours

H.L. Vaill

Farewell.

1. Hebrews 4:16.

FLORA GOLD VAILL TO HERMAN VAILL, 29 APRIL 1826
HLVC, ts.

[Addressed to:] Rev'd. Herman L. Vaill / East Haddam

Cornwall April 29—1826

My dear husband,

Sabbath morning.

This is probably the last sabbath that H. & I shall ever spend together on earth. solemn thought.[1]

If we are what we hope we are, the time will come when we shall meet, and enjoy an eternal sabbath in our Fathers Kingdom above, where there will be unalloyed happiness & where farewell sounds which are so unpleasant to us now, will cease. We expect Boudinot tomorrow by Stage from Hartford & some one will meet him there to bring him to Cl. Tuesday they expect to set out & spend first night in Washington in company with father & mother. The scene will be trying to us all, but we hope for Divine support & consolation.[2] I have enjoyed myself very well since I have been at home & although I feel

anxious to return to M. & to my husband again—still I shall feel a reluctance about leaving the parental dwelling which is so pleasant, &
so lonely, on mothers account in particular.

Your affectionate wife,
F. G. Vaill

1. The marriage had taken place a month earlier, on 28 March 1826.
2. A "#" is penciled into the typescript at this point.

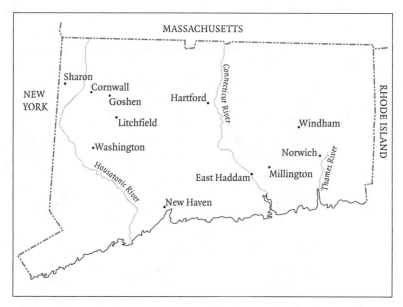

Map 1. Connecticut

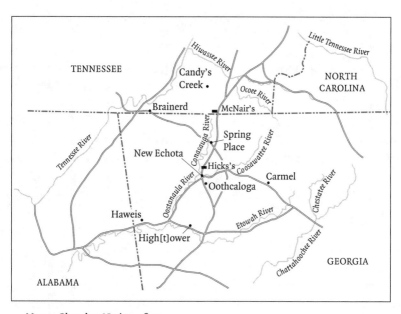

Map 2. Cherokee Nation, 1825

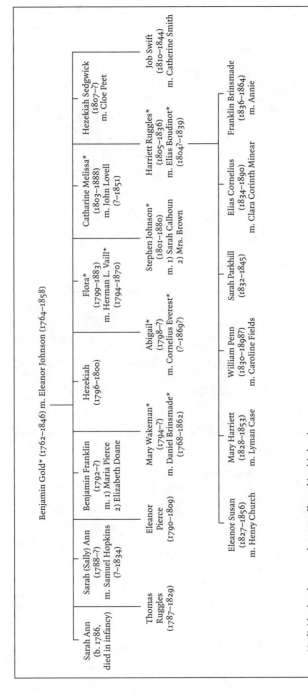

Gold Family Tree

Benjamin Gold* (1762–1846) m. Eleanor Johnson (1764–1858)

Sarah Ann (b. 1786, died in infancy)

Sarah (Sally) Ann (1788–?) m. Samuel Hopkins (?–1834)

Thomas Ruggles (1787–1829)

Benjamin Franklin (1792–?) m. 1) Maria Pierce 2) Elizabeth Doane

Eleanor Pierce (1790–1809)

Hezekiah (1796–1800)

Mary Wakeman* (1794–?) m. Daniel Brinsmade* (1768–1862)

Eleanor Susan (1827–1856) m. Henry Church

Mary Harriett (1828–1853) m. Lyman Case

William Penn (1830–1898?) m. Caroline Fields

Abigail* (1798–?) m. Cornelius Everest* (?–1869?)

Flora* (1799–1883) m. Herman L. Vaill* (1794–1870)

Stephen Johnson* (1801–1880) m. 1) Sarah Calhoun 2) Mrs. Brown

Sarah Parkhill (1832–1845)

Catharine Melissa* (1802–1888) m. John Lovell (?–1851)

Harriett Ruggles* (1805–1836) m. Elias Boudinot* (1804?–1839)

Elias Cornelius (1834–1890) m. Clara Corinth Minear

Franklin Brinsmade (1836–1864) m. Annie

Hezekiah Sedgwick (1807–?) m. Cloe Peet

Job Swift (1810–1844) m. Catherine Smith

*Individuals who wrote letters collected in this book.

Foreign Mission School, Cornwall, Connecticut, from a photograph taken late in the nineteenth century. (Courtesy of Cornwall Historical Society)

Daniel Brinsmade. (Courtesy of Gunn Historical Museum, Washington, Connecticut)

Daguerreotype image of Herman Vaill, probably taken in the 1840s. (Courtesy of Leila Vaill Fetzer Estate)

Daguerreotype image of Flora Gold Vaill, probably taken in the 1840s. (Courtesy of Leila Vaill Fetzer Estate)

Benjamin and Eleanor Gold's house, Harriett's childhood home and where her wedding took place, as it stands today. (Photo by Theresa Strouth Gaul)

An interpretive sign at the New Echota State Historic Site displaying a drawing, based on archaeological evidence and contemporaneous descriptions, of Elias and Harriett Gold Boudinot's house. (Drawing by Charles O. Walker; photo by David Gomez; courtesy of Georgia Department of Natural Resources, New Echota State Historic Site)

Front page of the *Cherokee Phoenix*, 13 March 1828, edited by Elias Boudinot from 1828 to 1832. The newspaper printed its columns in English and Cherokee.

A reproduction of Harriett Gold Boudinot's tombstone standing in the graveyard at the New Echota State Historic Site. The words "We seek a rest beyond the skies" are inscribed across the bottom of the stone; according to Elias's letter of 16 August 1836, Harriett wished to have the hymn beginning with those words sung to her in her final illness. The original gravestone, made out of New England limestone, is retained by the site. (Photo by David Gomez)

This miniature image is of Elias Boudinot, according to unidentified handwriting on the back. (Courtesy of Henry M. Boudinot Estate)

This miniature of Harriett Gold Boudinot made from her oil portrait is probably the one requested by Elias Boudinot in his letter of 20 May 1837. (Courtesy of Henry M. Boudinot Estate)

PART 2

Cherokee Letters, 1827–1839

ELIAS AND HARRIETT GOLD BOUDINOT TO
HERMAN AND FLORA GOLD VAILL, 5 JANUARY 1827
HLVC, m.

[Return address:] Carmel Cher. Na / Feb 23, 1827 [Addressed to:]
Rev. Herman L. Vaill / East Haddam / Millington Society /
Connecticut [Postage:] 25

High Tower January 5th 1827

Dear Brother & Sister,

Your good letter dated Nov. 17th 1826 has just reached us, & we are
extremely happy in being able to answer it without any delay & indeed
why should not we be punctual, as you must know, we have none of the
ponderous reasons which have occationed your delay—none of your
tradings, journeyings, weddings &c &c & if we postpone writing, until
we should make some sort of trade, in order to report to you at what
pr. Centum we had lost or gained, or until we should perform some
Journey, or should wait until some illegible had committed the gross
crime of matrimony; it would be so mighty long before you hear from
us, that I reckon[1] you would not a little be mad at us. So you see we
had better write to you now, though we have no great news to tell you.
We rejoice with you that you have a Boy to your liking.[2] May he thrive,
& grow, & be come a great blessing to his parents, who purchased him
so dearly; & when you shall become old (if that should be your lot) &
infirm, & your hair shall change, your limbs shall totter, may he then
be your stay & your support. You will perceive by the date of this where
we are. High Tower is on one of the branches of Coosa, about 30 miles
from its junction with Oostahnalee. about 4 years ago, a mission was
established here under the American Board of Commissioners, —Mr
Proctor[3] who first commenced the establishment, has been obliged
to leave it, on account of the vacancy of the Mission at Carmel. This
of course [end of page 1] has lain destitute for some time & indeed
the Mission has declined much, & the Society School hardly exists. We
came here the 1st day of December, to take charge of it for this winter only. The Mission find us, & we have $20 pr month. I expect to
begin the School in a few days. I cannot tell how I shall succeed—it is
quite discouraging. We have good deal of company sometime, & I am

afraid, that my dear wife does rather more than she aught to do. Every Sabbath we have preaching & I am generally the Interpreter. Mr. Worcester[4] of Brainerd spent some time with us—while here we commenced systematizing the Cherokee language, & forming rules for the foundation of the Tenses. I presume the Cherokee verbs are the most complicated in the world—nothing like it in any language, whether learned or Savage, unless we except those spoken by the Indians generally. You will form a slight idea of the almost infinite forms in the Cherokee verbs, when I tell you that we have discovered 29 Tenses in the Indicative mode, in all the verbs, & 30 in some; & that in the verb To tie, there are not less than 178 forms, only in the present Tense Indicative mode. Mr. Worcester however proceeds rapidly in acquiring the language—he intends to preach in it—the blessing of God attend him. I have nearly finished, my part of the sheet—so I am obliged to be concise in every thing. We shall expect to hear from you again before a great while. Let no future Trade, Journey, or Wedding prevent [end of page 2] you from writing & rejoicing the heart of

Your Indian Brother
E. Boudinott

Dear Br. & Sister,

Should I like you, wait for a leisure hour I know not when you would hear from me, You see I have not much room, & I shall not much more than answer some of Sister F's questions—leaving other things for other letters which you may see at C. You wish for some account of our family. I will then tell you briefly—beginning with my Parents. My Cherokee Father often reminds me of my own Father by his cheerfulness & I think is remarkable for his amiable, kind, & affectionate disposition. Sister M. says he used to often to speak of me before I came here—said I was going to leave all my friends to come and do them good, & they must love me a great deal & both he & My Dear Cherokee Mother frequently say that I am like an own child to them.[5] Mother is a very feeble woman. But never idle if she is able to be off her bed. She cuts & makes all the clothes for her family except the coats for the men. She is remarked by all who know her for her amiable kind & friendly disposition. Our oldest Br—named Stand is a young man about 21—has a decent education, & is much esteemed in the Nation.[6] Nancy is our eldest Sister. She is 19 or 20. Not many of her age smarter for business. She is also amiable & [missing] in her disposition. a member of the church at [Haweis[7] Next] is Br Thomas. He attends school & in his appearance often [reminds] me of Gold Hopkins.[8] Next is Sister Mary. Now living with Mr. Remley's family at Echota. She has always been a great favorite with me—is remarkably lively has a good mind & it will not be saying too much, to say I know of no girl of her age & advantages superior to her. She wishes to write to my Mother & probably will before long Next is Betsey our youngest sister at school. She reads & spells well, is a very pretty girl & I think bids fair to make a smart woman. The next is John Alexander Petrie, formerly called Henry. He was selected by the Missionaries & named by the request of Mr. J.A. Petrie of Charleston S.C. who wishes to give him a thorough English education.[9] Mr. Boudinott received a letter a few weeks since from Miss Sarah A. Petrie. She calls him their little Brother & expreses very great affection & interest for him. Alexander is yet young just beginning to read. We cannot now tell what he will make—but he is as promising as any boys of his age I ever saw. He is very pleasant, active & ambitious. The youngest of all is a daughter & is yet a babe—name Susan. Had I time & room I could tell you many things relative to our family which would be interesting. [end of page 3] I love them all much & I may say—we love each other. You also wish to know what I have to eat At Father Watie's we had coffee, Sugar, Tea milk corn & wheat bread, Beef—Pork—Venison & an abundance of fowls & I sometimes made puddings, Pies, & Cakes—Butter, Cheese, Apple Sauce & Pickles are not as plenty as they probably will be hereafter. At this place we have not a great a variety—but do very well. I am Baking rice pudding for dinner today & I think it will be very good. I not only rise early enough to get my own food but sometimes for ten or fifteen besides. Now Sister Flora—although I shall tell you nothing of the little ones I can tell you much more. Indeed your family & work are insignificant compared with mine. Since we came here, untill the two last weeks I had no assistance except Sister Betsey when out of school & our family has averaged most of the time 8 or 10. Christmas time we had several interesting meetings & company from abroad. For four days I had from ten to 15 to wait upon. I do my cooking principally in the room where we live as we have 8 of the school-children who live with us but do their cooking in the Kitchen.[10] I do my baking in iron Bake Ovens. Sister N. is now with us & is a great help to me out of school. We only came here for this winter & expect to return to our Parents next month. We are not yet settled, when we are we will let you know.

★ ★ ★

At Oogillogy I spent considerable time in sewing for other people — such as making bonnets & the like[11] — but here I can hardly find time to do my own mending — but notwithstanding all my cares I can truly say I am contented & never passed my days more pleasantly than while I have been in this Nation. My health is generally good, my appetite excellent — not for particular things only, but for whatever is set before me.[12] The country here differs much from Conn. appears to me as I expected a new country would. Nothing appears strange, but as though I had always lived here. I think the climate more pleasant & healthy than Conn. We have heard the Frogs sing every day since Jan & some evenings this month, (Feb) we have set with our doors open as you do in June. But a few days extreme cold weather so that one or two not far from here were frozen to death. While writing this I have confined myself as it were in fetters — but as I have several other letters to answer soon you can see them when you go to C. & obtain other information. Your Cheerful & affectionate Sister

H.R.G.B.

[LM 2] I saw br. Potter at Haweis last Sept. He wished me to give his respects to you both. Please write to C. soon as you receive this & tell our parents all is well I am
[LM 1] writing to them but understand we have several letters at Father W's. so I wait a few days longer. It is about six months since I wrote them H.

[LM 3] Last week, I had a very unexpected visit from Cousin Sarah. She cam[e with] the intention to spend a week but her Husband was called into the Creek Nation & was obliged to send for her in three days [missing] sent her in their Coach with a driver & little black girl, to take care of Clarinda.[13] She came in company with Br. [missing] Sister Nancy on their return from Haweis. While She was her we took time to do a little necessary sewing. Cousin S health [missing] good. My love to all friends. Visit our Parents often & do every thing for their comfort. O my dear precious Mother. How shall we [ever] repay half her kindness to us. Your Cherokee Sister

1. The k in this word is written above the line and appears in lighter ink, perhaps from Harriett's pen, the ink from which is considerably lighter than that from Elias's in this letter. This suggests that Harriett might have proofread Elias's letters.

2. Charles Benjamin Vaill, born 11 September 1826.

3. Isaac Proctor opened the Hightower mission and school in 1822.

4. Samuel Austin Worcester (1798–1859), an ABCFM missionary who went on to work extensively with Boudinot in translating the Bible into Cherokee. Bass describes his life and relationship with Elias. See Kilpatrick and Kilpatrick for his contributions to the *Cherokee Phoenix*.

5. Elias's parents were Oo-Watie (1773–1842), or David Watie, and Susanna Reese (ca. 1786–1832).

6. Elias's younger brother, Stand Watie (1806–71), went on to play a prominent role in Cherokee politics. A signer of the Treaty of New Echota, he escaped assassination after removal and assumed leadership of the Ridge-Boudinot-Watie faction after the deaths of his brother, cousin John Ridge, and uncle Major Ridge. Influential in allying the Cherokees with the Confederacy during the Civil War, Watie attained the rank of general, the only southern Native American to do so. He was the last confederate general to surrender at the end of the war.

7. A mission near present-day Rome, Georgia.

8. Possibly Harriett's nephew, son of Samuel and Sarah (Sally) Gold Hopkins. They had a son named Benjamin Gold Hopkins who would have been sixteen years old, the approximate age of Thomas Watie.

9. Taking a benefactor's name was a common practice among Cherokees receiving missionary educations. Named "Gallegina" or "Buck" at birth, Elias himself had adopted the name of his benefactor, Elias Stockton Boudinot, the New Jersey philanthropist and member of the Continental Congress. Elias had met him in 1817 on his way to Cornwall.

10. It was common practice for the mission school students to live with the missionaries. This allowed them to observe firsthand and participate in the gendered division of labor and the values of family life the missionaries promoted; see Perdue, *Cherokee Women* 162–67, for discussion of the gendered values inculcated by missionary schools.

11. Harriett's skills with the needle would have been valuable in Cherokee society. Most Cherokees at this time dressed in Western dress, and the women were anxious to learn to spin, weave, and sew so that they could participate in the commercial economy that otherwise largely excluded them (Perdue, *Cherokee Women* 117).

12. Probably a reference to Harriett's pregnancy. Her first child, Eleanor, was born five months later on 4 May 1827.

13. Sarah Northrop Ridge, whose marriage to John Ridge in 1824 had caused another scandal in Cornwall; Clarinda was the Ridges' daughter. John Ridge was Elias's first cousin, thus Harriett was now related to Sarah by marriage. As one of the wealthy elite of the Cherokees, John Ridge was a plantation owner and slaveholder. See Perdue, *Slavery*, for more information on slavery and the Cherokees.

ELIAS AND HARRIETT GOLD BOUDINOT
TO HERMAN VAILL, 21 NOVEMBER 1827
HLVC, m.

[Return address:] Springplace C. N. / Nov. 29, 1827 [Addressed to:] Rev. Herman L. Vaill / East Haddam / Millington Society / Connecticut

New Echota November 21st, 1827

My Dear Brother,

You will receive the enclosed short Prospectus for a weekly paper to be published in this place, and under the direction of the Cherokee Legislature.[1] You know that such a paper have been had, for some time, in contemplation; and you are also aware of the reasons which has induced us to commence i[t]. It is altogether an uncertain experiment, for its future existence must entirely depend on the indulgence & good will of those who are friendly to us. We have nothing to recommend our paper, but its novelty & our good intentions. We do not wish to be thought as striving to rival other papers of the day, by exhibiting to the public, learning, talents & information, for these we do not profess to possess. We have therefore to crave the indulgence of the [Critic?] and suitable allowance of all our readers. Our object is simple, and in our opinion requires no great attainments. It is, as you will notice in the foregoing Prospectus, the benefit of the Cherokees, who, you know, are uninformed. I have taken the liberty, Dear brother Vaill, to address this to you, knowing that you take a deep interest in whatever concerns us, and are a well wisher to all the Indians. You will therefore do the Cherokees a great favour if you will present this Prospectus to all whom it may concern, and obtain as many Subscribers as you possibly can, if any are to be had in Connecticut, the land of intermarriages.

I am happy to tell you that we are in a tolerable state of health. Our little Eleanor has been unwell, but is now lively & peart. She is now a great deal of company for us. [end of page 1] All who see her say, "she is the handsomest child I ever saw." You must not think that I brag. I went to Brainerd the other day, and found a small bundle which our Mother Gold sent to Harriett, by one Miss Fields who is gone as missionary to the Choctaws. I must close & leave a small space for my wife. Your brother

E. Boudinott

★ ★ ★

Dear Br [and Sis]ter,

I have many things to say—but must make my sentences short. To day our people have had corn husking & I have had a quilting The men husked about 600 bushels of corn—but on account of the unpleasant weather I had but few quilters. It has been snowing most of the day—seems quite like New England weather. I am now making preparations to remove to New Echota as we expect to go next week. Mr. Worcesters Family are to live but a few steps from us. We shall do nothing about building before spring. I am much attached to this neighborhood. almost all the people here are our relations. When we get to N.E. there will be four families living within sight of each other. One of them Mr. E. Hicks lives in a handsome framed house which cost him 15. hundred dollars. It need not however have cost more than 5 hundred in N. England & thus it is with many other things here; the prices are more than double. If you are disposed to send a box—I choose not to particularize many things. Whatever is useful to you or would make you comfortable, would be the same to me. You know what I had. Were my Parents able as they once were I should be apt to wish for many things which my sisters had—but had rather suffer any inconvenience than than they who have done so much, should now in their old age deny themselves any thing more. Any kind of clothing would be very acceptable. Flannel is as useful here as in N. End. I should like to visit you but is not likely we shall in several years if ever—am more attached to this than my native home. The place of my birth is dear to me but I do love this people & with them I wish to live & die. Write soon & you may expect a long letter in return for I have much to tell you, & hope you are enjoying a revival of religion. Pray for the Cherokees that they may all be brought to the truth. I intend to write to my Parents & other friends in a few days. Your affectionate sister,

Harriet.

[RM 2] The Georgians make us but little trouble at present, though they are determined to have the land.[2] We are about 100 miles from Athans in Georgia, & about 160 miles from Macan. E.B.

1. Funded with money raised by Elias on his northern speaking tour and printed in specially cast types in the Sequoya syllabary, the *Cherokee Phoenix* began its run on 21 February 1828 with Elias as editor. The prospectus, printed in October 1827 and enclosed in this letter to Herman Vaill, announced that "the great and sole motive in establishing this paper, is the benefit of the *Cherokees*" (Boudinot, "Prospectus"; italics in the original). The bilingual paper, with its columns printed in English and Cherokee, provided a forum for information and argumentation relative to the Cherokees' political situation and, in the practice of the day, extensively reprinted miscellaneous material from other papers. Elias printed two hundred copies for Cherokee readers, and the paper also reached subscribers outside the Cherokee Nation. The paper's name changed to the *Cherokee Phoenix and Indian's Advocate* in 1829 and continued under Elias's editorship until 1832, when he resigned. Though he hoped to use the paper to foster open discussion about the removal debate, the Cherokee Council wanted the paper to articulate only the dominant, antiremoval position. The paper continued with a different editor until 1834 (Perdue, *Cherokee Editor* 15–16, 87–88). Perdue's *Cherokee Editor* reprints a large number of Elias's editorials.

2. Elias refers here to Georgians' increasing pressure on the U.S. government to fulfill decades-old promises to purchase Cherokee landholdings in the state.

ELIAS AND HARRIETT GOLD BOUDINOT TO HERMAN
AND FLORA GOLD VAILL, 23 JANUARY 1829
HLVC, m.

[Return address:] New Echota, C.N. / Feby 4 [Addressed to:] Rev
Herman L Vail / River Head / (Conn) [Postage:] 25

New Echota Jan. 23^d 1829.

Dear brother & Sister,

Your kind letter dated, <u>River Head</u>, your new place of residence, was duly received by us & we can assure you, it gave us much pleasure to hear from you, though at the same time, we sympathized with you in the loss of your dear Cath.[1] She was a lovely child, and perhaps your affections were too much on her, which is commonly the case with most parents. It is sometime since I wrote to you—the excuse I have to make is pressing business, & your unsettled state. As you are now settled, I cannot neglect you any longer—but I have to be short & in <u>mighty hurry</u>.

Perhaps few will properly know the extent of my duties, by merely seeing the Phoenix, which carries but little evidence of much labour. But I can assure you I have no time to be idle. My duties are complicated. I have no associate in the Management of the paper, so I have to select pieces [end of page 1] for publication, & this requires some time in order to be Judicious, & then I have to prepare what little editorial may be seen in the Phoenix, ~~illegible~~ in English & Cherokee, & ~~illegible you~~ to write one column a week original in Cherokee with so much other work, is no small matter—one cant write fast in Cherokee.[2] When printing days come I have to look over the proof sheets. I have also to receive all communications on business made to this establishment—subscribers names to register, some to discontinue, others to credit, & a particular account of receipts and expences to keep. When ~~all~~ this is done, a very little part of the week is left. If I have, what may be called a leisure day, I have a work of a different nature to perform, preparing tracts in the Cherokee language, with the Rev. S.A. Worcester. We are now publishing a small Hymn Book, about 50 pages 24s. a copy of which you will receive a week after this reaches you, perhaps at the same time. It is the first Cherokee book

Cherokee Letters, 1827–1839 {161

ever published.[3] Our attention here often will be directed to the translation of the gospel of St. Matt. about 11 chap. of which are now ready. You will see by the Phoenix that we have had a change of Printers. The Former Printer [end of page 2] Mr. Harris, who is a Methodist by religious profession has occasioned me a great deal of ~~illegible~~ vexation. He has been secretly circulating falsehoods, one of which is that the Cherokee Phoenix is under the influence of Mr. Worcester,[4] & has gone so far as to lodge charges ~~against~~ in the War Department. His conduct became intolarable. Before the commencement of the year I received full authority from the principal Chiefs to continue or dismiss what printers I pleased. I accordingly addressed a note to Mr. H. stating that he should be discontinued on the first day of Jan. I requested him to resign. He returned me a very in[solent] answer, & declared he would not deliver [the office?] except by force, whereupon I [obt]ained an order from the Asst. Prin. Chief by virtue of which he was dispossessed by the Marshall. He has ~~illegible~~ threatened to kick me, Mr. Worcester, Mr. Ross,[5] & a host of others I believe, but has not done it yet. Since his removal We get along a great deal better.

We are all well. Eleanor is a great girl now—begins to talk smartly. Mary[6] does [prime] she has real Indian black eyes. People say she is handsomer than Eleanor.[7] You must not think we brag [end of page 2]

I will now close, leaving little space for Harriet. In great haste, I remain your Indian

Brother,
Elias Boudinott

Dear Br. & Sr,

Accept my thanks for your punctuality in writing. Mr B. would keep this letter—that he might write a better one but I prevailed upon him to send it, as leisure hours with him are very scarce. I rejoiced to hear that my dear parents had a thought of visiting us. I think if their health is as good as when I left them, they may safely undertake the journey—in company with Mr Birdseye or perhaps one of their younger sons. Mr Worcester & wife came from Vermo[nt] in one horse Carriage & all their expenses amounted to about 20. dollars. I should be happy indeed to see any of my relations & they would be truly welcome

* * *

here. Do tell me in your next how Mr. Everest & wife feel. I remember I once had a Sister Abbey; kind & dear—whom I tenderly loved. Does she ever talk about Harriett with affection? Or are the feelings she cherished two years ago, still unalterable? those months were trying ones to me, yet I number among them some of the happiest hours of my life—when a consciousness of doing right was my only consolation. I have many things to say I will try to write a long letter to some of you before long. Mr. Chamberlain & Mr. Worcester with their wive dined with us last Monday.[8] Sister Polly lives with me & sends love to you—love to your little ones—your Affectionate Sister

Harriett[9]

1. She died 27 August 1828, shortly before her fourth birthday.

2. One observer commented of Boudinot's translation abilities: "I am told that Mr. Boudinott is the best translator in the nation, he having the best knowledge of the English language" (qtd. in an 1829 letter by Samuel Worcester to Jeremiah Evarts).

3. *Cherokee Hymns Compiled from Several Authors and Revised* (1829). Elias and Worcester went on to translate together *The Gospel according to Matthew* (1829), *The Acts of the Apostles* (1833), *The Gospel of Jesus Christ according to John* (1838), *The Gospel according to Luke* (1840), *The Epistles of John* (1840), *The Epistles of Paul to Timothy* (1844), and *The Epistles of Peter* (1848). Elias also translated *Poor Sarah, or, the Indian Woman* (1833), the authorship of which is sometimes mistakenly attributed to him.

4. Elias frequently had to defend the paper against the charges that the paper was under missionary control or actually edited by a white man (Perdue, *Cherokee Editor* 19).

5. John Ross (1790–1866) was the Cherokee Nation's principal chief from 1827 through 1866. Ross, popular with Cherokee traditionalists, remained staunchly antiremoval. After Elias began in 1832 to favor removal, Ross forced his resignation from the *Cherokee Phoenix* and later became his political nemesis. Elias published *Letters and Other Papers Relating to Cherokee Affairs: Being in Reply to Sundry Publications Authorized by John Ross* in 1837.

6. Mary Harriett was born 5 October 1828.

7. The last three words of this sentence are double underlined.

8. Refers to William Chamberlain (1791–1849), an ABCFM missionary, and his wife, Flora Hoyt Chamberlain (1798–1886), and Samuel and Ann Worcester (1799–1840). Bass describes the friendship that developed between Ann Worcester and Harriett (116–17).

9. Harriett's signature is written across the right margin at the top of the page next to Elias's.

BENJAMIN GOLD TO HERMAN AND FLORA GOLD VAILL,
29 OCTOBER 1829
HLVC, m.

[Return address:] New Echota C. N. / Oct. 30th 1829 [Addressed to:] Rev. Herman L. Vail / Lime / River Head / Connecticut [postage:] 25

Wensday, New Echota 29th October 1829

Dear & beloved Children,

We arrived here the day before yesterday in good health & good spirits—after a pretty long journey from Cornwall the 16th day of Septr 47 days on the road traveling every day except Sabbath & two half days being two rainy & one hole day being a very raney day—by the great goodness of Divine Providence we have been upheld & preserved all the way in good health & free from any meterial harm. the weather was drye & dusty untill we got to Fishkill where we spent the first Sabbath with our good old friend M^r [Swartant?] & on Monday we passed on to the side of the River & met our beloved Son T.R. Gold unexpectedly as we were riding along Just before we came to the ferry some one hallowed halo & behold it was Ruggles[1] from N. York—we passed the river together & spent the afternoon together in Newburgh & just at sunset took Tea together & parted with the Shake of the Hand—we passed on to Montgomery the next Town & put up—through the night it rained & laid the dust & so frequently rained we saw no more dust flying all the way to the Cherokee Nation—of course it was muddy & heavey traveling the greatest part of the way—but we took it patiently & slowly all the way & enjoyed ourselves well for the most part—we were much pleased with the country & people—many very fine Towns & viliges we passed through in the states of New York—Jersey—Pensylvany—Maryland & Virginia—then we came into Tenesee where the country appeared to be new—but the people kind & accommodating —we traveled about 400 miles in Virginia the north side of the blue ridge where we could see it for two or three hundred miles & we after spoke together of what you said in your last letter to us before we left home—Viz. that you should like to be in the bush when we were traveling along the blue Ridge & hear the Col singing some old tune & Mother taking out her snuff box to take a pinch of snuff—we did frequently amuse ourselves by a song & pinch of snuff as we passed along that country—we were on Harriotts track & heard of her & her Husband often in many places where the people appeared to remember them with much interest & told us many interesting things about them. we passed the Ferry at [Highvassy?] on thursday the 22 day of this month & set our feet on Cherokee ground & within about 100 rods arrived at the House of Mr Lewis Ross^2 one of the Councel of the Cherokee Nation & that [end of page 1] night rained & all the next day—so that we could not think of riding—but we found ourselves in a good harbour all they welcomed us in this nation—Mr Ross & his Lady were both of them at New Echota at the session of the Councel with one of their Children—still there ware four butiful children at home—the eldest a Daughter who had been attending school at Knoxvill Tenessee twelve years old a very interesting girl. Mr Ross is I believe a half breed Mrs Ross of the old Megs family of which was Post Master Genl. Mr Rosss House is a large & elegant white House as hansomely furnished & hansomely situated as almost any house in Litchfield County—he appears to be rich & no doubt he is so. he has around his House about 20 Negro slaves who paid good attention to us two nights & when we offered to pay a bill they told us that Mr Ross would not take any thing for entertainment of any people who had connections in the Nation—from there we went to the next public house about 22 miles M^r McNairs—a very grand Brick house & every accomodation around it; he is a white man & his wife a cherokee & a superior woman about half breed. while he sat at supper with the family my wife says to me who do you think M^{rs} McNair looks like I answered she makes me think of Mrs Weston our former Ministers wife—so she thought—the complexion about the same & the speach behaviour & every thing much alike indeed she appeared to be a Pious & fine woman & has a fine family of children they also made us welcome & would take nothing of us. Harriott also staid at those two last mentioned places when she came into the country—we passed on from thence to springplace about 22 miles the old Moravoan Missionary Station & put up & staid over night where they treated us kindly & would take nothing of us—next morning passed on & reached New Echota a little before sunset—about 20 miles—where we met our Dear children & friends in health & with feelings of Joy that may be better conceived than expressed—but all the way in the Nation we had no need of spending any money except at the ferriy—to be short the people all appear to be perfectly friendly & many places we have seen look indeed like civilisation & they tell us that many other parts which we have not yet seen are much better—we hope to be able to visit all the Missionary stations schools &c in the nation before we return—I think so far as I have seen that the land is very excelent—smoth land clear from Stone in most parts about level enough—well watered [end of page 2] the timber is of most sorts that we have in Connecticut white oak is the greatest part & of a butiful Quality—in some places it is the largest & hansomest that I ever saw in any country—but in general is of a suitable & convenient size—a good proportion of hansom walnut timber & considerable good chesnut timber—& while woods almost every where interspersed with large smoth & tall pine trees & pine of all sizes. New Echota is on a hansom spot of gound a little elevated—with a Councel House & Court House in the center & two or three Merchants Stores about half a dozen hansom framed Dweling Houses in sight which would be called respectable in Litchfield county & very decently furnished to be in any country & all new built say within 3 or [4] years.³ illegible & I have been in most of the Houses & find the families very polite & agreeable & pleasant & fit associates for any country. The National Councel & superior Court is now here in session & I have yesterday & to day attended both & seen important causes before them—have observed much order & decorum —in their Councel & Court are Quite a number of learned pollished & well Qualified Gentlemen fit to appear in any place in Connecticut. I have a fine opportunity at this time & have been Introduced to most of the members of the Councel & the Court—am mu[ch] pleased with the acquaintance I have already had—be sur[e so]me of the gentlemen are full blood Cherokees & in a rude State but easily to be seen of great natural powers of mind. It seems to me a very great pity that any part of our country should attempt or desire to arrest from this Nation a right which they possess by arts & treaties of the United States—rites I say which they have to the possession & Government of all the lands which they have not ceeded to the United States. I could go on to tell you many more interesting things which I have noticed in my Journey & that I have seen here but it is now evening & I have another letter to write & put in the Mail which is to close at eight o'clock & can only say that Mr B. & H. & Sedgwick[4] are all in good health the oldest little girl is as smart & pretty & healthy as can be found & the other is a bright well looking child—but has been for some time troubled with [end of page 3] a bilious complaint[5]—you must write us a good long letter & tell all the interesting things that transpire—give our kindest & best affections to your dear companion & kiss the dear little ones for us & if Mr Everest & our dear daughter Abby is within your reach remember us to them & their little ones—in haste we subscribe ourselves as ever your very affectionate Parents

B.& E. Gold

H.L— & F— G— Vail

★ ★ ★

It is now a long time since we have had the pleasure of receiving a letter from you. Do write us soon, & let us know how the people about you feel respecting the Great Indian Question. William Penn is very popular amongst us.[6] Yours EBoudinot

1. "Son T.[homas]R.[uggles] Gold" and Ruggles are the same person, the Golds' eldest son. He died in December of the same year, so this is the last meeting of parents and son.

2. The brother of John Ross, principal chief of the Cherokee Nation.

3. In the 1870s, an elderly man named White Horse reminisced about the appearance of New Echota in the 1830s. He described Elias and Harriett's house as "a large two story frame, with garden, orchards, and convenient out-house attached" (qtd. in Malone, "New Echota" 6).

4. Harriett's younger brother, Hezekiah Sedgwick (1807–?). Sedgwick apparently lived with Harriett and Elias for a period of time and assisted Elias in the publication of the newspaper.

5. A condition related to indigestion. In a letter written to his brother on

8 December 1829, Benjamin described his grandchildren as "two beautiful and interesting children: would pass in company for full-blooded Yankees. My wife says she thinks they are rather handsomer than any she has seen at the north" (qtd. in Gold 38).

6. Jeremiah Evarts, corresponding secretary of the ABCFM, published a series of twenty-four articles setting out his opposition to President Andrew Jackson's plan for Indian removal. The essays appeared in a newspaper called the *Washington Intelligencer* from August through December of 1829 under the pseudonym "William Penn" (Prucha, *Cherokee Removal* 8). See Prucha's *Cherokee Removal* for discussion and reprinting of the articles. Harriett and Elias gave the name William Penn to their first son, born a few months later.

BENJAMIN GOLD TO HERMAN AND FLORA GOLD VAILL,
14 APRIL 1830
HLVC, m.

[Return address:] New Echota, C.N. / Apr. 15 [Addressed to:] Revd H.L. Vaill / East Lyme / River Head Conn. [Postage:] 25

New Echota April 14—1830

Ever Dear children,

I think to give you one more letter before I leave the Cherokee Nation. My wife thinks on the whole that if we leave this country before another spring that we had better not stay here through the heat of summer—the warmer Climate rather seems to [(sorta)?] debelitate her constitution & she has to take a little opium now & then to brace her up—but for my part their good spring water & Coffee & as much good victuals as they give me—keeps me in pretty good Plyght without any medicine whatever—but if we can make out our visits as we had calculated—we now propose to set our faces towards home about the first of June. I wrote a letter to Mr Everest at Norwich some weeks since—which probably you have seen—which was somewhat particular. I have at this time a number of letters to write & can only just give you a short one. I hope [end of page 1] that within a few months to be in Connecticut & be able by the leave of Providence to visit you at your Home & tell you more particularly about our Journey & acquaintance with the Cherokee Nation. I like the Country much & I think I should prefer the Climate to that of New England. I think this is as healthy a region as ever I was acquainted with. I traveled much & seen the people in various parts. I rarely see or hear of a sickly person. I think if I was a young man that I should prefer settling here to any country that I am acquainted with—but my day is pretty much past & gone & I shall have about enough to do to visit my children—if my life should be prolonged as much as can be reasonably expected.[1] I have spent the time since I came to this Station in the most pleasant & agreeable manner—have just returned from a visit at High Tower [end of page 2] about 35 miles from this place—spent the sabbath with good Mr Buttrick one of the exelent of the earth. The Missionaries in this Nation are all faithful & good men & their companions & assistants all appear to be exelent people & suitable for the business. Mr Boudinott's family are all well. they send their tenderest & kindest love to you— their 3 little children grow & come on fine[ly] William Penn[2] among the rest is s[econd] to no boy of his age—little Mary looks out of as hansom pair of black eyes as ever was seen. Eleanor will be 3 years old the 4$\underline{th}$ May next—appears to know as much as any girl of her age— attends Miss Sawyers[3] school which is kept in the Courthouse about 30 rods from her Fathers House. Sedwick is clearing & fencing land for Mr B. at present & what he means to do in future I believe he tells no one—as ever your most affectionate Parents

B & E. Gold [end of page 3]

Dear Br & Sr,

I should be glad to fill a sheet for you, but you see I have only a little place. I feel as though the time was near when I must again say farewell to my dear Parents. I feel disappointed because they cannot stay longer, but Mother thinks prudence requires them to go. I trust I shall ever remember their visit with gratitude. They will tell you a great deal about us when they see you. I hope and pray that a kind providence may conduct them safely back again to meet their numerous friends who yet remain in the land of the living.

* * *

The children are much attached to their Grand Parents. I hardly know what I shall do with them when they are gone off you were about to call your last baby, <u>temperance</u>, because you dispensed with rum—what shall we do? We have had 3. without the assistance of a shot of rum—or any kind of ardent spirits. The truth is, we have not bought a drop since we kept house & I hesitate not to say, (without boasting) that my husband is, & <u>has ever been</u> a more temperate man—than any of his brothers in law on <u>my</u> side. I hope you will not stop writing us when our Parents leave us. I assure you, this is a trying season with us as a people. Mr. B. says <u>he</u> will write as soon as circumstances will allow. Very affectionately your Sister

Harriett R.G. Boudinott

1. Benjamin Gold lived another seventeen years to the age of eighty-four. He was sixty-seven when he made the journey to visit his daughter.

2. Born 4 February 1830.

3. Sophia Sawyer (1782–?) was an ABCFM teacher. A strong-willed woman, Sawyer taught the Boudinot children, resided in their home for ten months in 1834, and became their close friend. Harriett wrote a letter on her behalf to the ABCFM in 1834 (letter to Benjamin Wisner). For more on Sawyer's life and especially her influence on author John Rollin Ridge, son of John and Sarah Northrop Ridge, see Parins 14–18, 23, 25.

ELIAS AND HARRIETT GOLD BOUDINOT TO
BENJAMIN AND ELEANOR GOLD, 3 JUNE 1830
CornHS, THS, pm.

[Addressed to:] Col. Benjamin Gold / Candy's Creek

New Echota, June 3^d 1830.

Dear father and Mother,

We got home on the day we parted about an hour and a half before sun setting, probably about the time you got to Mr. McNair. I was fearful on mother's account that the creeks you had to cross would be too full—but we found holly creek was not as high as we thought it would be. I hope you got along safely. When I got home, according to your request, I kissed our dear little creatures. I told them it was grand ma's kisses. Ask Mary where grand ma is, she replies, <u>yon</u> and points towards the East. We all miss you greatly—you have left a vacancy here which cannot be filled—but we must be resigned—we perhaps may see each other again in this world.

I forgot to mention to father that I want him to call with your specimens of cloth &c. at the office of the <u>Adam's Sentinel</u>, Gettysburg Pa. & at the office of the "<u>Intelligencer</u>" Harrisburg Pa,[1] & request the editors' to notice the improvements of the Cherokees & give my respects to them. I exchange with them—you will there also see the Phoenix—wishing you safety in your journey and a happy arrival at home, I subscribe myself your son.

Eboudinot [end of page 1]

Dear Parents, I am glad of an opp to send you a line—we feel quite lonesome without you here. I shall think of you <u>very</u> <u>much</u> while on your long journey, & hope you will, by <u>all means</u> write <u>every week</u>. I hope Mr. Foreman will accompany you. Mr. Thompson is at Mr. W's & Mr. B. will go with him to, Hawie's tomorrow, I understand Mrs. Cossland, the moravian, who lives this side of Mr. Clanders, is dead—her complaint was consumption. We are all well here, Eleanor & Mary often talk of you—but Eleanor is quite reconciled to staying & going with Pa & Ma. Eleanor reads in "No Man" & her Pa has got her a new spelling Book. William is a good boy yet, says little about his grandparents, & I fear thinks less—but he will learn about you when he grows. Wishing you a pleasant journey under the smile of a kind providence I subscribe myself

your affectionate Daughter
Harriett.

⋆ ⋆ ⋆

My eyes are fairly well.

We intended to send this to Mr. Sweetland but hearing of you still at C. Creek we thought best to send now.

1. The *Adams Sentinel* was published in Gettysburg from 1826 to 1867. The *Pennsylvania Intelligencer* was published in Harrisburg, Pennsylvania.

[Return address:] [stamped] NEW ECHOTA / CHER. Na.
[Addressed to:] Rev. Herman L. Vaill / River Head / Connecticut
[Postage:] 25 [Noted:] one sheet

New Echota Jan 7. 1831.

Dear Br & Sr,[1]

To tell the truth I hardly know what to say to you after so long a silence. Indeed it is a great while since I have taken my pen to chat with you. In the first place, I thank you for your last very acceptable letter. I was almost ready to conclude you had struck us off the list of those you loved; but when your letter came, it shove such fears away, & brought you both so near, I could almost see you, and hear your cheerful voices. Perhaps by this time, Father & Mother are with you. If they should be there when you receive this, read it to them, & let them read it for themselves. I think a great deal about them, & wish I could call them back here again. I assure you, you have no idea how much they are beloved, & with what interest they are enquired after by the people of this Nation. I wish to tell them, we are as happy as ever, excepting the want of their company. Sometimes when going about the house, I am just ready to say, Mother, will you come here a minute? & she will recollect how many times I used to call her. Ask her if she does not remember how, when, a few days before she left, I called illegible her into the upper piazza to view our pleasant garden, & the prospect around. Tell Father we have our well in the back porch fixed with a very convenient windlace, like the Hightower fashion. I like it much better than the pump. Our water is so sweet & pure that I have almost substituted it for coffee & Tea—though the rest of the family use as much as ever. Our coffee sugar & Tea amounts to about 50_ dollars a year. It is becoming some what fashionable at least among the Missionaries here to dispense altogether with coffee & Tea as well as ardent spirits. They say partly for the sake of economy, & partly because they feel better without it. [end of page 2]

I wish Br & Sister Vaill, you could just step in, & sit, if it were but a few minutes with us this evening. Susan sits in one corner, mending her stockings, and I in the other writing this letter—while the children are all a bed & asleep.[2] Mr Boudinott has gone to Mr. Worcesters to pay off Mr S. of Tennessee for our years supply of pork. Br. S is at the Printing office—helping the printers who will have to work perhaps till day light to be ready for tomorrow's Mail. The extra sheet has crowded them this week. Mr. B. has just returned & gone to the Office to correct the proof sheets—says I must write for him that he should have no time—but I think he will write a little. He works very hard—especially when he has no communications. for he does much besides his charge of the Phoenix. His salary is also small, considering his expenses—but he is willing to makes some sacrifice for his country, & so must others who will do something for their nation at this peculiarly trying time. We know not what is ~~illegible~~ before us. Sometimes I fear the Cherokees will see evil days—but I think they will come off victorious in the end & that is all they want—they fear nothing; if but their country & freedom is spared them.

I have thought much of my Father's family of late, & especially my [dear] Sisters. I suppose you sometimes get together. Le[t] Harriett be remembered, though absent, I sometimes very much wish to compose one of your circle again. I do not mean, that I could be placed back among you; (that I could never submit to, unless providence made it as plainly my duty as it did to leave you) but that I could sit with you as I am; with the Husband of my choice—who not only professes, but is truly worthy of my warmest affections—m[y t]enderest love. Our little cherokees I will not say much about—only wish you could see them & judge for yourselves. Tell Father, I think he will have to make an heir of William Penn—for he is said, by all, to look like him & I think he has no other grand son who does resemble him. Now do not wait so long before you write us again & tell us all about yourselves & our family connexions & the little nieces & nephews. I know not how many you have—but I suppose somewhat about half a dozen.[3] Kiss them all for me, & let them know that their they have Cherokee Cousins.

Forgive me this poor letter from your affectionate Sister

Harriett [end of page 3]

Dear Brother & Sister,

I must also apologize to you for neglecting to write—but you must take the will for the deed. You will see by the public prints in what situation our affairs are. I think the matter is coming to a crisis, and I am glad it is. Very soon the virtue of the Republic will be put to the test. You see what Georgia is doing, & what she has threatened to do—[#] to resist the process of the Supreme Court of the United States—but I have no time to dwell upon the matter. We may, I think, with propriety, look for great things soon.

★ ★ ★

I should like to write a great deal if I had time and room—but Harriet, my Squaw, has been pretty particular. We hope we shall have the pleasure of hearing from you soon. Do not forget us, and remember the Cherokees in their afflictions.

Yours E Boudinot

[LM 1] Tell Gold Hopkins, if he is threatened with the Quinsy[4] again, I would prescribe a simple remedy, which he need not fear, & perhaps it might prove effectual with him, as it has with many others. Put hot embers into a small kettle, cover it with a board, having an auger hole in it—put brown sugar on the embers—then place an inverted funnel over the hole & let the end of it come into the mouth so as to steam the throat I know a person who was cured by this simple remedy who had not swallowed in two days.

H.

[LM 2] We were happy to receive a letter from Br Brinsmade by last mail. I rejoice to hear there is a prospect of sister Mary's recovery. I greatly desire a letter from her. Mrs Worcester is in a critical state of health—but I hope she may be spared—she is truly a valuable woman, & a Sister indeed she has been to me ever since our first acquaintance. Eleanor has had the Quinsy lately, was quite sick two or three days.

[RM 4] P.S. We have written upon a news paper sheet—but never mind that for we have no other.

1. The first page of this letter is written by Sedgwick Gold and is omitted here.

2. The identity of Susan is not certain. Elias did have a younger sister bearing this name.

3. Flora was pregnant with her fifth child at this time and would bear her sixth the next year.

4. An inflammation of the throat.

ELIAS AND HARRIETT GOLD BOUDINOT TO
HERMAN AND FLORA GOLD VAILL, 1 JULY 1831
HLVC, m.

[Return address:] New Echota C. N Ga / July 2nd [Addressed to:]
Rev. Herman L. Vaill / River Head / Connecticut [Postage:] 25

New Echota, July 1, 1831.

Dear brother & sister,

We owe you apology for not answering your very acceptable letter long ago. We might perhaps, if we were so disposed, make abundance of excuses, but to get out of the matter the sooner we will plead guilty. This, however, we might properly ~~illegible~~ say—we have been in hot water ever since our last to you, that is the masculine portion of us.[1] We have hardly known which ~~illegible~~ way to turn. Trouble upon trouble, vexation upon vexation. I allude to the Georgia affair. The war is becoming hotter and hotter every day, as you no doubt learn from the Cherokee Phoenix. From that source you obtain some knowledge of what ~~illegible~~ our neighbors, Christian & civilized, are doing. But the half is not told—it cannot be told. We tell enough, however, I believe, for our purpose, if the good people of the U. States can be induced to arouse, to feel and to act on this momentous subject.[2]

Why do our friends at the north appear to be [end of page 1] so careless? Do they not know that a piece of great wickedness is in a course of perpetuation? The last right and in some respects, the most important right of the Cherokees, is to be fought and contended for—their right to the land. It is true we have been abused persecuted and oppressed beyond measure—~~illegible~~ our rights have been outrageously wrested from us, yet we are on our lands—we have possession. Our enemies cannot complete their designs until they get the land—they intend to get it by force, and that before long too. Now will the people of the U. States permit such an outrage upon the property of the defenceless? If they do not mean to permit it, they must contend with their might. The enemy is at the door, and there is no time to be lost—the friend of justice and the oppressed must be up and doing. I wish every friend of the Cherokees, who ~~illegible~~ intend to second their efforts in the coming Congress of the United States, to be well aware of this fact, that the Georgians propose in the next Legislature to survey and to draw for our lands, and that they calculate [mark that][3] no opposition from President Jackson! ~~Well, [now] our safety, I believe, depends~~ This great evil can be averted if the people can but be induced to speak in their might. If the lands are secured to us we can bear the rest comparatively very well, & hope for the restoration of our rights in the change of ~~illegible~~ the administration of the Gen. Gov^t. [end of page 2]

But I ~~illegible~~ dwell too much on the subject—perhaps you know as much as I can tell you. One thing is certain there is a crisis approaching, both in the history of the Cherokees & the United States. Shall robbery be committed? The President must soon be brought under great responsibility. He knows it and [would?] be glad to [avoid it?]. Every effort therefore will be made to induce, by a series of mean acts and oppressions, the Cherokees to come to terms before the next Legislature of Georgia and session of Congress—or have the matter in a suitable train.

Last mail brought us a letter from our good parents, dated in New Haven. They say they have moved into that city principally to take care of Swift and his things while he is in College.[4] They intend to take in boarders also, and expect to maintain themselves in that way. They say they have so many grand children coming on, some of whom will wish to get an education in Yale, that they aught to be there to take care of them. They express a hope that some of our ~~Indian boys~~ papooses may go there. As to that we can say we have three [yet?] we do [not] know how it will be. William Penn, however, if we live and if he lives and is not a block head, and above all if we have the means at our command, will go to New England for <u>larning</u>. But you see it depends upon many contingencies.

Perhaps it may be best to inform you that I have some expectations of leaving home this fall. You may possibly see me at River Head. I mean <u>alone</u>. I have occupied more of this sheet than I intended to and have left very little space indeed for the S___w.[5] All our wives are known in Georgia by that name. I leave her enough, however, to tell her family news. The children are doing prime. Ask the old folks about them and take their word for it—it is just as they say. I hope you will not follow our example—~~illegible~~ civilized folks do not ~~illegible~~ retalliate—write soon therefore and oblige yours truly

E. Boudinot [end of page 3]

Dear Br & Sr,

Mr. B. has said with regard to the condition & prospects of our people, what I wanted say. I therefore need not repeat it. I will only say, I am astonished at the apathy which prevails in the States in regard to the Cherokees. The friends of the Indians seem sleeping while their enemies are diligently pursuing their work & the sufferings of the poor Cherokee are daily increased beneath the oppressor's rod. You say there are a few "Ancient Lords of the soil" still left in your town. Now Dr Brother do you treat them as ~~such~~ though they once were such? Do you with the most untiring diligence endeavor to instruct and enlighten them? I am sure if I were there I should be willing to be shut out from all other society that I might manifest my friendship to them—if by so doing I could be beneficial to their interests. I am not enthusiastic on this subject. How are the American people ever to atone for the injuries done the original inhabitants of this Country? With shame for my native State, I notice the proceedings of the late Connecticut legislature towards a remnant of the Mohegan Tribe of Indians. Could they not do a little?[6] I know not how to stop or write of any thing else, so greatly are my feelings interested & sympathies excited for the suffering Indians.

⋆ ⋆ ⋆

I have but little "family news" at present. My health has been poor for two months past. I shall write Mother more particularly about it. Br. Sedgwick paid us a visit and again left us for C. Path last April, & the next thing I heard of him he had started for Ohio.[7] I feel very anxious about him—perhaps he will go to N.E. He intimated to me that he should go to Ohio & return here again in the fall. Do write us soon. My love to all my friends & kiss the little ones for me. O how happy should I be to see you all—but know not when I shall unless you come to see me I think however if the nation should be established in peace here again & we should be spared, there is a prospect of my visiting new England—with wishes for your happiness I remain your affectionate

Sister Harriett.

[LM 3] Excuse this very hasty scrawl[8]

1. On two occasions in 1831, Elias was forcibly brought before the commander of the Georgia Guard and questioned (Perdue, *Cherokee Editor* 22–23). He wrote about his experiences in the *Cherokee Phoenix* in August and September of 1831.

2. In this sentence, Elias underlines "arouse" with one line, "feel" with two lines, and "act" with three lines.

3. The bracketed material and the brackets in this sentence appear in the manuscript.

4. Job Swift, Harriett's younger brother, graduated from Yale University in 1834.

5. Elias's deletion of the three interior letters of "squaw," following the nineteenth-century convention of obscuring obscenities in texts, suggests that he saw the word as pejorative.

6. Two white women who had opened a Sabbath school for Mohegans in Connecticut unsuccessfully sent a petition to the Connecticut legislature requesting funds for the construction of a chapel and the hiring of a permanent missionary (De Forest 483).

7. Creek Path was a mission station west of New Echota in Alabama.

8. Written in Elias's handwriting.

[Addressed to:] Rev. Herman L. Vaill / River Head / Connecticut
[Postmark:] Feb 29 Boston, MS

Boston,[1] Feb. 28, 1832

Dear brother & sister,

Perhaps you will think it somewhat ~~curious~~ strange that I have been so near you & have failed to call on you. Do not think I have neglected you. I wanted to see you greatly, but the great importance of my being in this city at this time rendered it necessary that I should pass you for the present. I will assuredly, if I live, give you a call. I will also see our brother Stephen and other friends in Cornwall, and Mr. Brinsmade & his family in Washington. That will be I think sometime in April.

My health has been very good since I left home. Harriet informs me in a letter dated 11th inst that she is well.[2]

Since I have been here I have become acquainted with Mrs. Appleton & her family—interesting & sociable.

Yours in haste
Elias Boudinot

1. Elias left on a trip to the north to raise funds for the *Cherokee Phoenix* in the fall of 1831 and returned in the spring of 1832 (Perdue, *Cherokee Editor* 25).

2. "Inst" refers to the current month; thus Harriett's letter was dated 11 February.

[Return address:] New Echota Ga / March 31 [Addressed to:]
Rev. Herman L. Vaill / River Head / Connecticut [Postage:] 25

New Echota March 29th [1832][1]

Dear Brother and Sister,

I now thank you for your very acceptable letter—received a long
time ago. I perhaps ought to have answered it sooner, but you know
it is the fashion in our family to wait a long time after we receive a letter before we answer it—and I have another reason.[2] My Husband is
from home & I have written him almost every week through the winter, which occupied nearly all the leisure time I could afford to devote
to writing. He has also written me nearly every week[3]—but as it happened I got no letter by last mail—so that instead of writing to my
Husband, I now scribble a few lines for you.

I was glad to hear of your health & prosperity, & that your little ones
were coming on so well. I infer from Mr. B's last letter, as well as from
your own, that ere this, you have—but I will leave it for you to tell me
what—as I hope to hear from you again before long. I am happy to
tell you that my health is as good as usual, & that all my family of little
ones are also well. Eleanor and Mary go to school & are remarkably
fond of their Teacher and their books. They can both read. E learns
every [end of page 1] morning one verse from scripture according to
the verse a day system. We receive the Verse—[Herald?] & Expositor—
& Miss Sawyer has adopted the plan in her school. We are invited to
attend the examination of her scholars to-morrow. I can hardly help
wishing you were here to witness the proficiency of the dear little creatures. Indeed I wish you could see us in our family, in our neighbourhood, and our Nation. You need not say that I possess that disposition
of bragging so peculiar to the Gold family—perhaps I do—but I now
only mean—I wish you to see how Indians can live—how families,
& how a nation of Indians can live. I should have added with regard
to Eleanor—that her Papa has ordered the Juvenile Rambler[4] for her
use—she now receives it & reads it with great pleasure. William Penn

has gone to his Grand Pa's. I wish much to see him—he has been gone 12 days. His Uncles learn him to walk like an old man to jump like a boy, & make bows like a gentleman. He is sometimes very amusing to us. Permit me to tell you just how he looks. He is very strait—has a high-projecting forehead, dark brown hair—large face, rosy cheeks & perfectly black eyes—& what is more than all, I think he has common sense—a mind capable of cultivation—& should his life be spared I hope he will be disposed to improve his natural talents—S4S or gah-sa gah the youngest, being only one month old—I shall not say much about her. She is probably like other children of her age. I love her. I cannot say we—for her Pa has not yet seen her—but if it is possible for a person to love an object he has not seen—I know he loves her. [end of page 2]

I think it is this day 6. years since I received the hand of Mr. Boudi-nott[5] & gave my own in the covenent of marriage. I now look back to that day with pleasure, & with gratitude. Yes I am thankful. I remember the trials I had to encounter—the thorny path I had to tread, the bitter cup I had to drink—but a consciousness of doing right—a kind affectionate devoted Husband, together with many other blessings, have made amends for all. Surely I have, ere this, entered upon the "sober realities of a married life" & if any tears have been shed for me on that account—I can now pronounce them useless tears. I hope you have already seen Mr. B. I know he intended to call on you & other members of the family. He said in one of his letters, he supposed Mr Everest[6] would not wish to see him. I think you mentioned that they would treat him well should he go there. If that is all, it is not my wish that he should go there—but I do wish that Br E. could see him with an unprejudiced mind—not knowing who he was. I know that Mr. B. has no bitter feelings towards Mr. E. & would meet [them] with perfect cordiality, if they felt the same—but I cannot [endure,] at least I am not willing to endure the thought that my worthy companion should be treated with coolness or neglect by any of my friends. I have been pleased to hear of the reception he has thus far met with among our family connexions in N. York & in Boston. He is worthy of it all—but my heart is warm & I cannot express half what I feel. You will excuse me for the freedom I have already used. I hope you &

Mr. Boudinott will have a <u>long pleasant</u> chat & that I may see him too before a great while. I begin to feel almost ashamed that I have written so much about myself & family—but when I began I was afraid that I should have to leave part of the sheet a blank & I knew Br. V. wouldn't like <u>that</u>, so I thought I would write down every thing just as it came into my head. It is now late in the evening & as I expect company tomorrow I must bid you good nig<u>h</u>t [end of page 3]

I could say much about our national affairs but neither time or room will allow me at this time. The decision of the S. Court has much encouraged the Cherokees,[7] & though troubles may yet be before them —they will continue firm. I fear Messrs Worcester & Butler[8] may yet have to stay another year in their confinement. [illegible] justice indeed if they do. Mrs. Worcester is very cheerful. You don't know what a good Sister she is to me. We are as one family. She is just your age Sister Flora.

★ ★ ★

Please write me again soon. My love to all the family who have not forgotten me. Neither time or absence <u>has</u> or ever can diminish my affection for you all. I sometimes feel as though I must fly to you—at the same time I am perfectly contented & happy here. Will you not sometime come & see how happily we live here? Your ever loving Sister

Harriett

[RM 4] I think I have not [illegible] [inscribed?] my letter <u>very</u> beautifully

1. The year of this letter's composition is not named, but references to Elias's absence from home and the Supreme Court decision place it in 1832.

2. Reference to the birth of Harriett and Elias's fourth child, called Sarah by family members, born 24 February 1832.

3. In a letter written during this trip to his brother, Stand Watie, Elias wrote, "Tell Harriet I have written to her almost every week—and generally very long letters. . . . Tell H. I do behave myself" (Dale and Litton 6).

4. The *Juvenile Rambler; or, Family and School Journal* was published in Boston beginning in 1832.

5. The actual anniversary date was 28 March.

6. Rev. Cornelius Everest, husband of Harriett's sister Abbey. There is no evidence that the Everests ever reconciled with Harriett and Elias.

7. The Supreme Court's decision in *Worcester v. Georgia* was a victory for the Cherokees in their struggle with Georgia. Elias's friend and collaborator in translation work, Samuel Austin Worcester, had been imprisoned for refusing to take the oath of allegiance that the state of Georgia required of whites living in Cherokee territory. The Supreme Court ruling held that individuals residing within the Cherokee Nation were not subject to Georgia's laws. Elias describes his reaction to the ruling in a letter to his brother (Dale and Litton 4–7).

8. Dr. Elizur Butler (1794–1857) was imprisoned along with Worcester.

ELIAS BOUDINOT TO BENJAMIN AND
ELEANOR GOLD, 16 AUGUST 1836
"Last Hours of Mrs. Boudinott," *New York Observer*, 26 November 1836; reprinted as "The Death of Harriet Gold Boudinot," *Journal of Cherokee Studies* 4.2 (1979): 102–7.[1]

New Echota, GA., Aug. 16, 1836

My Dear Father and Mother,

By the last mail I addressed a hasty letter to brother Swift, apprising him of the dangerous illness of Harriet, and requesting him to communicate the same to you in such a way as he might think best, to lessen the weight of affliction which a future letter would in all probability inflict upon your parental hearts. In fact, in order that you might be saved from conflicting hopes and tears, in regard to her recovery or death, I stated to him that her case was a hopeless one, and that you need not look for any other information but that which would apprise you that she was no more. Presuming that you have, by the help of God, prepared your minds to hear what was too plainly to be expected, I now perform the sad office of communicating to you the death of your daughter and my dear companion. Yes, Harriet is no more—she died yesterday morning, 19 minutes after 1 o'clock, and about 3 o'clock in the afternoon, we consigned her mortal remains to our mother earth, there to lie until God shall raise the dead. As a last duty, therefore, in fulfillment of the promise I made in the letter alluded to, I undertake to give you some account of her sickness and death.[2]

But what you will most desire to hear, I have no doubt, are her religious exercises during her sickness. I am enabled to satisfy you in this respect, in some measure, although not to the extent you would have been satisfied, if her extreme bodily suffering, which continued to the last, and which affected her mind towards the close, had not prevented her from saying many things she desired to say, and if some good christian friend had been present to converse with her during her whole sickness—for I must confess, that on account of my extreme anguish, I did not converse with her as much as I should have wished. I have noted down, however, several things she said in reference to the state of her soul, and which I have no doubt will have a tendency to alleviate your afflictions.

When she first considered her case critical, she told me that she had not such views of the state of her soul as she wished. There was darkness, which she prayed, and desired me to pray, might be removed. "I have lived," she said, "so unprofitably. I have done so little for Christ, that I can hardly dare to hope that God will receive me into his glorious kingdom. At times I have been almost ready to give up my hope in Christ, and to seek anew with tears and repentance, that which is so necessary in a dying hour. But then, I have thought if I was not the child of God, he would not have given me those blessed manifestations of himself, which it has been my joy to experience at times. If I had no regard for his honor and glory, I would not have felt as I have felt when I have heard his glorious name profaned or lightly spoken of, or his holy Sabbath violated." I said—"I suppose you do not distrust him now, and you believe that he is just and generous and will do all things right." "Yes, I believe he is a glorious being, and I am willing to commit my all to him. But I long for more light—for an assurance in his mercy. I owe my wretchedness and my entire dependence upon the mercy of God through the merits of the blessed Redeemer." She then requested me to read a portion of Scripture and pray with her, which I did. During that time she appeared to be absorbed in spiritual contemplations and referred to some passages that I read as having once afforded her great happiness and consolation.

A day or so after, she was taken with great distress and anxiety, and other unusual sensations which she considered as indicating her speedy dissolution. She told me she should die, and prayed me to be faithful to our dear children—"Read the bible and pray with them daily, and teach them to keep the Sabbath. The violation of that holy day around us has been the source of great affliction and anxiety to me, and I trust our dear children will be kept from such violations of God's commandments." She said to Mary, who stood at the head of the bed sobbing, "you told me, Mary, that you wanted to be a christian—you must ask God to give you a new heart—you must pray to him continually. Cannot you pray now for your mother. Come, my dear, go to your room and pray for your ma." The little girl retired, as she was requested. To William, she said, "I want you to be a good boy—to be a good man when you are grown, and to do a great deal of good while you live. Be kind to your little brothers. "It has been my sole wish and prayer to God," she continued, addressing herself to all the children, "that you may become christians, and be useful in the world, and be finally happy in the world to come. Be kind to each other and love one another." To brother S., who stepped in at that moment, she said, brother S., I have but a short time to stay with you in this world," and added some word of exhortation which has now escaped my recollection.[3]

It was not until on the 12th, that I relinquished every hope of her recovery. On that day, she was quite free from pain, and appeared unusually placid—there was a benignity and smile about her countenance that I had never noticed before. On my sitting by her, and taking hold of her hand she said, "there is a beautiful hymn which a friend used to sing, beginning with 'We seek a rest.'"[4] "Would you like to hear it sung?" "Yes, it is a sweet hymn—I wish some one could sing."

On that day, I enquired of her in what state her mind was—she replied, "better; I feel that I have given myself and my children to God. I know he is gracious, and will do all things right. Tell my friends, that although I have not a positive assurance of my acceptance through Christ, yet I feel that I can trust in his righteousness and merits alone for salvation, and I hope he will not forsake me and permit me to pass the dark valley of death alone. I can review all my supposed good deeds and former attempts to serve him, and lay them all at the foot of his Cross as worthless and filthy rags. He is just withholding from me the light of his blessed countenance, on account of my past unworthy life, and because I have not served him with more ardor and sincerity. If God should raise me and lengthen my poor existence here, O may my life and actions testify to the goodness and mercy of my Redeemer." She then requested me to read the last words of Dr. Payson. Having read some of the rapturous expressions of that good man, contained in his life, page 365, she said—"These were the words of Doctor Payson. I cannot say, I feel as he did, but I do feel something as he did." [5] At the same conversation, I think she said, "this world is a world of sickness and death—millions are called away daily to their final accounts. Oh! what a glorious thing the plan of redemption is, to redeem us from the evils of sin. If we could only realize and know what this redemption secures to us beyond these earthly tolls, afflictions, sickness and death—if we could only know what heaven is,"—I told her that we cannot know what heaven is, only that it is a glorious place—it is impossible for those feeble senses to realize what God has prepared for our who love him; she said, "No man shall see God and live." [6]

On the 13th, she enquired of father whether he still prayed for her. He said that he did daily and to her health, but if not, that he would give her the light of his countenance and receive her into his blessed kingdom. She observed, "that is the way I wish him to pray. I should like to live, if it is God's will, on account of my dear children, that I may do good to the Cherokees; but he knows best and will do all things right." A question being asked whether she still remembered her Redeemer, she said, "Oh yes, he is all my hopes and confidence."

She requested me, when I wrote to her northern friends to mention an incident that happened a few days before we left Cornwall. She alluded to a little female meeting that was held in Mr. Stone's house, and mentioned, I think, as being present, Mrs. Birdseye, Mrs. S. Gold, and Miss Carter. "What a blessed time that was," she said, "it was almost a heaven upon earth. Tell them I have remembered it with delight, and shall remember it to my death."

She often spoke of her christian friends, and expressed a desire that they could be present to pray with her and encourage her in her dying hours. "I suppose, however," she said, "Harriet Newell was even less 'favored' in this respect than I am." [7] She frequently mentioned Mr. Butrick's name, and wanted to know whether he would not think of her and come and see her. I told her he did not know that she was sick. You would like to see all good people, would you not? "Yes, I love them all. I love them, because they love God. I have been much deprived of their company of late, and consequently of religious privileges, and that has been a source of much affliction to me. No one has come to preach to us. I do not feel hard towards them, but consider it just that God should deprive me of his ordinances and other religious privileges for my past neglect of them." She then desired to talk to Mr. J. Field—who had come the evening previous. Having gotten brother S. to interpret for her, she urged the importance of religion, as that alone would prepare us for death and for heaven, that holy and blessed place. She said, "Life is short, at the very longest. We all must die, sooner or later. Those who live a hundred years would feel and know it. Such a life is but a speck compared to eternity, to which we are all approaching. I have thought of you, your family connections, and I have loved you all, and my first concern, and I hope to meet you in heaven." She closed by observing that her mind and body were very weak, which prevented her from saying many things she wished to say.

In the afternoon of the 13th, Mr. and Mrs. Northrop,[8] Mr. and Mrs. Ridge, and Miss S. Ridge arrived. She had previously expressed a great desire to see Mr. N., whose prayers and conversation she should highly prize. She said she blessed and thanked God that he had permitted Mr. Northrop to come and see her. Although after that, on account of her extreme weakness and sinking condition, she was able to say but little, yet Mr. N. had some conversations with her, which he will himself rehearse to you when he sees you. He has also a message from her to deliver to you personally, recommending the religion of Jesus Christ as the only thing that can soothe a dying bed.

In the evening her greatest distress commenced. I thought the last struggle had come, and, added to her bodily suffering, there seemed to pass over her mind a desponding cloud. In the agony of her distress she was heard to exclaim, "Lord have mercy upon me—my friends, pray for me! Oh, it is terrible to have even one doubt or one cloud!" She would occasionally say, "Patience! patience!" A friend told her to look to the Saviour, he would not leave her nor forsake her. "You feel that you can trust him, and believe that he will do all things right?" "Yes,

yes." She afterwards, the next day, told Mr. N. that at these times of extreme bodily pain and suffering, Satan, the great adversary of her soul, was trying to take advantage of her weakness, by suggesting doubts and fears, but she had been enabled to look to the Saviour, and that all the clouds which oppressed her were removed—that there was then a clear sky between her and her Saviour. This was but a few hours before she died, and but a short time before she became unable to speak.

Early in the morning of the last day, 14th, after the most distressing night she had had, she requested a number of her friends to come to her bed. Upon my inquiring how she did, she said, "I am in great distress, (meaning her bodily distress,) I hope this is the last night I shall spend in the world—then, how sweet will be the conqueror's song!"[9] I inquired whether her darkness was removed. "Yes." You can look to the Redeemer and consider him yours? "Yes." "You are happy notwithstanding all your bodily pain and affliction?" "I am happy." "Tell father Watie," she said, "to pray that my death may be easy, and that it may be to the glory of God." Her paroxysm returned, and here the conversation ended.

After this she was still able to say something at intervals. At one of these times when she could talk, William happened to step in. She caught hold of his hand and laid it upon her breast, and addressed him as follows: "My dear William; this body and soul are about to separate. My soul will go to God, and my body will be laid in the grave, in the cold ground. Now, William, I want you to be a good boy, to repent, and to love the Savior, so that when you die you may go to that good place. But if you do not repent, oh William there will be mourning, mourning, mourning."

After this I recollect nothing she said, although I believe she still talked a little with Mr. Northrop. She began to decline rapidly. Her paroxysms returned oftener, and each left her weaker than the preceding, until her mind became wandering, her speech declined into a whisper, and her articulation became indistinct. Still, it was apparent, from the incoherent expressions which now and then became audible, and from the composure, that was depicted in her countenance, that seemed to say, "All is well," that her mind was upon heavenly things.

To this succeeded, seemingly, an entire want of consciousness, but still nature resisted, and yielded only inch by inch, until respiration became more difficult and rattling, one convulsion followed another, one gasp another, and her breath became short and shorter, and the immortal spirit forsook its earthly home to join the righteous and just men made perfect, and "to sing the conqueror's song."

In the afternoon our friends and neighbors collected to pay the last tribute of respect to the remains of one who was respected in life and beloved in death. In the procession were the members of our family, our friends and connections and other Cherokee acquaintances, our neighbors, Brigadier General Dunlap, Major Payne, Major Kennedy, Captain Vernon, and other officers, and nearly one half of the privates of the U.S. volunteers stationed at this place. She is buried on a hill near the little spring occupied, I think, by Mr. Tarvin, when you were here, as you go out to Oogillogy. As I have not a foot of ground that I can call my own, I had to ask of the proprietor the privilege of depositing her beloved remains on his land, and I have consigned her ashes to his protection.

So died your beloved daughter, and we mourn for her, but not as others mourn who have no hope. Our loss is her everlasting gain, but nature must yield and give vent to tears when the most endeared link of the social tie is broken. To me, the loss is irreparable, left, as I am, with six helpless children, at an age when they most need the care, the oversight, and instruction of a mother. May God be my strength and my wisdom—may he keep me from repining, and enable me to own and acknowledge the justice of this tremendous stroke! Pray for me and these motherless children; pray that the great affliction may be sacrificed to our souls—that the prayers of our dear departed friend may be heard, and her exhortations blessed, and that we may yet have occasion to praise God for this instance of his inscrutable providence.

To you, the death of your beloved child, although perhaps you had but little hope of ever seeing her in the flesh, must be a source of great affliction; to you, especially, my dear mother! The child of your prayers, upon whom you doted when an infant—who was beloved to you even when she left her paternal roof to unite her destiny to a "son of the forest" is taken away from you. Although far separated from you, you must feel the anguish mothers feel when they see the earthly tie that binds them to their children broken. But you have no reason to repine—you may rejoice that God gave you such a child, that he accounted her worthy, as we have every reason to believe, to enter into his glorious kingdom even before her aged parents. To her brothers and endeared sisters, the death of my dear Harriet must have been most painful. But I would exhort them to acknowledge God's hand in this afflictive dispensation. May we all have the heart to say: "The Lord gave and the Lord hath taken away, and blessed be the name of the Lord."[10] And in view of the dissolution which awaits us all, may we pray: "Let me die the death of the righteous, and let my last end be like hers."

And now, my dear parents, I must close. I hope you will not forget me, although the link that bound me to you is gone. But there are other links, dear to you—for their sakes, and the sake of our departed friend, you will still consider me as being near to you, and I trust I shall still be worthy of your regard and affection.

I am, as ever, your dutiful son.

Elias Boudinott[11]

1. The material prefacing the letter as it appeared in the *New York Observer* is given below. The editor of the *New York Observer* wrote the "Editor's Note," and the person who introduces Elias's letter is not identified.

(Editor's Note: Failing to overcome the popular support for John Ross, John Ridge, Elias Boudinot and other members of the Treaty Party themselves negotiated a removal treaty which was signed on December 29, 1835, at New Echota. The treaty was highly favorable to the Cherokees and the signers hoped that when it was understood it would be accepted by the majority. However, it was not. In addition to his political problems, Elias Boudinot also suffered a tragic personal loss in the death of his wife which is described below.)

LAST HOURS OF MRS. BOUDINOTT

For the New York Observer.

Messrs. Editors—The death of Mrs. Boudinott, who died in August last, has been noticed in the papers, but no particular account has been given. I am, therefore, requested to present to you for publication the following sketch, consisting principally of extracts from Mr. Boudinott's letter to her parents. You will be kind enough to give this a place in your column, for the benefit of her numerous acquaintances, and perhaps it will not prove uninteresting to those who knew her by reputation, and who take an interest in all those whose spirit of charity—sympathy for suffering humanity, and more especially whose love for him, who died for the world, leads them forth, forgetful of self, to devote their lives in acts of good to others.

Mr. Elias Boudinot, with whom she linked her fortunes, is well known to the public, before whom he has been acting for the last ten years, in defense of the rights of the Cherokees and in the cause of all the sons of the Forest. Mr. B. was educated at the Foreign Mission School, in Cornwall, Conn. He has appeared before this community as the advocate of Indian rights; and for several years was the Editor of the Cherokee Phoenix, the first and only paper ever published by a son of the Forest, independent of the white man's aid and talents.

Mrs. Harriet Boudinott was the youngest daughter of Col. Benjamin and Eleanor Gold, of Cornwall, Conn. She chose that "good part," while yet young, early imbibed the Missionary spirit, and aimed at engaging in that cause when age should permit and opportunity be given.

The Foreign Mission School being established in her native place, called for her warmest sympathies. Through this School, she became acquainted with the character of the Indian, and felt the wrongs with which he was oppressed. She also, at this time, became acquainted with several intelligent sons of the Forest, among whom was Mr. B. With him she chose to cast her lot, and to the last, he has proved himself worthy of the trust. Since that, for the last ten years, with the exception of a few months which she passed in visiting her Northern friends, her life has been spent in the bosom of the Cherokee Nation, where she has been an eye witness of Indian wrongs. She was devoted heart and soul to the welfare of that race, into which she was adopted; and while laboring in their behalf, and mourning over their deplorable condition, she delighted in being one of them and in sharing with the oppressed, rather than with the oppressor.

It was always the desire of Mrs. B. to be where she could do good. Her highest happiness consisted in the ability to minister to others. She sought the bed of sickness and cottage of the poor. Her days of childhood and youth were passed in the bosom of her father's family, and in one of the delightful valleys of New England. She was the favorite of a large family of brothers and sisters, and a wide circle of friends; she could but be happy. But she was not satisfied with such a lot, when she must be so much the passive recipient of happiness; she therefore sacrificed a thousand earthly comforts and sought a place where she might better exercise her benevolence. She found it among the Cherokee; and there she found more joy and satisfaction for her generous soul, than even under her paternal roof. She has now found rest where the oppressor's arm can never have power. Though she condemned herself for not having done more, she has left us a bright example for imitation. Her career was short, but she only wished to live longer, that she might do more for Him, in whom she placed her hopes of a bright immortality.

The following extracts from Mr. B's letter, present her to us in the last great trial, and in the full triumph of the christian.

2. The editor of the *New York Observer* here inserted a note: "(We here omit the particulars which follow, respecting her health previous to her first sickness, the nature of her disease, its progress, etc.)" The exact cause of her death is unknown. She delivered her fifth child, Elias Cornelius, on 1 August 1834 and her sixth child, Franklin Brinsmade, on 15 May 1836, exactly three months before her death; it seems likely that her death was in some way connected to the latter's birth. (Gabriel incorrectly asserts that Harriett delivered a stillborn son, her seventh child, in May [158]).

3. It is likely that "brother S." is Stand Watie, Elias's younger brother. Later in the letter, Elias mentions that this individual acted as an English-Cherokee interpreter for Harriett, heightening the probability that it is Stand and not Harriett's brother Sedgwick.

4. Hymn 98 of John Newton's *Olney Hymns* (295). "We seek a rest beyond the skies" is inscribed on Harriett's gravestone. A reproduction of the gravestone stands today at the New Echota State Historic Site, and the original is part of the collection there.

5. Elias refers to the memoir of Edward Payson (1783–1827), which records his last utterances as "Peace! peace! Victory! victory!" (423); "I am going, but God will surely be with you" (423), a comment to his wife and children; and "Faith and patience hold out" (423–24), a response to a question about his spiritual state.

6. Exodus 33:20.

7. Harriet Newell, who married a missionary to India, died on the Isle of France off the coast of southeast Africa at the age of nineteen. She, too, longed for her family and the presence of Christians at her deathbed (Woods 247). Elias's description of Harriett's death bears many formulaic similarities to Samuel New-

ell's letter conveying news of his wife's death, suggesting the conventionality of such epistles (Woods 238–53).

    8. At this point in the article, the editor inserts a footnote:

> Mr. and Mrs. Northrop were at this time on a visit from the North to their daughter, Mrs. Ridge, who was another young lady whose sympathies were awakened in behalf of the sons of the forest, with one of whom she chose her destiny, rather than with the white man.
>
> Mr. Ridge is the son of Major Ridge, who commanded a detachment of 500 Cherokees, under General Jackson in the last war. Many in this city have heard his eloquence in behalf of his oppressed countrymen.

    9. The last lines of Hymn 37, "Begone, Unbelief," by John Newton, based on Romans 8:37, are: "And then, O! how pleasant, / The Conqueror's Song" (249–51).

    10. Job 1:21.

    11. The article ends with the following text: "There is much in the life of Harriet Boudinott of high interest; and like those of Harriet Newell, her memoir would be entertaining and useful presenting an elevated character in the domestic relations as well as in that of a missionary sent forth by her divine Master, to speak salvation to those in darkness. Should it be thought best hereafter, such a memoir may be expected."

ELIAS BOUDINOT TO HERMAN AND
FLORA GOLD VAILL, 28 AUGUST 1836
HLVC, m.

[Return address:] [illegible] / 28 Augst [Addressed to:]
Rev. Herman L. Vaill / East Lyme / River Head P.O. / (Con.)
[Postage:] 25

Creek Path, Aug 28, 1836.

My dear brother & Sister,

    I suppose you have heard of the severe stroke God has laid upon me—in taking away my dear Harriet—yes, your dear Sister is no more. I wrote to Swift, before she died, but when we considered her case hopeless, and requested him to inform you all. I have since written, with great difficulty, on account of illness and weak eyes, a long letter to our good father & mother, giving a particular account of her death, particularly of her Religious exercises. I refer you to that letter, for I cannot now write. If I could see you I would have plenty to say, and tell you all about my loss. You know what I have lost—what these dear children have lost—it is irreparable. May God sustain us all under this severe affliction.

H. died on the 15th just 1 year to the day after we arrived from the North.[1] She suffered extreme bodily pain throughout her whole sickness, and it had considerable effect upon her mind. She complained of darkness [du-?][2] [end of page 1] the fore part of it—but towards the latter, she said her darkness was removed, that there was a clear sky between her & her Redeemer. The morning before she died, after the most distressing night she had had, she called us to her bed. Upon my enquiring how she did, she replied that she was in great distress, (meaning her bodily distress). "I hope," she said, "this is the last night I shall spend in this world, then how sweet will be the Conqueror's Song." Are your doubts & darkness removed? "Yes." Can you look to the blessed Redeemer, and call him yours? "Yes." Are you happy notwithstanding all your bodily pain & affliction? "I am happy."

But my dear bro. & sister I must refer you to my letter to our dear parents, as I am in a poor condition to write at this time, for the reason I have already stated. We mourn for our dear friend, but not as others mourn who have no hope. We have every hope that can console us. But pray for the living—pray for me who am left with 6 helpless children, bereft of a mother, and consequently [end of page 2] that care and attendance which none but a mother can give. Pray for them—pray that the prayers of their ^{dear departed} Mother may be answered, and her exhortations blessed to their spiritual good. O may we all profit by this severe dispensation of God's providence. May we learn our own end.

I have brought the children here and shall leave them a while. Mr. & Mrs. Potter are very kind and are willing to do any thing for them. I wish to do what is best for them, but what will be [best?] & practicable I cannot yet say. This affliction came, ~~illegible~~ to all human appearance, in a most ~~illegible~~ ^{deplorable time}—just at the time when we are calculating to break up & go to the west. The Lord be my strength &

my wisdom. Farewell. Write to me & give me some advice what I ought to do for the children. I have tho^t some of taking a part of them to the North.

Yours as ever
Elias Boudinot [end of page 3]

Mr. Potter sends love to you & says he used to know you in South [Farms?]

All my plans are now disconcerted. I really do not know what to do. You cannot imagine the extent of my bereavement. I cannot express it—it is beyond the power of language to express. When I think of that dear individual—for ten years my endeared companion—one who was willing in youth to leave her paternal home & her friends for me—now no more—whose face I am never to see in this ~~illegible~~ world.

* * *

Oh it is more than human nature can bear. But the Lord keep me from repining. Pray for me my dear bro. & Sister. Pray for these children she has left with me & may we finally join her in our father's Kingdom.

E.B.

1. Harriett had cherished hopes of visiting her family for years. In a fragment of a letter dated 27 May [1833?], Harriett wrote to her father: "With regards to coming to Conn. I refer[d] of course to Mr. Boudinot. He says it is impossible to answer that question explicitly now. But this much you may depend on, if our lives are spared. Should the Nation remove, which, without doubt they will do, we should of course share with the rest in receiving an equivalent for our title here, & should that be sufficient, we should with great pleasure spend a part of it in visiting our northern friends before we go far to the West. O how happy should I be to see you my dear Parents, Brothers & Sisters. I would be thankful for the interview, & hope it would not be less profitable than pleasant" (letter to Benjamin Gold). Sophia Sawyer, teacher of the Boudinot children, comments in a letter written on 27 December 1834 that the Boudinot family, including children, left New Echota for New England around the beginning of that month (letter to David Greene). In February of 1835, Elias and other members of the Treaty Party were in Washington, D.C., arguing their position before the U.S. government, as were members of Ross's party (Peyer 209). See also Elias's letter to his brother dated 28 February 1835 from Washington (Dale and Litton 10–12).

2. Typescript in the Herman Landon Vaill Collection reads "in," but it appears to me that Elias intended the word—perhaps "during"—to continue on the next page. It did not.

ELIAS BOUDINOT TO JOB SWIFT GOLD, 26 OCTOBER 1836
HLVC, m.

[Return address:] New Echota Ga / Octr 27 [Addressed to:]
Mr. J.S. Gold / 88 Nassau Street / New York [Postage:] 25

New Echota, Oct. 26, 1836.

My dear brother,

I have the pleasure to acknowledge the receipt of your letter of 25 Sept. I also received at the same time other letters from other friends, and yesterday one from Stephen. All these I have answered by this mail.

You cannot think how consoling it is to my deeply wounded heart to receive such testimonials of sympathy and kind feelings, especially from the friends of my dear Harriet, who has now left ^{me} to enter upon scenes of Blessedness which our limited imagination cannot comprehend. Why should we mourn on her account? On ours we might.

You have ere this seen my letter to our parents, giving some detailed account of her sickness and death. She gave us a consoling evidence that she was prepared for that voice which has called her away. I was desirous that the substance of that account might be published in some news paper, if it was thought proper by her friends. You know the feeling, that once existed in regard to her. Perhaps an account of her last days may correct the remains of that feeling, if any exists.

A notice of her death has, I presume been published in the Herald, if in other papers I should like to receive copies. Here [end of page 1] her memory is honored in the recollection of all who knew her, from the highest to the lowest. Perhaps no one in this Country has ever commanded such universal respect as she did. No one has ever entered into our humble dwelling, which many did, of the highest respectability, on account of our position here, without going away impressed with the sense of respect which nothing but virtue & propriety can ever command.[1] Even the people of Georgia, not ~~illegible~~ unfrequently carried away with overwrought passions and prejudices against our race, such as personally knew her, or had heard of her from report have testified to her worth and unsullied character. Some who best knew her have said, "they never knew such a woman." Are there any in her native country, in her native village, who can bring aught against her? Let such ~~illegible~~ come here where she spent the best ten of her years, and allege their charges against a woman who was emphatically the favorite of this Country.

To lose such a friend is indeed a great and heavy affliction. But it is the will of God and it is our duty to submit, and to pray that this affliction might be sanctified to ~~illegible~~ us. I trust it will. I trust it will teach us our dependence, and our own dissolution which will soon occur at the longest. May we be ready [end of page 2]

In regard to the children I have concluded to send four to the north, but shall not be able to do so until the Spring. My Calculation is to go with them myself. In the mean time I shall spend the winter here in preparing claims for the Cherokees. This will give me full employment, and may be somewhat profitable.

I am now very desirous to see you all, to talk over matters, which have been, I have no doubt, the theme of your conversations lately. May you be prospered in your health & in your business. [I] shall always ~~illegible~~ take an interest [in] your affairs, and as long as I shall remember with the tenderest affection my dear Harriet, which will be to the day of my death, I shall remember her dear parents, her brothers & Sisters.

My love to your wife & believe me to be as ever your affectionate bro.

E. Boudinot

1. Sophia Sawyer, the Boudinot children's teacher, resided with the Boudinot family for ten months in 1834, when she described Harriett as "one of those modest, amiable, lovely females, who never displeases any one, & makes every [illegible] & thing pleasant around her" (letter to David Greene). Upon hearing of Harriett's death, she wrote in 1836, "Mr. Boudinott is a man, as you know, of the finest sensibilities—very domestic in his feelings and habits—has lost one of the most lovely women in the world—at a time too, the most trying in the history of nations or individuals six children hanging now solely on a father's care—the

eldest has entered her tenth year—the youngest only a few months old. I fear for him amidst the wreck of his nation" (letter to David Greene).

ELIAS BOUDINOT TO BENJAMIN AND ELEANOR GOLD,
22 MARCH 1837
CornHS, THS, pm.

[Return address:] [stamped] Brainerd, Ten. / March 22
[Addressed to:] Col. Benjamin Gold / Cornwall Bridge / (Con.)
[Postage:] 25

Brainerd Ten. March 22, 1837

Dear father & mother,

I received your letter sometime ago and I have neglected to answer it thus long. Your letter found me sick in bed, in a very low spirits. When I got able to be about I went to Creek path, to see my children. I staid there a week or so then returned to New Echota then from there to this place, in pursuit of my little boy Franklin. He is now here in the care of Miss Sargent[1] for the present, Sally Ridge having married, and returned back to New Echota. They had proceeded this far on their way to Arkansas. She is married to one G. M. Paschal. I have accordingly made other arrangements for the poor little fellow—the good people at Creek path will take him and take care of him as long as they continue there, which however cannot be long. I must then trust to providence. I know God will provide for him & take care of him. All this reminds me of my great loss, which cannot be retrieved. But my children are in as favorable circumstances as I could wish. They are the favorites in Mr. Potters School. Cornelius is a Pet in the family—but the poor boy is afflicted with lameness in one of his limbs, and I am afraid will be a cripple as long as he lives. I sent him to Huntsville, Ala. to an eminent physician, and I trust he may be benefited. Franklin is a Pet of the family here, and he is very healthy. The other children are doing [end of page 1] well and are making good proficiency in learning. After due deliberation I ~~illegible~~ have concluded to take Eleanor only to ~~illegible~~ the North, at least for the present. We are calculating to go about the first of May, in Company with sister Elizabeth &

Sarah Bell, who intend to go to Ipswich Seminary and Miss Sargent, formerly teacher here, returning to see her friends in Vermont.[2] I will not write much now. I trust you still enjoy good health and that you will be prospered in your old age. I shall never forget you—I cannot forget you, while I have the remembrance of those happy days I enjoyed with your dear daughter, my honored and beloved wife—now beyond the reach of earthly trials & affliction. And that remembrance will last to the last moment of my earthly existence. Remember me also, as I know you will and wish for my happiness and the happiness of the dear children left in my hands without a mother to guide them in their tender years. Pray for us.

My love to all friends
Yours as ever
Elias Boudinot

1. Delight Sargent (1800–1893), a native of Vermont, began her work as a teacher with the ABCFM in 1827. She served at the Brainerd, Creek Path, and Red Clay missions.

2. Sister Elizabeth is Elias's younger sister, Elizabeth Watie, also called Betsey by Harriett in her letter of 5 January 1827. Sarah Bell went on to marry Stand Watie, Elias's younger brother, in 1843.

ELIAS BOUDINOT TO BENJAMIN AND
ELEANOR GOLD, 20 MAY 1837
HLVC, m.

[Return address:] New Echota Ga / May 21 [Addressed to:] Col. Benj. Gold / Cornwall Bridge / (Con.)

New Echota. May 20th 1837

My dear Father and Mother,

Sometime since I wrote from Creek Path to Sister Mary, Giving her at large my circumstances then, resulting from the loss of my dear wife, and apprising her of my intention to change my situation. You will have read that letter before this reaches you, and formed an opinion in regard to the propriety or impropriety of the course I intended to pursue. It is true I was very desirous to see you and consult you first, because I have too much respect for you to do any thing which you would not approve. But in this case the person who has now become the Mother of my dear Children is so unexceptionable, so universally acknowledged to be like your dear daughter Harriet, I have ventured at the step before receiving any intimation of your opinions. I hope it will meet with your approbation, for I can assure you, and all your friends in this Nation will assure you, your dear grand children could never expect a better friend, a better mother.

You may remember Miss D. Sargent who was the teacher at Brainerd when you visited that station She is about my age, of small person, excellent acquirements and most lovely disposition. She was the ~~illegible~~ favorite of all the Missionaries, and accounted the very best teacher that has been in this Nation. Her father, Doct. Sargent, resides in Pawlet, Vermont. She will, at my request, write to you shortly. The children are de- [end of page 1] lighted with her and feel that they have a home once more.

I enclose you a letter which I received from Mary the other day. It will show you a little how they feel, and how Mary improves. She did not begin to write, I believe, until late last ~~winter~~ fall, and the letter I enclose has not a single correction whatever, even the punctuation, and not even copied. Mary bids fair to make a ~~illegible~~ scholar.[1] So do the others. Sarah is a substantial little girl of great independence. Eleanor is now quite a large ~~illegible~~ girl, learns well, and will look very much like her mother when she grows. William also will bear strong resemblance to her & to your family. Cornelius is still lame and I think will resemble William. Frank is a little fellow to himself the darling and pet of his ~~illegible~~ new Ma, and of the whole family at Creek Path. I think, if he lives, he will make a better looking man than either of his brothers. He has a high arching noble forehead, with black quick and sparkling eyes—of a good gentle disposition, but susceptable of great animation and feeling, so far as a little boy can be judged. In fact, I have reason to be thankful, as all my friends tell me, that I have such promising children, and I tell you this because you are so deeply interested in their welfare. And let me tell you again, they could never have a better, and a more competent friend to enoble them to improve their natural advantages, than their new Ma.

You will have learnt already that I have relinquished my journey to the east, for reasons which will occur [end of page 2] to you at first thought, and which I believe I mentioned to Mary in my letter. You know it is a long tedious and expensive journey, which cannot be undertaken, except with an object to justify it. That object does not now exist, at least to the extent that it did before. I am still desirous that Eleanor should go and live with her aunt Mary, and I trust she may be disposed to do so, when Mr. Potter goes to New England, although I have understood lately that she was rather disposed to go to Arkansas. I expect to leave for that Country early in the fall, and I must be making my calculations shortly.

I wrote the other day to Swift by private conveyance, particularly in reference to two subjects. In regard to placing a marble slab at H's grave, and in regard to a miniature copy of her portrait, which I was desirous might be taken and sent to me by Dr. Lillybridge, who will return about the first of July. Will you please urge this matter. I have funds plenty in Swift's hands to pay for the expense. Write to me also about the other matter and let me know what you wish.

I hope I shall not be forgotten by you. It is true I have made a new connection, but I can never, as I shall never forget you, for your own sakes & for the ~~illegible~~ sake of my first and endeared friend H. I shall be happy to hear from you, to receive letters from you & to correspond with you as usual. Farewell.

> With most sincere salutations to yourselves
> and all our friends I remain as ever yours
> Elias Boudinot

P.S. Write and direct "Hellicon P.S. Marshall Co. Ala."

1. Sophia Sawyer, the teacher of the Boudinot children, commented on Mary four years earlier in 1832: "Mary is a superior child in all things—she has just entered her fifth year, can read correctly in the Testament on any common readings Your attention would be directed to her among fifty children Her punctuality to her lesson as it regards recitation & committing & her general conduct as it respects attention, is such as would give credit to a scholar of twenty years" (letter to David Greene). Mary went on to attend Mt. Holyoke Female Seminary in 1846–48.

[Return address:] Kidran Ark / June 27 [Addressed to:] Gen.
Danl. B. Brinsmade, / Washington, / Connecticut. [Postage:] 25

Park Hill, Cher. Na. June 26, 1839.

Genl D. B. Brinsmade,

Dear Sir,

I hasten to communicate to you the afflictive intelligence of the death of a beloved friend and christian brother of mine, and your brother-in-law, Elias Boudinot. Under circumstances peculiarly trying to surviving friends, he has been taken from among us. He has fallen by the hands of assassins! He was living in my house, not having completed his own, which is about a quarter of a mile distant. There he was, last Saturday morning, when some men came up, inquiring for medicine. He set out with them to come and get it, and had walked but a few rods, when he was heard to shriek, and his hired men, at and near his house, ran to his help; but before they could reach the spot, the deed of blood was done The murderers were pursued a few rods into the woods, where they joined a party of armed men on horseback, and made their escape. They seemed first to have stabbed Mr. Boudinot in the back with a knife, and then finished their dreadful work with a hatchet, inflicting seven strokes, two or three of which sunk deep into his head. He lived until we received word, and arrived at the spot to see him breathe his last, but he was insensible to surrounding objects, groaning only, but without motion or speech.

The same morning Mr. John Ridge, living more than 60 miles from the place, was dragged from his bed, and stabbed to death at his own door, the murderers inflicting [end of page 1] many wounds, and then brandishing their knives, and laughing with exultation at the deed they had done. On the same day, also, at the distance of 40 or 50 miles from home, and 30 or more from this place, Maj. Ridge, the father of John, was waylaid and shot. These circumstances shew that the conspiracy was very extensive. Others, which I have not time to name, shew the same fact in a strong light. Undoubtedly the part which they took in relation to the treaty has been the cause of these inhuman assassinations. I would that my beloved friend Mr. Boudinot, had had no part in that transaction; yet I have no doubt of the sincerity of his own conviction that he was doing right, and hazarding his life for the good of his people. He was a great and good man—a man who, in an uncommon degree, exhibited the spirit of the Gospel. To me he was a dear friend, a most intimate companion, and a most valued helper. He fell by violence, but he rests in peace, and will rise, we confidently trust, to a glorious immortality.

Mr. Boudinot had requested his wife, if he should be taken away, to go with the children to their friends and hers in New England, which she intends to as soon as circumstances allow. You will probably see her and them before many months at least. In the mean time she will probably write to you herself before long.[1]

You will communicate this melancholy intelligence to Col. Gold and to the different branches of the family. But be so kind as not to suffer this letter or any part of it, [end of page 2] to be put in print.

Mrs. Worcester wishes to be affectionately remembered to Mrs. Brinsmade, with whose correspondence she was familiar while her sister lived—one very dear to us all. Give my own and Mrs. Worcester's affectionate remembrance to Col. and Mrs. Gold, and assure them of our deep sympathy in their afflictions.

> I am truly yours,
> S.A. Worcester.

June 27. We have news direct from Ridge's. The previous account of the circumstances of his death was exaggerated. The effort seems to have been to spare rather than to wound the feelings of his family. A part of the same company who killed John Ridge at four o'clock in the morning, killed his father at a distance of near 40 miles at ten o'clock the same [morn]ing. He was on a journey.

It is doubtful whether Mrs. Boudinot can consistently leave the country before another spring. The settlement of his worldly affairs seems to require her to remain for some time.

1. A crosshatched line runs above the word "long."

Works Cited

Adams, John D. *Elias Cornelius Boudinot: In Memoriam*. Chicago: Rand McNally, 1891.

Altman, Janet Gurkin. *Epistolarity: Approaches to a Form*. Columbus: Ohio State University Press, 1982.

Anderson, Rufus. *Memoir of Catharine Brown, a Christian Indian of the Cherokee Nation*. 1824. Reprint, Signal Mountain, Tenn.: Mountain Press, n.d.

Anderson, William L., ed. *Cherokee Removal: Before and After*. Athens: University of Georgia Press, 1991.

Andrew, John. "Educating the Heathen: The Foreign Mission School Controversy and American Ideals." *American Studies* 12.3 (1978): 331–42.

Angus, Patricia Monture. "Native Americans and the Literary Tradition." In *Native North America: Critical and Cultural Perspectives*, edited by Renée Hulan, 20–46. Toronto: ECW Press, 1999.

Apess, William. *On Our Own Ground: The Complete Writings of William Apess, a Pequot*. Edited by Barry O'Connell. Amherst: University of Massachusetts Press, 1992.

Barton, David, and Nigel Hall, eds. *Letter Writing as a Social Practice*. Philadelphia: John Benjamins Publishing, 2000.

Bass, Althea. *Cherokee Messenger*. 1936. Reprint, Norman: University of Oklahoma Press, 1996.

Bergland, Renee L. *The National Uncanny: Indian Ghosts and American Subjects*. Hanover: University Press of New England, 2000.

Berkhofer, Robert F., Jr. *Salvation and the Savage: An Analysis of Protestant Missions and American Indian Response*. Lexington: University of Kentucky Press, 1965.

———. *The White Man's Indian: Images of the American Indian from Columbus to the Present*. New York: Knopf, 1978.

Bieder, Robert E. *Science Encounters the Indian, 1820–1880*. Norman: University of Oklahoma Press, 1986.

Boudinot, Elias. *An Address to the Whites Delivered in the First Presbyterian Church, on the 26th of May, 1826*. Philadelphia: William F. Geddes, 1826. In *Cherokee Editor: The Writings of Elias Boudinot*, edited by Theda Perdue, 68–83. 1983. Athens: University of Georgia Press, 1996.

———. Editorial. *Cherokee Phoenix*, 28 Jan. 1829. In *Cherokee Editor: The Writings of Elias Boudinot*, edited by Theda Perdue, 103–6. 1983. Athens: University of Georgia Press, 1996.

———. "Georgia and the Missionaries." *Cherokee Phoenix*, 16 July 1831. In *Cherokee Editor: The Writings of Elias Boudinot*, edited by Theda Perdue, 128–31. 1983. Athens: University of Georgia Press, 1996.

———. Letter to David Green. 1 Aug. 1837. American Board of Commissioners for Foreign Missions Papers 18.3.1, vol. 8. Houghton Library, Harvard University, Cambridge, Mass.

———. *Letters and Other Papers Relating to Cherokee Affairs: Being in Reply to Sundry Publications Authorized by John Ross*. Athens, Ga., 1837. In *Cherokee Editor: The Writings of Elias Boudinot*, edited by Theda Perdue, 159–233. 1983. Athens: University of Georgia Press, 1996.

———. "Prospectus." 1827. In *Cherokee Editor: The Writings of Elias Boudinot*, edited by Theda Perdue, 89–90. 1983. Athens: University of Georgia Press, 1996.

———, trans. *Poor Sarah, or, the Indian Woman*. New Echota, C.N., 1833.

Boudinot, Elias, and Samuel A. Worcester, trans. *The Acts of the Apostles*. New Echota, C.N., 1833.

———. *Cherokee Hymns Compiled from Several Authors and Revised*. New Echota, C.N., 1829.

———. *The Epistles of John*. Park Hill, C.N., 1840.

———. *The Epistles of Paul to Timothy*. Park Hill, C.N., 1844.

———. *The Epistles of Peter*. Park Hill, C.N., 1848.

———. *The Gospel according to Luke*. Park Hill, C.N., 1840.

———. *The Gospel according to Matthew*. New Echota, C.N., 1829.

———. *The Gospel of Jesus Christ according to John*. Park Hill, C.N., 1838.

Boudinot, Harriett Gold. Letter. n.d. Cornwall Historical Society, Cornwall, Conn.

———. Letter to Benjamin Gold. 27 May [1833?]. Cornwall Historical Society, Cornwall, Conn.

———. Letter to Benjamin Wisner. 4 July 1834. American Board of Commissioners for Foreign Missions Papers 18.3.1, vol. 8. Houghton Library, Harvard University, Cambridge, Mass.

Boudinot, Mary. Letter to Benjamin Gold. 24 Sept. 1845. Cornwall Historical Society, Cornwall, Conn.

Brinsmade, Mary. "The Priest, the Judge and the General, Being an Account of the First Three Generations of the Brinsmade Family in Judea." Ts. Gunn Memorial Library, Washington, Conn.

Broughton, Trev Lynn, and Linda Anderson, eds. *Women's Lives/Women's Times: New Essays on Auto/Biography*. Albany: State University of New York Press, 1997.

Brown, David. Letter to Jeremiah Evarts. 29 Sept. 1825. American Board of

Commissioners for Foreign Missions Papers 18.3.1, vol. 5. Houghton
Library, Harvard University, Cambridge, Mass.

Bunyan, John. *A Holy Life, the Beauty of Christianity, or, An Exhortation to Christians
to Be Holy*. London, 1684.

Burnham, Michelle. *Captivity and Sentiment: Cultural Exchange in American Literature,
1682–1861*. Hanover: University Press of New England, 1997.

Butrick, Daniel S. "Cherokee Mission." *Religious Intelligencer* 10.18 (1825):
280–81.

———. Letter to Elias Boudinot. 9 June 1839. Ts. John Howard Payne
Papers 9. Newberry Library, Chicago.

———. Letter to Jeremiah Evarts. 7 Nov. 1824. American Board of
Commissioners for Foreign Missions Papers 18.3.1, vol. 4. Houghton
Library, Harvard University, Cambridge, Mass.

———. Letter to Jeremiah Evarts. 13 Dec. 1825. American Board of
Commissioners for Foreign Missions Papers 18.3.1, vol. 5. Houghton
Library, Harvard University, Cambridge, Mass.

———. Letter to Jeremiah Evarts. 13 Mar. 1826. American Board of
Commissioners for Foreign Missions Papers 18.3.1, vol. 4. Houghton
Library, Harvard University, Cambridge, Mass.

———. Letter to John Howard Payne. n.d. Ts. John Howard Payne Papers 9,
101–2. Newberry Library, Chicago.

Casper, Scott E. *Constructing American Lives: Biography and Culture in Nineteenth-
Century America*. Chapel Hill: University of North Carolina Press, 1999.

Castiglia, Christopher. *Bound and Determined: Captivity, Culture-Crossing, and White
Womanhood from Mary Rowlandson to Patty Hearst*. Chicago: University of
Chicago Press, 1996.

Chamberlain, Betsey. *The Life and Writings of Betsey Chamberlain, Native American
Mill Worker*. Edited by Judith A. Ranta. Boston: Northeastern University
Press, 2003.

Chamberlain, Paul H. "The Foreign Mission School." Cornwall: Cornwall
Historical Society, 1968.

"The Cherokee and His Beautiful Bride." *Atkinson's Saturday Evening Post* 18.0
(28 Sept. 1839): n.p.

Child, Lydia Maria. *Hobomok, and Other Writings on Indians*. Edited by Carolyn
Karcher. New Brunswick, N.J.: Rutgers University Press, 1986.

Church, Mary Brinsmade. *Elias Boudinot: An Account of His Life Written by His
Grandaughter [sic]*. Ts. Gunn Memorial Library, Washington, Conn.

Cook, Elizabeth Heckendorn. *Epistolary Bodies: Gender and Genre in the Eighteenth-
Century Republic of Letters*. Stanford: Stanford University Press, 1996.

Cooper, James Fenimore. *The Last of the Mohicans: A Narrative of 1757; The Writings*

of James Fenimore Cooper. Edited by James Franklin Beard, James A.
Sappenfield, and E. N. Feltskog. Albany: State University of New York
Press, 1983.

———. *The Wept-of Wish-ton-Wish.* New York: P. F. Collier, n.d.

"Cornwall Mission School (Con.)." *Gospel Advocate and Impartial Investigator* 3.48
(9 Dec. 1825): 382–83.

"Cornwall School." *American Eagle* 2.91 (31 May 1824): 1–2.

Dale, Edward Everett, and Gaston Litton, eds. *Cherokee Cavaliers: Forty Years of
Cherokee History as Told in the Correspondence of the Ridge-Watie Family.* 1939.
Reprint, Norman: University of Oklahoma Press, 1995.

Decker, William Merrill. *Epistolary Practices: Letter Writing in America before
Telecommunications.* Chapel Hill: University of North Carolina Press, 1998.

De Forest, John W. *History of the Indians of Connecticut from the Earliest Known Period
to 1850.* 1851. Reprint, Hamden, Conn.: Archon Books, 1964.

Delly, Lillian. "Episode at Cornwall." *Chronicles of Oklahoma* 52 (1973): 444–50.

Derounian-Stodola, Kathryn Zabelle, and James Levernier. *The Indian Captivity
Narrative, 1550–1900.* New York: Twayne, 1993.

Dierks, Konstantin. "The Familiar Letter and Social Refinement in America,
1750–1800." In *Letter Writing as a Social Practice,* edited by David Barton and
Nigel Hall, 31–41. Philadelphia: John Benjamins Publishing, 2000.

Dippie, Brian W. *The Vanishing Indian: White Attitudes and U.S. Indian Policy.* 1982.
Reprint, Lawrence: University Press of Kansas, 1991.

Ditz, Toby L. "Formative Ventures: Eighteenth-Century Commercial Letters
and the Articulation of Experience." In *Epistolary Selves: Letters and Letter-
Writers, 1600–1945,* edited by Rebecca Earle, 59–78. Brookfield, Vt.: Ashgate,
1999.

Dwight, Edwin Welles. *Memoirs of Henry Obookiah.* New Haven: Nathan Whiting,
1819.

Earle, Rebecca, ed. *Epistolary Selves: Letters and Letter-Writers, 1600–1945.*
Brookfield, Vt.: Ashgate, 1999.

Ehle, John. *Trail of Tears: The Rise and Fall of the Cherokee Nation.* New York:
Doubleday, Anchor Books, 1988.

Evarts, Jeremiah. Letter to Henry Hill. 9 Feb. 1826. American Board of
Commissioners for Foreign Missions Papers 11, vol. 2. Houghton Library,
Harvard University, Cambridge, Mass.

———. Letter to Henry Hill. 2 Apr. 1826. American Board of Commissioners
for Foreign Missions Papers 11, vol. 2. Houghton Library, Harvard
University, Cambridge, Mass.

Faery, Rebecca Blevins. *Cartographies of Desire: Captivity, Race, and Sex in the
Shaping of an American Nation.* Norman: University of Oklahoma Press, 1999.

Favret, Mary A. *Romantic Correspondence: Women, Politics, and the Fiction of Letters.* Cambridge: Cambridge University Press, 1993.

Filler, Louis, and Allen Gutman, eds. *The Removal of the Cherokee Nation: Manifest Destiny or National Dishonor?* Boston: Heath, 1962.

"The Foreign Mission School, Cornwall, Connecticut." N.p.: n.p., 22 Jan. 1825.

"The Foreign Mission School, Cornwall, Connecticut." N.p.: n.p., 17 June 1825.

Foreman, Grant. *Indian Removal: The Emigration of the Five Civilized Tribes of Indians.* Norman: University of Oklahoma Press, 1932.

———. "The Murder of Elias Boudinot." *Chronicles of Oklahoma* 12 (1934): 19–24.

French, Thomas. *The Missionary Whaleship.* New York: Vantage, 1961.

Fuller, Wayne E. *The American Mail: Enlarger of Common Life.* Chicago: University of Chicago Press, 1972.

Gabriel, Ralph Henry. *Elias Boudinot, Cherokee, and His America.* Norman: University of Oklahoma Press, 1941.

Gannett, Lewis, and Michael Gannett. *The Schools of Cornwall.* Cornwall, Conn.: Cornwall Historical Society, 1984.

Gerber, David. "The Immigrant Letter between Positivism and Populism: American Historians' Uses of Personal Correspondence." In *Epistolary Selves: Letters and Letter-Writers, 1600–1945*, edited by Rebecca Earle, 37–55. Brookfield, Vt.: Ashgate, 1999.

Gilroy, Amanda, and W. M. Verhoeven, eds. *Epistolary Histories: Letters, Fiction, Culture.* Charlottesville: University Press of Virginia, 2000.

Godbeer, Richard. "Eroticizing the Middle Ground: Anglo-Indian Sexual Relations along the Eighteenth-Century Frontier." In *Sex, Love, Race: Crossing Boundaries in North American History*, edited by Martha Hodes, 91–111. New York: New York University Press, 1999.

Gold, Theodore S. *Historical Records of the Town of Cornwall, Litchfield County, Connecticut.* 1877. 2d ed. Hartford: Hartford Press, 1904.

Goldsmith, Elizabeth, ed. *Writing the Female Voice: Essays on Epistolary Literature.* Boston: Northeastern University Press, 1989.

Hall, Nigel. "The Materiality of Letter Writing: A Nineteenth Century Perspective." In *Letter Writing as a Social Practice*, edited by David Barton and Nigel Hall, 83–108. Philadelphia: John Benjamins Publishing, 2000.

Hansen, Karen. *A Very Social Time: Crafting Community in Antebellum New England.* Berkeley: University of California Press, 1994.

Harris, Sharon M. Introduction to *American Women Writers to 1800*, edited by Harris, 3–30. New York: Oxford University Press, 1996.

Harris, Susan K. *The Cultural Work of the Late Nineteenth-Century Hostess: Annie Adams Fields and Mary Gladstone Drew.* New York: Palgrave, 2002.

———. "Personal Letters in the Cultural Work of the Late 19th-Century Hostess." Paper presented at the American Literature Association Conference, Long Beach, Calif., 31 May 2002.

Harvey, Joseph. *The Banner of Christ Set Up.* New Haven: Nathan Whiting, 1819.

Haynes, Carolyn. "'A Mark for Them All to Hiss At': The Formation of Methodist and Pequot Identity in the Conversion Narrative of William Apess." *Early American Literature* 31.1 (1996): 25–44.

Hodes, Martha. *White Women, Black Men: Illicit Sex in the Nineteenth-Century South.* New Haven: Yale University Press, 1997.

———, ed. *Sex, Love, Race: Crossing Boundaries in North American History.* New York: New York University Press, 1999.

Hodgson, Adam. *Remarks during a Journey through North America.* New York: Samuel Whiting, 1823.

Horsman, Reginald. *Race and Manifest Destiny: The Origins of American Racial Anglo-Saxonism.* Cambridge: Harvard University Press, 1981.

How, James. *Epistolary Spaces: English Letter Writing from the Foundation of the Post Office to Richardson's Clarissa.* Burlington, Vt.: Ashgate, 2003.

"A Journey in New-England." *Evangelical and Literary Magazine* 5.9 (1822): 463–73.

Kauffman, Linda. *Discourses of Desire: Gender, Genre, and Epistolary Fictions.* Ithaca: Cornell University Press, 1986.

———. *Special Delivery: Epistolary Modes in Modern Fiction.* Chicago: University of Chicago Press, 1992.

Kilpatrick, Jack Frederick, and Anna Gritt Kilpatrick. *New Echota Letters: Contributions of Samuel A. Worcester to the "Cherokee Phoenix."* Dallas: Southern Methodist University Press, 1978.

Kline, Mary-Jo. *Guide to Documentary Editing.* Baltimore: Johns Hopkins University Press, 1987.

Konkle, Maureen. "Indian Literacy, U.S. Colonialism, and Literary Criticism." *American Literature* 69.3 (1997): 457–86.

"Last Hours of Mrs. Boudinott." *New York Observer,* 26 Nov. 1836. Reprinted as "The Death of Harriet Gold Boudinot." *Journal of Cherokee Studies* 4.2 (1979): 102–7.

Lemire, Elise. *"Miscegenation": Making Race in America.* Philadelphia: University of Pennsylvania Press, 2002.

Luebke, Barbara F. *Elias Boudinot, Cherokee Editor: The Father of American Indian Journalism.* Ph.D. diss., University of Missouri, 1981.

———. "Elias Boudinot, Indian Editor: Editorial Columns from the *Cherokee Phoenix*." *Journalism History* 6 (1979): 48–53.

Maddox, Lucy. *Removals: Nineteenth-Century American Literature and the Politics of Indian Affairs*. New York: Oxford University Press, 1991.

Malone, Henry T. "The *Cherokee Phoenix*: Supreme Expression of Cherokee Nationalism." *Georgia Historical Quarterly* 34 (1950): 163–88.

———. *Cherokees of the Old South: A People in Transition*. Athens: University of Georgia Press, 1956.

———. "New Echota—Capital of the Cherokee Nation, 1825–1830." Ts. Herman Landon Vaill Collection, Yale University Library, New Haven, Conn.

Martin, Robert G., Jr. "*Cherokee Phoenix*: Pioneer of Indian Journalism." *Chronicles of Oklahoma* 25 (1947): 102–18.

McLoughlin, William G. *After the Trail of Tears: The Cherokees' Struggle for Sovereignty, 1839–1880*. Chapel Hill: University of North Carolina Press, 1993.

———. *Cherokee Renascence in the New Republic*. Princeton: Princeton University Press, 1986.

———. *Cherokees and Missionaries, 1789–1839*. New Haven: Yale University Press, 1984.

Murphy, James E., and Sharon M. Murphy. *Let My People Know: American Indian Journalism, 1828–78*. Norman: University of Oklahoma Press, 1981.

Namias, June. *White Captives: Gender and Ethnicity on the American Frontier*. Chapel Hill: University of North Carolina Press, 1993.

Narrative of Five Youth from the Sandwich Islands. New York: J. Seymour, 1816.

Nelson, Dana D. *The Word in Black and White: Reading "Race" in American Literature, 1638–1867*. New York: Oxford University Press, 1993.

Newton, John. *Olney Hymns in Three Books*. London: J. Nisbet, 1826.

Norton, Mary Beth. *In the Devil's Snare: The Salem Witchcraft Crisis of 1692*. New York: Knopf, 2002.

———. *Liberty's Daughters: The Revolutionary Experience of American Women, 1750–1800*. Boston: Little, Brown, 1980.

Parins, James W. *John Rollin Ridge: His Life and Works*. Lincoln: University of Nebraska Press, 1991.

Payson, Edward. *Memoir, Select Thoughts, and Sermons of the Late Rev. Edward Payson*. Compiled by Asa Cummings. Portland: Hyde and Lord, 1849.

Pearce, Roy Harvey. *The Savages of America: A Study of the Indian and the Idea of Civilization*. 1953. Berkeley: University of California Press, 1988.

Perdue Theda. *Cherokee Editor: The Writings of Elias Boudinot*. 1983. Athens: University of Georgia Press, 1996.

———. *Cherokee Women: Gender and Culture Change, 1700–1835*. Lincoln: University of Nebraska Press, 1998.

———. "Rising from the Ashes: The *Cherokee Phoenix* as an Ethnohistorical Source." *Ethnohistory* 24 (1977): 207–18.

———. *Slavery and the Evolution of Cherokee Society, 1540–1866*. Knoxville: University of Tennessee Press, 1979.

Peyer, Bernd. *The Tutor'd Mind: Indian Missionary-Writers in Antebellum America*. Amherst: University of Massachusetts Press, 1997.

Plane, Ann Marie. *Colonial Intimacies: Indian Marriage in Early New England*. Ithaca: Cornell University Press, 2000.

Powell, Timothy. *Ruthless Democracy: A Multicultural Interpretation of the American Renaissance*. Princeton: Princeton University Press, 2000.

Price, Kenneth M., and Susan Belasco Smith, eds. *Periodical Literature in Nineteenth-Century America*. Charlottesville: University Press of Virginia, 1995.

Prucha, Francis Paul. *American Indian Policy in the Formative Years: The Indian Trade and Intercourse Acts, 1790–1834*. Cambridge: Harvard University Press, 1962.

———, ed. *Cherokee Removal: The "William Penn" Essays and Other Writings*. Knoxville: University of Tennessee Press, 1981.

Review of "An Address to the Whites," by Elias Boudinot. *North American Review* 23 (Oct. 1826): 470–74.

Ridge, John. Letter to Albert Gallatin. 27 Feb. 1826. In *The Cherokee Removal: A Brief History with Documents*, edited by Theda Perdue and Michael D. Green, 34–43. Boston: Bedford, 1995.

Ridge, John Rollin. *The Life and Adventures of Joaquin Murieta*. 1854. Reprint, Norman: University of Oklahoma Press, 1955.

Ryan, Susan M. *The Grammar of Good Intentions: Race and the Antebellum Culture of Benevolence*. Ithaca: Cornell University Press, 2003.

Samuels, Shirley. *Romances of the Republic: Women, the Family, and Violence in the Literature of the Early American Nation*. New York: Oxford University Press, 1996.

Satz, Ronald. *American Indian Policy in the Jacksonian Era*. Lincoln: University of Nebraska Press, 1975.

Sawyer, Sophia. Letter to David Greene. 26 Dec. 1832. American Board of Commissioners for Foreign Missions Papers 18.3.1, vol. 8. Houghton Library, Harvard University, Cambridge, Mass.

———. Letter to David Greene. 27 Dec. 1834. American Board of Commissioners for Foreign Missions Papers 18.3.1, vol. 8. Houghton Library, Harvard University, Cambridge, Mass.

———. Letter to David Greene. 21 Sept. 1836. American Board of

Commissioners for Foreign Missions Papers 18.3.1, vol. 8. Houghton
Library, Harvard University, Cambridge, Mass.

Scheckel, Susan. *The Insistence of the Indian: Race and Nationalism in Nineteenth-
Century American Culture.* Princeton: Princeton University Press, 1998.

Schultz, Lucille M. "Letter-Writing Instruction in 19th Century Schools in the
United States." In *Letter Writing as a Social Practice*, edited by David Barton
and Nigel Hall, 109–25. Philadelphia: John Benjamins Publishing, 2000.

Seaver, James E. *A Narrative of the Life of Mrs. Mary Jemison.* Edited by June
Namias. 1824. Reprint, Norman: University of Oklahoma Press, 1992.

Sedgwick, Catharine Maria. *Hope Leslie; or, Early Times in the Massachusetts.* Edited
by Mary Kelley. 1827. Reprint, New Brunswick: Rutgers University Press,
1987.

Sheehan, Bernard W. *Seeds of Extinction: Jeffersonian Philanthropy and the American
Indian.* Chapel Hill: University of North Carolina Press, 1973.

Sheidley, Nathaniel. "Hunting and the Politics of Masculinity in Cherokee
Treaty-Making, 1763–75." In *Empire and Others: British Encounters with
Indigenous Peoples, 1600–1850*, edited by Martin Daunton and Rick Halpern,
167–85. Philadelphia: University of Pennsylvania Press, 1999.

Smith, Sidonie. *A Poetics of Women's Autobiography: Marginality and the Fictions of
Self-Representation.* Bloomington: Indiana University Press, 1987.

Sorisio, Carolyn. *Fleshing Out America: Race, Gender, and the Politics of the Body in
American Literature, 1833–1879.* Athens: University of Georgia Press, 2002.

Stanton, Domna C., ed. *The Female Autograph: Theory and Practice of Autobiography
from the Tenth to the Twentieth Century.* 1984. Reprint, Chicago: University of
Chicago Press, 1987.

Stanton, William. *The Leopard's Spots: Scientific Attitudes toward Race in America,
1815–59.* Chicago: University of Chicago Press, 1960.

Starr, Edward C. *A History of Cornwall, Connecticut: A Typical New England Town.*
New Haven: Tuttle, Morehouse, and Taylor, 1926.

Stepan, Nancy Leys. "Race and Gender: The Role of Analogy in Science." In
The Anatomy of Racism, edited by David Theo Goldberg, 38–57. Minneapolis:
University of Minnesota Press, 1990.

Strong, William Ellsworth. *The Story of the American Board.* Boston: Pilgrim Press,
1910.

Tilton, Robert S. *Pocahontas: The Evolution of an American Narrative.* New York:
Cambridge, 1994.

Walker, Cheryl. *Indian Nation: Native American Literature and Nineteenth-Century
Nationalisms.* Durham: Duke University Press, 1997.

Walker, Robert Sparks. *Torchlights to the Cherokees: The Brainerd Mission.* New York:
Macmillan, 1931.

Wallace, Anthony F. C. *The Long, Bitter Trail: Andrew Jackson and the Indians.* New York: Hill and Wang, 1993.

Warrior, Robert Allen. *Tribal Secrets: Recovering American Indian Intellectual Traditions.* Minneapolis: University of Minnesota Press, 1995.

Watts, Isaac. *Hymns and Spiritual Songs.* Hartford: J. Loomis, 1836.

Webster, Noah. *The American Spelling Book: Containing an Easy Standard of Pronunciation.* 1783. Boston: Isaiah Thomas and Ebenezer T. Andrews, 1802.

Wesley, John, and Charles Wesley. *Hymns and Sacred Poems.* 1740. Philadelphia: A. Bradford, 1743.

Wiegman, Robyn. *American Anatomies: Theorizing Race and Gender.* Durham: Duke University Press, 1995.

Wilkins, Thurman. *Cherokee Tragedy: The Story of the Ridge Family and of the Decimation of a People.* New York: Macmillan, 1970.

Woods, Leonard. *Memoirs of the Life of Mrs. Harriet Newell.* Lexington, Ky.: Skillman, 1815.

Worcester, Samuel A. Letter to Jeremiah Evarts. 4 May 1829. American Board of Commissioners for Foreign Missions 18.3.1, vol. 5. Houghton Library, Harvard University, Cambridge, Mass.

———. Letter to Rufus Anderson. 22 Dec. 1825. American Board of Commissioners for Foreign Missions Papers 18.3.1, vol. 5. Houghton Library, Harvard University, Cambridge, Mass.

Wyss, Hilary. *Writing Indians: Literacy, Christianity, and Native Community in Early America.* Amherst: University of Massachusetts Press, 2000.

Young, Mary. "The Cherokee Nation: Mirror of the Republic." *American Quarterly* 33 (1981): 502–24.

Index

Agriculture, Cherokee, 5, 11

Altman, Janet, 40

American Board of Commissioners for Foreign Missions (ABCFM), 4, 82 (n. 5). *See also* Foreign Mission School; Mission schools

American Eagle, 8, 87 (n. 6), 108 (n. 4). *See also* Bunce, Isaiah

American Indians: civilization and conversion of, 4, 20; and assimilation, 4, 22; and intermarriage, 11; stereotypes of, 11–13; as authors, 50–51, 71 (n. 31). *See also* Cherokees

American Spelling Book, 79, 81 (n. 2)

Anderson, Rufus, 101 (n. 2)

Andover Theological Institute, 8

Apess, William, 50

Assimilation, 4, 22. *See also* Boudinot, Elias: and assimilation

Autobiography, 23–24

Bachelors of Cornwall Valley, 10, 87 (n. 6)

Backus, Charles, 96, 103 (n. 11)

Ball plays, 19–21

Banner of Christ Set Up, 102 (n. 9)

Beecher, Lyman, 82 (n. 5)

Benevolence, 7, 9, 21, 51, 56–57, 68 (n. 11), 74 (n. 40)

Biography, 63, 64, 193 (n. 11)

Boudinot, Annie, 76 (n. 44)

Boudinot, Caroline Fields, 76 (n. 44)

Boudinot, Clara Minear, 76 (n. 44)

Boudinot, Delight Sargent, 65, 66, 199, 200

Boudinot, Eleanor Susan, 75 (n. 44), 168–71 passim, 180, 198, 200–201

Boudinot, Elias, 2; education of, 6, 8, 20, 92; childhood and adolescence of, 6, 8, 82 (n. 3); and missionaries, 6, 21–23, 71 (n. 33), 74 (n. 40); names of, 6, 67 (n. 8), 157 (n. 9); health of, 8, 82 (n. 3), 193, 198; Christian beliefs of, 19–21, 92; and assimilation, 20–22, 50, 61; and experience of prejudice, 22, 55, 181; as husband, 53–54, 173, 181, 197–98 (n. 1); and wife's death, 62–63, 64–65, 183–90, 193–95, 196–97, 198–99, 200, 201; removal of to Arkansas, 65; death of, 65, 75 (n. 44), 202–3; second marriage of, 65, 199–200; biraciality of, 69 (n. 18); as teacher, 153; as father, 154, 159, 162, 176–77, 194, 197, 198–99. *See also* Gold-Boudinot courtship; Gold-Boudinot engagement; Gold-Boudinot wedding

—and Cherokee politics: official roles of, 49; reputation of, 52, 59, 61, 65; and Georgia Guard, 58, 175, 178 (n. 1); and opposition to removal, 58–59, 174, 175–76; and Treaty of New Echota, 60–61, 65, 74 (n. 40), 195, 202–3; and support of removal, 60–61, 74 (n. 40); and John Ross, 74 (n. 39), 163 (n. 5)

—as editor of *Cherokee Phoenix*: and establishment of paper, 49, 158–59, 160 (n. 1); editorial duties of, 49–50, 71 (n. 34), 161–62, 171, 173; and criticism of United States, 50–51; and reception of paper, 52, 191;

and opposition to removal, 58–59; resignation of, 60, 160

—letters: as writer of, xiv–xv, 48, 162; from, 153–54, 158–59, 161–62, 170–71, 175–77, 179, 183–90, 193–95, 196–97, 198–201; postscripts from, 167, 174

—as writer: writings other than in *Cherokee Phoenix*, 6, 45, 163 (n. 3); translations by, 45–46, 50, 154, 161–62, 163 (nn. 2, 3); critical reception of, 50–51

Boudinot, Elias Cornelius, 75 (n. 44), 192 (n. 2), 198, 200

Boudinot, Elias Stockton, 6, 67 (n. 8)

Boudinot, Franklin Brinsmade, 75 (n. 44), 192 (n. 2), 198, 200

Boudinot, Harriett Gold: obituary of, xiv, 63–64, 183–93, 196; and Foreign Mission School, 5; and suitors, 33, 80; as missionary, 44, 46, 56, 63–64, 91, 131, 191–92, 193; health of, 62, 106, 125, 177–78, 183–90, 192 (n. 2); death of, 62, 183–90, 193–94, 196; memoir of, 63–64, 193 (n. 11); romanticized story of, 66; and education, 79; religious beliefs of, 83, 91, 139–40, 160, 184–88; and visit to New England, 178, 194, 195 (n. 1). *See also* Gold-Boudinot courtship; Gold-Boudinot engagement; Gold-Boudinot wedding

—married life of: domestic conditions of, 46, 52–53, 71 (n. 34), 154, 155–56, 159–60, 172; and adjustment to life in Cherokee Nation, 46–47, 51–57, 61–62, 154–56; and attitudes toward marriage and husband, 53–55, 173, 181–82

—and Cherokees: affection for, 46, 160; and Cherokee politics, 56–57, 58, 60, 61–62, 64, 170, 173, 177, 180, 182

—relationships: with sisters, 38, 53–54, 100, 139–40, 163, 173, 178; with Watie family, 46, 154–55, 186, 187, 188; with parents, 140, 143, 157, 159–60, 169, 171, 172

—letters: as writer of, 27–28, 45–48, 51–57; to, 79–80, 90–101, 141–42; from, 83–87, 138–40, 154–57, 159–60, 162–63, 171, 172–74, 177–78, 180–82; marginal insertions in, 136–37, 169–70

Boudinot, Mary Harriett, 75 (n. 44), 162, 168–71 passim, 180, 185, 200, 201 (n. 1)

Boudinot, Sarah Parkhill, 75 (n. 44), 181, 182 (n. 2), 200

Boudinot, William Penn, 75 (n. 44), 169, 171–88 passim, 200

Brainerd, 154, 200

Brainerd, David, 96, 114

Brinsmade, Daniel, 5, 82 (n. 4); and Gold-Boudinot engagement, 31–33, 37, 40, 81, 84, 89–90, 107–8

—letters: from, 89–90, 107–8; marginal insertion in, 122; to, 202–3

Brinsmade, Mary Gold, 5, 37–40 passim, 66, 107 (n. 1), 174, 201, 203; and Gold-Boudinot engagement, 104–7, 111, 112, 122, 128

—letters: from, 104–7; to, 116–22

Brown, Catharine, 101 (n. 2)

Brown, David, 16–17, 92, 101 (n. 2)

Bunce, Isaiah, 8–10, 13, 14, 37, 68 (n. 11), 88 (n. 11), 108

Butler, Elizur, 182, 183 (n. 8)

individual *Gold and Boudinot family members*

Fields, Caroline. *See* Boudinot, Caroline Fields

Foreign Mission School: history and curriculum of, 4–7, 68 (n. 9); criticisms of, 8–9, 14, 19, 103; and intermarriages, 8–10, 13–14, 19, 81–82, 85, 87 (nn. 2, 4, 5, 6), 88 (n. 11), 121; and Gold-Boudinot engagement, 14, 81–82, 85, 88 (n. 11), 121; closing of, 45; effects of intermarriages on, 93–98, 110, 117–18, 125–26

Fox, Emily, 13

Gabriel, Ralph Henry, xi, 23, 69 (n. 20)

Gambold, John, 18

Gender. *See* Women

Georgia, 48, 58–60, 63, 64, 160, 174, 175–76, 197

Georgia Guard, 58

Godbeer, Richard, 11

Gold, Abigail (Abbey). *See* Everest, Abigail (Abbey) Gold

Gold, Benjamin, 5, 10, 13, 99, 103 (n. 14), 128, 173, 176, 189–90, 199, 201; as patriarch, 35–36; and Gold-Boudinot engagement, 35–36, 89, 98–99, 105–6, 109–11, 113, 116, 128, 129–35 passim; visit to Cherokee Nation, 52, 164–67, 168–69; Harriett Gold Boudinot's affection for, 140, 142, 157, 159–60, 166, 169, 171, 172; description of grandchildren, 168

—letters: from, 128–29, 164–67, 168–69; to, 129–32, 170–71, 183–90, 198–201

Gold, Catharine. *See* Lovell, Catharine Gold

Gold, Eleanor, 25–26, 176, 189–90, 199, 200; and Gold-Boudinot engagement, 35–36, 84–85, 88 (n. 9), 89, 98–99, 105–6, 109–11, 113, 116, 119, 128–35 passim; Harriett Gold Boudinot's affection for, 140, 142–43, 157, 159–60, 166, 169, 171, 172; visit to Cherokee Nation, 164–67, 168–69

—letters: to, 170–71, 183–90, 198–201

Gold, Harriett. *See* Boudinot, Harriett Gold

Gold, Hezekiah Sedgwick, 129, 167, 169, 178

Gold, Job Swift, 86, 88 (n. 15), 178 (n. 4), 201

—letters: to, 196–97

Gold, Mary. *See* Brinsmade, Mary Gold

Gold, Samuel, 116

Gold, Sarah (Sally). *See* Hopkins, Sarah (Sally) Gold

Gold, Sedgwick. *See* Gold, Hezekiah Sedgwick

Gold, Stephen: and burning of effigies, 1, 14, 37, 43, 85; and Gold-Boudinot engagement, 1, 43–45, 101, 115, 118, 124, 135–36; and threats against Elias Boudinot, 14, 37, 111

—letters: from, 81–82; to, 103–4

Gold, Swift. *See* Gold, Job Swift

Gold, Thomas, 123

Gold, Thomas Ruggles (brother of Benjamin Gold), 123

Gold, Thomas Ruggles (son of Benjamin Gold), 134, 164, 167 (n. 1)

23; formal properties of, 23, 24, 48; material properties of, 23, 26, 53, 70 (n. 25); cultural function of, 23, 30–31; critical assessment of, 23–24; conventions of, 24, 28; postscripts in, 24, 28–29; intertextuality of, 24–25; multiple audiences of, 24–25; multiple authorship of, 24–25, 28, 48; postage on, 25–26, 27–28, 108; evolutions in, 26

Life-writing. See Autobiography

Lovell, Catharine Gold, 29, 39, 42, 90, 123, 134; marriage of, 34, 136, 138; and Gold-Boudinot engagement, 109–13, 125–26

—letters: to, 81–82, 83–87, 104–8; from, 109–14, 124–26; marginal insertions in, 128–29

Lovell, John, 136

Lowery, Lydia, 101 (n. 2)

Major Ridge. See Ridge, Major

Marriage: history of white-Indian, 11; parental involvement in, 35–36; of mutuality, 54. See also Boudinot, Elias; Boudinot, Harriett Gold; Gold-Boudinot engagement; Intermarriage; Lovell, Catharine Gold

Matrilineality: of Cherokees, 5, 6, 15–16, 22

McAlpine, Silas Hurlbut, 12

McLoughlin, William G., 5, 17

Memoir. See Biography

Memoir of Catharine Brown, 101 (n. 2)

Memoirs of Henry Obookiah, 4, 96, 101 (n. 7)

Memoirs of the Life of Mrs. Harriet Newell, 63–64

Minear, Clara. See Boudinot, Clara Minear

Ministers. See Everest, Cornelius; Stone, Timothy; Vaill, Herman

Miscegenation. See Intermarriage

Missionaries. See American Board of Commissioners for Foreign Missions; Boudinot, Elias: and missionaries; Boudinot, Harriett Gold: as missionary; Foreign Mission School; Mission schools; *and individual missionaries*

Mission schools: in Cherokee Nation, 5, 6, 153, 154, 157 (n. 10), 166, 178, 200. See also Foreign Mission School

Mohegans. See Mohicans

Mohicans, 177, 178 (n. 6)

Moravian missionaries, 5, 18, 166

Morse, Jedediah, 6

Mt. Holyoke, 75 (n. 44), 201 (n. 1)

Narrative of Five Youth from the Sandwich Islands, 96, 101 (n. 6)

Native Americans. See American Indians

New Echota, 49, 159, 166, 167 (n. 3)

Newell, Harriet, 63–64, 131, 186, 192 (n. 7)

New Haven Register, 10

New York Observer, xiv, 63, 190

North American Review, 45

Northrop, John, 8, 85, 112, 125, 136, 187–88

Northrop, Mrs., 8–9, 44, 70 (n. 28), 85, 87 (n. 5), 88 (n. 11), 89, 104, 110, 125–26, 135, 187

Northrop, Sarah. See Ridge, Sarah Northrop

Northrop-Ridge marriage, 8–13, 18–

Travel, 162, 164–66
Treaty Party, 60, 190, 195 (n. 1)
Treaty of New Echota, 60–61, 65, 74
    (n. 40), 195, 202–3

Vaill, Flora Gold, 5, 36, 39, 40, 42;
    and Gold-Boudinot engagement,
    134–37
—letters: marginal insertions in, 80–
    81, 128–29; to, 81–82, 83–87, 89–
    90, 104–8, 109–14, 123–24, 153–57,
    158–60, 161–63, 164–67, 168–
    69, 172–74, 175–78, 179, 180–82,
    193–95; from, 134–37, 142–43
Vaill, Herman, xi, 5, 13, 25; and Gold-
    Boudinot engagement, 21, 29, 33–
    34, 37, 38, 91–101, 116–22, 129–32,
    141–42; as letter writer, 25–26, 28–
    29, 37, 38, 40, 172, 180; letters of
    criticized by Gold family, 25–26,
    34–35, 40–43, 106, 108, 109–10,
    112–13, 128, 135; as recipient of
    letters, 27, 46; and support of prin-
    ciple of intermarriage, 80, 92, 117,
    130, 131, 141
—letters: from, 79–81, 90–101, 116–
    22, 129–32, 141–42; to, 81–82,
    83–87, 89–90, 104–8, 109–16, 123–
    26, 128, 132–43 passim, 153–82
    passim, 193–95
Vanishing Indian myth, 62, 66

Washington, George, 5
Watie, Buck. See Boudinot, Elias
Watie, David, 6, 55, 154, 181, 186,
    188
Watie, Stand, 75 (n. 43), 155–56, 157
    (n. 6), 185, 187
Watie, Susanna Reese, 6, 154
Webster, Noah, 79, 81 (n. 2)
William Penn essays. See Evarts, Jere-
    miah: as author of William Penn
    essays
Women: and civilization, 7; and
    race, 11–12; and family, 38–39;
    and criticism of men, 40–42. See
    also Cherokees: and gender roles;
    Cherokees: and matrilineality; and
    individual women
Worcester, Ann, 58, 163, 174, 182
Worcester, Samuel A., 22, 58, 65,
    74 (n. 40), 159, 162, 163, 182, 183
    (n. 7); collaboration with Elias
    Boudinot, 50, 161, 163 (n. 3); and
    Cherokee language, 154
—letters: from, 202–3
Worcester v. Georgia, 58, 59, 182, 183
    (n. 7)
Wyss, Hilary, 20

Yale University, 42, 176, 178 (n. 4)